The Headship Game

The challenges of contemporary
school leadership

Brian Fidler and Tessa Atton

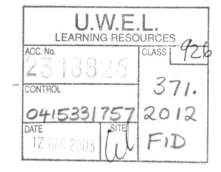

 RoutledgeFalmer
Taylor & Francis Group

LONDON AND NEW YORK

First published 2004
by RoutledgeFalmer
11 New Fetter Lane, London EC4P 4EE

Simultaneously published in the USA and Canada
by RoutledgeFalmer
29 West 35th Street, New York, NY 10001

RoutledgeFalmer is an imprint of the Taylor & Francis Group

Typeset in Goudy by
HWA Text and Data Management, Tunbridge Wells
Printed and bound in Great Britain by
TJ International Ltd, Padstow, Cornwall

British Library Cataloguing in Publication Data
A catalogue record for this book is available from the British Library

Library of Congress Cataloging in Publication Data
Fidler, Brian.
   The headship game : the challenges of contemporary school
leadership /
Brian Fidler & Tessa Atton.
       p.   cm.
1. School principals–Great Britain. 2. School management and
organization–Great Britain. 3. Educational leadership–Great Britain.
I. Atton, Tessa. II. Title.
LB2831.926.G7F53 2003
371.2′012–dc21   2003013933

ISBN 0–415–33175–7 (hbk)
ISBN 0–415–27781–7 (pbk)

Contents

Illustrations

Figures

Tables

Introduction

Cover design

Our publishers produced the cover design and sent it to us for approval. We agreed that chess was probably a very good choice of game to illustrate the kind of game that we had in mind when we suggested the title. We were not seeking to be frivolous by taking a gaming analogy for the career of headship but trying to suggest that this too has its rules, norms, expectations and gambits which are seemingly well-known to a few but quite obscure to the many.

Chess captures the idea of a series of planned moves being needed to move from beginning to successful conclusion and a great deal of thought being needed at each stage. However, we agree that the element of luck and the part that good fortune can play in a headship career is probably largely absent from chess (at least when the players are experienced). This is an important distinction. Whilst thought, reflection and advice can improve the chances of making the 'right moves', the headship game is not as predictable as chess.

Chess has a large number of possibilities but each piece is allowed only a certain range of moves, the play is in two dimensions and there are only 32 pieces that take part. Also chess is a game for only two players and each is the opponent of the other. Each of these limitations is different in the case of headship. In the career of headship there are even more possibilities than the large number in chess and yet there are patterns that appear to lead to success and checks that need to be foreseen. In headship the opponents are not so easily identified and much the biggest 'opponent' may well be circumstances and chance rather than any individual or individuals.

We were pleased with the allusion to chess in that the headship game is an intellectual game and that moves need to be thought about in advance, and their likely consequences foreseen, before committing to them.

There are winners and losers both on the way to headship and within headship but perhaps the situation to which chess provides an insight is stalemate. This has recently been noted in a small number of schools where heads and staff have reached an accommodation. Each would like to make moves but is thwarted by the other and the resulting stalemate means that the school is the net loser.

Origin of the book

Following our previous book on *Poorly Performing Staff in Schools and How to Manage Them* (Fidler and Atton 1999) where we briefly examined unsuccessful headteachers, we explored the idea of producing a companion book on poorly performing headteachers. We abandoned this for a number of reasons – it was difficult to collect evidence, there was no clear audience and more importantly we became acutely aware that quality of performance was not the same as perceived success. We did, however, realise that there was no book which explored headteachers' careers from the perspective of preparation and learning. Too many accounts do not conceptualise the process and assume that learning is based on factual transmission or experience rather than a complex process of experiential learning informed by theoretical constructs.

We have collected examples of vignettes of headteachers' experiences in chapters 4, 5, 6, 9, 10 and 11. These include a range of examples covering both successful and less successful practice. We have chosen them because we think that they illustrate scenes which provide a learning example for others. In the early sections we provide theoretical material and conceptual models as an aid to theorising about the job of headship. We hope that the combination of this material and the vignettes will provide a means of foreseeing and dealing with difficulties in practice. Thus in places there is some echo of our original intentions to identify causes of unsuccessful headship and examine ways of supporting heads in trouble. However, our main intention is to provide guidance – both conceptual and practical – to ensure a fit between the skills and attributes of a potential leader and the needs of a particular school. Although this is not a guarantee of successful headship, there are many examples of unsuccessful headship that result from a fit which was flawed from the start.

Taking up a headship for the first time is a particularly stressful experience. It is clear that better preparation can lessen and prepare for this anxiety but not eliminate it. One of the purposes of the vignettes and the examples from published research is to try to anticipate situations which may arise so that the possibilities and consequences can be foreseen to some degree. Much professional knowledge is tacit. Individuals are not conscious of their thought processes and have difficulty articulating them when they try. We hope that the stimulation of the theoretical material, research findings and vignettes will help to make the thoughts and reactions of the reader more explicit.

We hope that individuals and groups will read the vignettes and consider their reactions. Would they operate like this in these circumstances and if so would they have made other associated changes and actions that might have changed the course of events in the examples we give? We do not wish to suggest that there is one right answer in any situation and certainly not that we have identified it or that the vignette exemplifies it. On the other hand there are patterns that appear to be successful in particular external contexts and internal situations and deviations from these need to be thought through carefully to ensure that they are workable. Such considerations include:

- Rational – logically is this the appropriate course of action, taking as many considerations into account as possible including the predictable reactions of others? Is this part of a consistent predictable pattern which will engender continuity and confidence or is this an ad hoc action which breaks out from the predictable previous pattern? Does this represent the start of a new trend?
- Emotional – how will I feel as I carry this out and how will I feel afterwards? How will others feel?
- Perceptual – how might this appear to the superficial observer or if it is viewed in isolation?
- Symbolic – how might this have an impact beyond the scale of its importance as assessed rationally? Is this desirable and how might it be exploited?
- Principles and values – what underlying values does this involve and the results indicate or be taken to indicate?
- Trust – will this action increase trust in me or decrease it? Will my actions and my declared values be seen to be consistent?
- Precedent – could it be seen to set a precedent? Do I intend it as a precedent? How might a precedent be avoided if I envisage this as a more pragmatic decision reflecting particular circumstances?
- Political – will this provoke a political reaction because it is viewed as upsetting the current balance of power?

There also needs to be a consideration of the timescale for the results – immediate, short-term and long-term. There may be a different judgement according to the three timescales. Certain events need an immediate reaction. Although in a crisis it is the immediate which must drive actions, many possible crises can be foreseen and contingency plans formulated. These are better able to take account of short- and longer-term effects.

Coverage and readership

This book examines the career of headship. The first aspect of this is the progression through a series of posts towards headship and the acquisition of the skills and knowledge necessary for headship. The second is the selection, appointment and induction into headship. This leads on to a consideration of the stages of headship when in post and the increasing numbers of second headships. At any stage heads may encounter difficulties and require support. Finally there are some thoughts on life after headship.

There are conceptual ideas from the literature on professional knowledge and learning, leadership, management and headship which we have included. There are also research findings on headship from the early 1990s suggesting a series of career stages. We have tried to assess the confidence which should be placed in the generality of the results in the light of how the research was conducted.

The text is accompanied by many vignettes of examples from recent practice which illustrate incidents that headteachers meet. The early examples are from research published in the past and the current examples are mainly in chapters 4,

5, 9 and 10. We hope that these bring the conceptual ideas to life and give them an authenticity with which others can identify.

We hope that this book will be read by and of value to a number of groups:

- Those aspiring to headship
- Headteachers, particularly new headteachers
- Trainers, advisers, consultants and others who work with headteachers on leadership development
- Advisers and consultants who support headteachers
- Governors who appoint headteachers and receive professional advice from them.

Inevitably readers will take away from this study what interests them and what fits into the conceptual framework which underlies their understanding of the topic. Whilst accepting this, our intentions for the differing groups are the following. We hope that aspiring heads will gain an understanding of the contributions to their learning of experience through a series of posts in school and more formal qualifications before headship. It should also make them more aware of the demands on heads and the pitfalls. We hope that this does not discourage them but makes them more realistic and determined to be well prepared to take on the task.

We hope that those who work with headteachers on development or support will gain an enhanced understanding of the demands of headship and the skills, competencies and personal attributes which are needed. We have offered some insights into leadership and management learning through an appreciation of the conceptual and knowledge structures which professionals build through their experience. We think that the strengths and limitations of these mental frameworks are inadequately appreciated.

Governors have a pivotal role in the English school system. These mainly lay people are responsible for appointing headteachers, for taking the advice of headteachers to formulate school policies and rely on the professional skills of headteachers to carry out the policies that are set. We hope that a more comprehensive understanding of the task of the headteacher will help them appreciate the importance of headteacher selection and provide pointers to the criteria and evidence which they need to carry out the selection successfully.

The perspective on headship of each of these groups identified above is not the same. This will be especially true of the process of headteacher selection. Where perspectives are likely to differ we have attempted to examine the process from both perspectives with the guidance of an underlying theoretical approach to provide the continuing thread between the two.

Finally we hope that the book will be of interest and value to headteachers themselves, particularly newly appointed heads. The theoretical analysis and vignettes can stimulate their thinking and reappraise the understanding which underlies their current practice. Since we have covered the complete career we hope that there will be material of value for heads at all stages whether newly appointed, in their early years, in mid-term, looking for stimulation and challenge, preparing for their next headship or, as so many do, looking for a portfolio of work to take on after their early retirement.

We should like to stress the importance of headteachers helping promising members of their staff develop the knowledge and skills to aspire to headship. These are not acquired in a short course of training before applying for headships. They develop over a number of years particularly whilst holding middle management, deputy head and acting headship positions. Headteachers both appoint teachers to those positions and are also well-placed to stimulate the learning of those individuals whilst they carry out their duties.

Although this is a book mainly for practitioners, we hope that it will be suitable for those studying leadership and management on advanced courses. The first major sections of the text contain extensive references to the literature which can be followed up. It brings together material from a number of sources which inform and provide insights into headship. This material has not been brought together before to provide a preparation for, and an overview of, the career of headship. Thus we hope the book will be of value to those studying headship and other scholars who wish to acquire an overview of the career of headship in England and Wales.

Content of the book

We have collected together conceptual ideas from the literature and research findings from published sources. We have also developed ideas on how to carry out such processes as application for posts where there is little currently written and we have suggested tracks to headship and models for how to deal with the tensions of headship where none previously existed. We see this as a contribution to preparing for headship and supporting headteachers in post.

We have selected from this theoretical and conceptual writing and empirical research evidence what we consider is relevant to

- heads and prospective heads
- schools and those who govern and administer them
- those who educate, train and develop headteachers.

Where there are clear differences between the perspectives of these groups, specifically as regards selecting heads and dealing with poor performance, we have taken the perspective of the active party – governors and LEAs. However, we suggest that consideration of those processes from the perspective of other parties should be of value to heads and prospective heads even where they are on the receiving end of such actions. This extra knowledge should enable them to plan their actions better.

In some sections there is little recent empirical work, e.g. headteacher selection, and in others little at all, e.g. applications and references, so we have originated some reasoned prescriptive writing as guidance in a field where some is needed to clarify expectations. The writing is intended to be non-sexist and rather than always duplicating he and she and using plurals we have also used she to represent both male and female genders.

Theoretical and conceptual writing has been taken from many sources but the empirical research findings have mainly been taken from the UK and particularly England and Wales. This is consistent with our contingent view of leadership since we believe that differences between educational systems can so change expectations and basic assumptions that to combine findings from different education systems in other countries can only serve to confuse unless ways of differentiating the relevant expectations and assumptions can be formulated. For example Daresh and Playko (1992) in comparing heads in the UK with US principals make the point that in the US

> there is a tendency to look at the role of the school-based leader (principal) as a person allied with a formal administrative responsibility quite distinct from the roles and expectations of classroom teachers.
>
> (Daresh and Playko 1992: 146)

Whilst in the UK they recognise that the

> relationship between classroom teachers and the headteacher is maintained, and the headteacher is viewed as a member of the instructional team and not as an *outside administrator*.
>
> (Ibid., our italics)

Stott and Walker (1992) comparing Singapore with the UK point out

> There are of course systemic and cultural differences between the two countries. Management expectations, willingness to comply with central directives regardless of the implications, and the absence of effective unions, for example, all contribute to a substantially different contextual situation.
>
> (Stott and Walker 1992: 154–5)

Outline of the chapters

The book begins with a brief historical account of changes to schooling and the associated leadership issues since the Second World War. This reveals the changing external context in which schools operate and the preoccupations of headteachers at different periods of time. This is very relevant to the research findings on headship since, inevitably, the findings are partly dependent on the timing of the data collection. For example, research in the mid-1980s was heavily influenced by the effects of the teachers' industrial action of the time (e.g. Mortimore and Mortimore 1991a, 1991b) whilst later research was influenced by the introduction of the Education Reform Act in 1988 (e.g. Day and Bakioglu 1996).

In chapter 2 we examine the development of leadership thought. This has moved from assumptions that leadership characteristics are innate, through their being learned behaviours to the present formulation. This assumes that there may be personal characteristics which have been formed by heredity, early life experiences and early professional experiences. These characteristics provide the potential for leadership that can be developed. This implies that not everyone can become a leader but also that leaders can and should develop in order to be more effective. There is a critical assessment of transformational and charismatic leadership. We are sceptical of the extent to which appointed headteachers should be expected to demonstrate leadership of this kind. We examine a range of current approaches to leadership in education and propose an integrated and hierarchical arrangement of leadership theories that may be useful in different situations.

One of our contributions to the study of headteachers' careers is to collect together material on professional knowledge and its acquisition by headteachers and prospective headteachers. We consider it vital that prospective headteachers learn about leadership and management in their career before headship. Although there is much rhetoric about learning from experience, this is an activity which is not well-understood. There are five chapters which deal with learning, the job of the headteacher and its contemporary demands, selection and career preparation before headship.

Chapter 3 discusses the role of perception and knowledge in decision-making. This introduces the complexity of leadership knowledge which also has implications for how it is acquired. We point out that theoretical perspectives on organisations can help to make perceptions of situations more systematic. This may have implications for both how knowledge is acquired and also how it is stored and retrieved from memory. This chapter also has research evidence on the sources of learning which educational leaders have identified as playing a part in their development.

This is followed by a consideration of the different ways of examining the job of headteacher and the skills and knowledge that these indicate will be needed by headteachers. We examine some recent advertisements for headteachers to see what this tells us about the work of the previous head and what selectors have in mind.

In chapters 4 and 5 we study the external and internal demands on contemporary headteachers. We have collected many examples which are condensed to short vignettes that present the essentials of the particular situation. These examples are based on actual practice and we have only changed names and sometimes locations in order to preserve the anonymity of the individuals involved.

Application and selection are both essential to appointing an appropriate headteacher to a specific post. Both applicants and selectors need to consider the process from the other's perspective to maximise the chances of fit between headteacher and school. In chapter 6 we study selection. We illustrate the scale of the process by statistics on the number of headteacher appointments. We offer a structured process for selecting headteachers and analyse how the knowledge and skills of candidates could be assessed. We also examine the complexities of induction of new heads and the part that mentoring by existing headteachers can play. We consider that mentoring can have advantages for both parties which justifies the time that it takes.

In the following chapter we examine career paths to headship. We particularly note the formative influence of acting headship and suggest that this has further potential to be used in more systematic ways to prepare prospective headteachers for their work. Finally, we briefly study the application process for headships.

In chapter 8 we examine recent major studies of headship and particularly those which have suggested from their findings that there may be stages in the careers of headteachers. We have assessed and compared this evidence and propose a composite formulation of career stages from prospective candidate for a headship through to retirement. Our own later vignettes were not collected with quite this formulation in mind but a number indicate stages within it.

Chapters 9 and 10 include a substantial number of vignettes which cover the life cycle of a headteacher. Chapter 9 studies the period of applying through to taking up the post whilst chapter 10 covers the period from the first day to the end of the first headship. These vignettes from current practice illustrate the demands of the job of headteacher and the pressures which may be encountered at each stage of a headship career. We hope that these vignettes will alert potential headteachers to the requirements of current headship and that current head-teachers will be able to prepare for current and further stages in their career. Whilst many of the vignettes are concerned with problems which have been encountered by headteachers we hope that these will forewarn and allow readers to better understand the stance that they would take to these issues and consider alternative actions.

The vignettes are for illustrative purposes, they are not intended to be repre-sentative of the work of headteachers. They greatly over-emphasise problems that can arise. However, we believe it is hard examples like these which provide valuable learning. Trying to appreciate how such examples arise and how they might have been handled differently should be both taxing and worthwhile. We think it will be particularly valuable to envisage the sequence of often slowly developing events to see how their course might have been changed. We believe it is unlikely to be the actions of only one person that led to the final situation.

The vignettes are based on actual examples but have been anonymised in order to protect the identity of individuals and schools involved. Mainly the source of evidence has been the headteacher concerned and so this gives a particular perspective. Where it has been possible to check factual details we have verified these but the reactions, emotions and feelings are recorded from the head's perspective.

Chapter 11 covers three topics. The first looks at choosing a second headship and expanding the headship role to include more than one school. Taking a second headship has been found to remotivate and increase the satisfaction of those who move on from a first headship. Other ways of providing reinvigoration during headship are briefly examined so that heads can appreciate the range of choices which they could make. Lately there have been many opportunities for temporary headships – usually for schools which have particular problems. A range of examples of temporary headships are illustrated. Finally in this section we explore professional work after headship. Many heads take early retirement but wish to keep professionally active and this section explores some possibilities.

Chapter 12 analyses the stresses and challenges that heads might experience. There is a brief account of the latest study that examined stress in headteachers and how they coped with it. The major part of this chapter sets up a model to illustrate what we have called a trio of tensions. The trio consists of the head-teacher, the governing body and the school (staff, pupils and performance). We have suggested what seem likely patterns which lead to tensions at different stages of a head's career and we make suggestions about the considerations which heads might apply before such events in order to forestall them or use to deal with them if they occur. The value of the model is to give a simplified overview of the situation to aid planning. This chapter also gives some of the findings from research which examined what happened to heads who were found to be performing poorly.

The final chapter examines changes which might be made to the role of headteacher and how candidates prepare for headship. The first recommendation is that the expectations of what headteachers should be able to achieve should be lessened.

A period of consolidation should follow large-scale change. This would reduce the level of pressure on schools and headteachers to more acceptable levels. We also make suggestions from the evidence in the book for improving the learning of prospective headteachers at earlier stages in their career. Finally, again building on the evidence in the book, we suggest that fixed term contracts for headteachers should be reconsidered. This would legitimate more movement of headteachers between schools. It would prevent headteachers remaining in the same post for a very long time since there is so much evidence that this is rarely in the best interests of schools and their staff and pupils. It would also enable heads who see themselves as able to perform a particular task in a school over a limited number of years to do this and move on to a similar task in another school as a norm rather than an exception.

Finally, we should like to thank all the unnamed individuals who have con-tributed to the vignettes and to our developing understanding of headship.

Part I

History and theories of leadership

1 Recent developments in headship

Introduction

This section aims to give an overview of how headship has changed over the last 50 years and particularly since 1988. The period has been chosen to follow trends before and after the Great Debate of 1976 since this was the first noteworthy occasion when central government and the Prime Minister began to focus on education and particularly the state of schools.

It is important to have some understanding of educational history to understand

- Swings in policy
- Similar situations
- Any sense of progression.

A swinging pendulum is a useful analogy to help make sense of many changes in social policy. Many policy constraints have the features of dilemmas. This means that there are competing possibilities and both cannot be chosen simultaneously. At a point in time one has to be pre-eminent. One of these is the seat of power. The Education Act of 1944 created three seats of power in education: central government, local government and schools. At that time power was shared between all three. Since then there have been changes. The movement of power has been different in different areas of responsibility in education (see Tables 1.1–1.3).

It is quite clear that the net reduction in power has been at local government level.

There are similar dilemmas in social trends (excellence v. equity) and educational orthodoxy (mixed ability teaching v. streaming/setting). A knowledge of what has happened in the past provides a guiding star for future changes. Whilst the past is unlikely to be replicated, there is much repackaging of previous ideas. Unless some way of reconciling the conflicting demands can be discovered there is likely to be oscillation between which of the competing pressures is regarded as the most pressing at any particular time.

Table 1.1 Curriculum

	Pre-1988	1988	By 2002
Prime responsibility	School	Government	Moves to delegate more curriculum decision-making to school level

Table 1.2 Finance

	Pre-1988	1988	By 2002
Prime responsibility	LEA	School	Growth of earmarked budgets for priority areas and LEA co-ordinated schemes

Table 1.3 Parental choice of school

	Pre-1988	1988	By 2002
Indicator of preference	LEA	Parents	Competition for children reduced in emphasis in government publications

If choices are a way of resolving dilemmas, then much change results from dissatisfaction with previous choices. When the downside of the new choices becomes evident, unless there is new thinking, there may be a return to a previous situation with few new features in place. This is likely to perpetuate the cycle. For example, in the 1950s and 1960s the lack of motivation of secondary school students with a curriculum which allowed them little choice was noted. Student curricular options were created so that students would have some choice of the curriculum subjects they studied in the later years of schooling. When the National Curriculum was introduced in 1988 the virtues of a common curriculum for all students was a guiding star. This reduced student choice and trends in absenteeism and lack of motivation of student groups became evident. This has led to calls for more curricular choice for students including vocational curricula.

A trend which has not begun to be reversed at the time of writing is the tension between the academic aims of schooling and the social and behavioural aims. The pressure since 1988 has been on the academic aims. The cross-curricular strands which were to broaden the curriculum were not pursued and the time for cultural subjects, P.E./sports and social aims was reduced. It is clear, however, that employers need other skills in addition to academic ones and that social cohesion in society needs to be increased. Citizenship as a curriculum subject is a first indication of this. Thus a sense of history suggests that before long the inadequacies of pursuing test results whilst failing to prioritise the more social aims of schools will be recognised as needing to be reversed.

These few examples have been included to draw attention to the need for heads of institutions to be aware of the context in which they operate and the trends which may be at work in directing future changes. A sense of what has happened in the past may also be valuable in implementing current changes. There is a tendency to assume that previous research evidence on past changes is no longer relevant. This needs a more discriminating approach. The move to setting children by ability in primary schools in order to achieve better test results begins to replicate the streaming of children into ability groups in the past. Issues concerning the effects of social class, lack of movement between sets etc. will reappear unless there is monitoring of these potential effects as part of the changes. In this way there could be some learning from history rather than just repeating the same practice.

Before the Great Debate of 1976

Following the Second World War and the implementation of secondary education for all in the 1944 Education Act, much of the preoccupation at both central and local government was of 'roofs over heads'. This was ensuring that school building and teacher training could keep pace with the demand for school places and teachers resulting from raising the school leaving age in 1947 and 1976, the increase in the birth-rate and the trend to greater participation in nursery and sixth form education.

The main structural changes were in secondary schools where the change to comprehensive schools gradually took place. The tripartite system of grammar, technical and secondary modern schools was taken as the initial model in most LEAs. Schools were expanded in size both because there were economies of scale and also because a large cohort of 16-year-olds was needed to generate a viable sixth form able to offer a wide range of subjects in all-ability schools. Schools became larger – schools with 2,000 or more pupils – and split site. To use existing buildings from separate secondary modern and grammar schools when comprehensive education was introduced, the combined school often had upper and lower schools where a number of year groups were on one site and the remainder were on another. Such large schools led to a number of management structures. Some schools divided children into house structures to provide a smaller unit that a single head of house could oversee. Others divided responsibilities into a number of groups of years – lower, upper and sixth form.

Where mergers of schools took place, the more highly qualified teachers were in grammar schools and tended to be appointed to many of the senior positions in the new comprehensives. Pastoral structures were set up both to provide discipline and support on a more human scale and also to provide jobs for senior staff from secondary modern schools. Whilst these were initial appointments, as replacements were made these distinctions disappeared.

As comprehensive education came in, the need for 11+ tests disappeared and removed a large external influence on primary schooling and left them free to innovate. Project work, integrated teaching days and mixed ability teaching developed.

Middle schools taking children from 8–12 or 9–13 were set up in some areas. These were a combination of a pragmatic response to the stock of school buildings, the need to take all the age group into one building and a more educational rationale. The educational rationale was to provide a more gradual transition from the single class teaching of primary schools to the specialist teaching of the secondary school. For a variety of reasons including the key stages of the National Curriculum such schools have been disappearing for some time. However, the educational transition that they were intended to facilitate remains (see Table 1.4). The transition after a six week vacation at age 11 is enormous and probably requires action by both primary and secondary schools. This is an issue which has been raised many times before but satisfactory solutions have proved difficult.

The change to comprehensive education was controversial in principle but also ushered in other changes, e.g. size and organisation of schools. These took place in the 1960s accompanied by much questioning of social trends, optimism about the value of education and rapidly increasing spending on education. The first reaction was from academics and others who challenged comprehensive schools and the associated changes to primary schools following the ending of selection tests at 11. The first of the infamous Black Papers appeared in 1967.

The Great Debate and control of the curriculum

The 1944 Education Act had high and liberal aspirations for the curriculum but specified only that education was to be suitable for different 'ages, abilities and aptitudes' of children and contribute to their 'spiritual, moral, mental and physical development'. The only formal requirement was for the teaching of religious instruction and to start the day with an act of collective worship. Control of the curriculum had been delegated to LEAs and schools. A Labour minister, George Tomlinson, in the late 1940s is reputed to have said 'the minister knows nowt about curriculum' when asked about the government's view, and it was a Conservative minister, Sir David Eccles, in the 1960s who coined the phrase 'secret garden' to describe such school control.

His efforts to take some control of the curriculum centrally were thwarted. As a result the Schools Council for Curriculum and Examinations was set up and funded to provide curriculum development in 1964. Whilst teaching materials

Table 1.4 Transition from primary to secondary

	Primary	Secondary
Size	Small	Large
Location	Close to home	More distant often involving transport
Organisation	Class teaching all week	Specialists for brief periods
Academic teaching	Mixed ability	Setting by ability
Pastoral	Class teacher	Class tutor and year head

were produced as a result of these projects, their adoption was left to individual schools to decide. LEAs sometimes funded particular projects for their schools to make take-up more attractive and possible.

Government attempts to influence curricula had their counterparts overseas and in other parts of the educational system. The launch of the Sputnik by the Russians in 1957 is said to have sparked panic in US education. There was a widespread view that America was falling behind in the space race and this was in part because education in the USA had to be updated. This spawned a whole series of curriculum development projects in the 1960s and 1970s which added to knowledge of the management of change in schools.

The largest constraint on the secondary school curriculum was the examination system. Although secondary modern schools were intended to be free of examinations they soon began to offer a range of examinations to the more able of their leavers as it was becoming clearer that certification of attainment at the end of schooling would be increasingly needed for entry to work or further education. In 1958 an examination, Certificate of Secondary Education (CSE), specifically for secondary modern schools was proposed. Whilst there were to be externally set and marked papers similar to GCE, there was also to be a Mode 3 type of examination by which papers were internally set and marked with external moderation.

The later years of secondary education were organised to allow children to study for external examinations in their final two years of compulsory education. The range of subjects was set for GCE but innovation through Mode 3 was possible for CSE. This led to streaming and setting by ability in order to study for examinations of particular levels of difficulty.

The so-called Great Debate was inaugurated by the Prime Minister of the day, James Callaghan, in a speech at Ruskin College, Oxford in 1976. HMI had been commissioned to appraise the state of the education system. In an unpublished report 'The Yellow Book' they identified failings in primary schools, secondary schools, teacher training and vocational education. In addition to the Black Papers criticising education, the constraints on public spending following the first rise in world oil prices following the second Arab–Israeli war in 1973 and the poor economic performance of the UK were contributing factors to what was to be a concerted attack on the education system which still goes on.

The publicity which accompanied an investigation by Robin Auld QC in 1976 into the working practices of one junior and infants school in London, William Tyndale, also contributed to public unease about the state of schooling. Although these events reflected on schools in London the problems were taken to be widespread.

An HMI publication catalogued a number of failings in schools. This was referred to as the 'Yellow Book' but was never published although excerpts were published in the popular press (HMI 1976). The subsequent more systematic surveys of education in primary schools in 1978 (HMI 1978) and secondary schools in 1979 (HMI 1979) did not quite substantiate some of these findings but by then the Great Debate had been launched. A series of publications and regional conferences made it clear that more central intervention in schools was inevitable.

LEAs introduced schemes of school self-evaluation as a way of demonstrating that schools were accountable. However, research showed that schools were not very good at identifying weaknesses and even less good at devising ways of improving them.

A core or common curriculum was suggested in various government documents from 1980 but it wasn't until the Education Reform Act of 1988 that a National Curriculum was introduced. This with a few differences reflected the same subjects that were in the 1904 secondary school regulations. Although there was belated recognition of cross-curricular themes, these were not to be tested by SATs and were generally sidelined.

Leadership challenges

Thus until the 1960s the head's job was to run the school on the resources provided by the LEA. Responsibility allowances to provide salary payments for those who took on management responsibilities, such as heads of department, were introduced in the 1960s. Children and staff had to be allocated to classes and, in secondary schools, a timetable and examination schedule agreed. For many years it was an aspiration to reduce primary school classes to 40 and secondary school classes to 30. With an expanding birth-rate until 1964, teacher training was struggling to keep up.

In secondary schools there was a choice of curriculum projects and examinations. Some schools, in preparing for the raising of the school leaving age to 16 in 1976, ran link courses with their local FE college. Until the 1970s the 'leading professional' was the predominant model of headship. In the 1970s the increasing size of secondary schools and the management of those with responsibility posts led to the 'chief executive' being proposed as an increasingly appropriate model for secondary headship. This envisaged the headteacher as a manager of managers. The headteacher and multiple deputy heads as a management team began to be seen in larger secondary schools.

In the late 1970s and early 1980s a falling birth-rate from 1964 led to contraction in the school population and a spate of school closures and mergers. Schools tried to keep pupil numbers up where possible to prevent the possibility of closure and merger. Thus a concern for the public image of the school and attracting pupil numbers was around well before the Education Reform Act.

During the mid-1980s there was prolonged industrial action by teachers in support of a pay claim which led to an imposed contract of employment and revised salary negotiating machinery. The action affected schools in different ways and made management and leadership very difficult in many schools for a protracted period. This was at a time when secondary schools were combining GCE and CSE examinations into the General Certificate of Secondary Education (GCSE).

The composition and powers of governing bodies which had been set up in 1944 were progressively changed in 1980, 1986 and 1988. The changes gave more explicit powers to governing bodies and widened membership to include parents and teaching staff, and reduced the dominance of LEA nominations. Headteachers had to adapt to more powerful governing bodies, particularly in secondary schools.

It was the 1988 Education Reform Act (ERA) which took away from schools much curriculum decision-making by imposing a National Curriculum and in return gave them greater financial powers. Historically headteachers had control of capitation allowance, which amounted to about 5 per cent of the school running costs, and had played a part in selecting staff in conjunction with the local authority. Following ERA they and the governing body had control of some 90 per cent or more of the finances to run their school. The power to appoint head-teachers and other staff passed to governing bodies although these powers had been held by a small group of voluntary-aided schools since 1944.

Probably the most controversial feature of the ERA was to give parents a greater opportunity to choose (or more accurately express a preference for) the school for their children and to make the finance of schools directly dependent on the number of children in the school. Comparative league tables of exam and test results by school were published from 1992. Promotion and marketing were now features of management and leadership of schools, joining staff, finance and curriculum management. This was one aspect of an increase of market forces in education. Other aspects were compulsory competitive tendering and the opening to competition of many local authority services. Thus schools could choose the contractors for cleaning and grounds maintenance for example and redeploy any savings to other areas of educational expenditure.

The movement of power in education to central government and schools was at the expense of the powers which had previously resided at LEA level. The opening of local authority services to competition from private contractors further reduced the role, influence and size of LEA staff. This led to an increased feeling of isolation for many headteachers.

Whilst the consumers' power to influence schools had been increased by parental choice of schools and their representation on governing bodies, the professional influence of LEAs declined. In 1993 the inspection of secondary schools by a newly formed Office for Standards in Education began and was followed a year later by inspections of primary schools on a four-yearly cycle. These played a part in returning the attention of headteachers to teaching and learning from their preoccupation with controlling budgets which had required substantial amounts of time following financial delegation after 1988. The publicity given to inspection reports and their public availability increased accountability pressures on schools. These also introduced for the first time systematic procedures for dealing with schools said to be failing or in danger of failing to provide an adequate level of education for their pupils – so called 'failing schools'. These amounted to about 2 per cent of schools.

The management training of headteachers has expanded since schemes financed by central government were introduced in 1983. These have culminated in the National Professional Qualification for Headship (NPQH) before headship, Headteachers Leadership and Management Programme (HEADLAMP) for newly appointed heads and Leadership Programme for Serving Headteachers (LPSH) since the mid-1990s. First initiated by the Teacher Training Agency they are now operated by the National College for School Leadership set up in 2000.

It is easy to think that the situation was very calm before the last decade but, as this brief analysis shows, this wasn't the case. This also has implications for what we know of headship and leadership. Research done at a particular point in time tends to pick up the concerns of the time in addition to more general findings about headship and leadership. Thus falling rolls and mergers, teachers' industrial action or the effects of the Education Reform Act all loom large in recent research findings on headship.

2 Development of leadership thought and its application to schools

Introduction

The first section traces the development of leadership and management thought. This is mainly derived from the organisational and business literature. Although there have been some approaches to leadership which are purely educational, e.g. instructional leadership, most of the development of leadership thought in education has been derived from this more general literature which is summarised here. In particular the recent interest in transformational and charismatic leadership in schools has emerged in this way.

The following section examines the emerging distinction between leadership and management in organisational and business scholarship before a final section examines recent thinking in educational leadership and we produce our own hierarchy of leadership theories in education which we consider provides a theoretical structure to leadership in schools. This provides a more sophisticated framework for thinking about school leadership than is current when only one theory is presented as the solution to all problems. Our treatment allows leaders to choose the theory or theories which address the particular facets of school leadership which are appropriate to a specific situation.

The development of organisational leadership and management thought

Although the word leadership will mainly be used in this section the literature until fairly recently has not had a clear distinction between leadership and management, and, as we shall see in the next section, agreement is not universal on the distinctions.

Bryman (1992) traces four stages in the development of leadership thought since the Second World War.

- Trait (up to the late 1940s)
- Style (late 1940s to late 1960s)
- Contingency (late 1960s to early 1980s)
- New Leadership (since early 1980s).

In each case the development of the next phase appears to be motivated by the limitations which have been exposed by research of the previous theoretical formulation. A successor is formulated that is new, relatively simple to understand and appealing in terms of some important features of leadership. Each does not directly build on its predecessor nor is there necessarily a complete rejection of the previous stage. Each stage contains some truth but the next takes account of features which were seen as important at the time and which the previous stage did not deal with adequately.

The progression through the stages can be seen to have been guided progressively by the following quests:

- Identification of good leaders
- Consideration of whether the supply of leaders was fixed or variable
- Increasing interest in leadership effectiveness developing into a search for 'One Best Way'
- Increasing importance attached to the role of leaders in organisational change.

Trait approach

The trait approach was based on the assumption that leaders were marked out by certain defining characteristics. Although this may have begun with the assumption that such characteristics were innate, such as physical characteristics, the search continued and included a range of abilities and personal characteristics which may have been acquired and developed in life and work before leadership.

The key features of this approach were:

- Leadership abilities resided in the person
- These abilities were present when leadership was first exercised.

In common parlance 'leaders were born and not made'. As we have indicated this oversimplifies the assumptions which increasingly took account of development through early education and life experiences to produce leadership abilities.

The list of attributes was very general and not very discriminating in being able to pick out leaders from those who did not lead. This led to a reaction in the next phase which concentrated on behaviours and particularly those which could be developed in leadership preparation.

Leadership styles

A number of variants of what came to be called the leadership grid were formulated of which two principal dimensions were:

- consideration or concern for people and
- initiating structure or concern for results (see Figure 2.1).

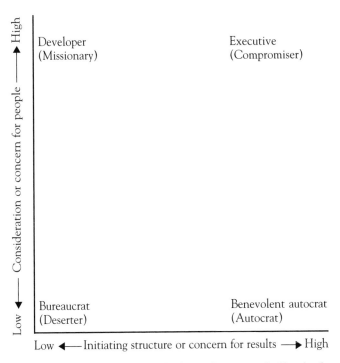

Figure 2.1 Effective (and less effective) leadership styles on a grid of levels of concern for people and results (Reddin 1987)

Sophisticated instruments were compiled to assess the degree to which individuals manifested these two behaviours in their work. A great deal of quantitative research was carried out by the Ohio State group in the USA using a particular leadership questionnaire and others took up this formulation based on the two dimensions, e.g. Blake and Mouton (1985). Reddin (1970) introduced an effectiveness dimension and adapted a version of his questionnaire for education.

The key features of this approach were:

- Individuals could develop these behaviours since they were manifest as actions rather than innate qualities
- High levels of both behaviours would provide the best leadership styles.

The search for 'One Best Way' was overtaken by a contingency approach – it all depended on circumstances.

Contingency theory

This recognised that 'One Best Way' was unrealistic and that what was appropriate leadership depended on circumstances. There were a number of attempts to identify the features on which leadership effectiveness depended and what were appropriate leadership responses. Some took the earlier work on traits and examined which features of situations suited particular leadership traits, e.g. Fiedler's (1967) work with such features as the relationship between leader and subordinates, the leader's formal position and power, and the degree of task structure. Others were based on the two sets of behaviours of the leadership grid, e.g. Hersey and Blanchard (1988).

The contingency principle has not been seriously questioned but the leadership theories that tried to encapsulate the principle and apply it in particular situations were not seen to offer sufficient help in choosing a leadership approach. At that time the assessment of the predictive value of the theories was carried out in a very demanding quantitative way. The reaction to this, transformational and charismatic leadership, by contrast has only been assessed in less demanding qualitative ways. New Leadership concentrates on what leadership is rather than what those in formal leadership positions do.

New Leadership

Bryman identifies a different conception of leadership emerging in the 1980s. The range of approaches he brings together as New Leadership. This introduced emotional and symbolic elements to theories of leadership. Principal theories within New Leadership are transformational and charismatic leadership. The two are closely connected but whilst some see charisma as central to transformational leadership and most see it as a central element, some writers ascribe little importance to it.

Transformational leadership began with J. Mcgregor Burns (1978) who contrasted it with transactional leadership in a political context. Whilst transactional leadership motivates by the offer of material rewards for success and punishes failure, transformational leadership seeks to inspire followers to exceed their own and the leader's expectations.

There are three major changes in the thinking encapsulated in New Leadership:

1   Leaders are distinguished by being recognised as such by followers
2   Followers have an impact on the leader
3   Leaders have some particular personal characteristics but also exhibit behaviours which might be developed.

The first of these moves away from either identifying leaders by personal traits they possess or behaviours that they exhibit in favour of the effect that they create on followers. Leaders do not exist in the abstract, only when recognised by followers. This implicitly accepts a situational approach in that it is followers in a particular situation who identify a person as a leader by his or her impact on them. As Bryman (1992) points out this raises some difficulties in organisations where individuals are appointed to executive positions. As the leadership model currently promoted for headteachers is transformational leadership, this brings with it an unanticipated difficulty. School governing bodies may appoint headteachers that they expect to be leaders, but whether they are or not depends on the school staff. However, as most writers agree that both forms of leadership – transactional and transformational – are required, it may be less difficult to appoint transactional leaders.

The second point adds to the effect of the leader on followers, a reciprocal effect on the leader. The leader needs followers and in some senses is dependent on them thus the leaders cannot ignore his or her effect on followers and may need to tailor behaviour to keep their support. Over time a leader may be significantly affected by the reaction of followers. The danger is shown by certain national political figures in that they come to believe the adulation of followers. The lack of critical appraisal encourages behaviour which becomes increasingly dysfunctional.

The third point assumes that successful leaders have potential in the form of personal attributes but that these can be used to develop behaviours which are likely to be recognised as leadership. For example, personal characteristics contributing to charismatic leadership have been identified (House 1977) as a

- high level of self-confidence
- tendency to dominate
- need to influence others
- strong conviction in the integrity of one's own beliefs.

Whilst the corresponding behaviours of charismatic leaders are:

- role modelling the values and beliefs to which they wish followers to subscribe
- personal image building to create an impression of competence and likely success
- expressing high ideals for the organisation's future
- setting high expectations for the achievements of followers
- expressing confidence in the abilities of followers and expectations that they will succeed
- arousing motives such as: a need for affiliation or achievement; a need to overcome an obstacle or adversary; a need for personal excellence in one's work.

In terms of developing charismatic leadership the following skills have been suggested as capable of development (Conger and Kanungo 1988):

- critical evaluation and problem detection skills (to find promising opportunities)
- visioning skills, e.g. a course in creative thinking
- communication skills, particularly linguistic skills
- impression management skills, e.g. modelling (use of exemplary behaviour), appearance, body language and verbal skills
- empowering skills, e.g. using high expectations, more participation in decisions, freeing employees (relaxing rules), setting meaningful goals and rewards.

Factors have been identified which cause followers to attribute charismatic leadership in the business world (Conger and Kanungo 1987, 1988). Such leaders

- have a vision of what they want the organisation to achieve which is different to the status quo
- are prepared to take personal risks to achieve the vision and hence are seen as trustworthy
- are opportunistic in terms of recognising the right time for action
- denigrate the present position and propose their vision as the solution
- express confidence in their own ability and take account of the needs of followers
- use personal power often based on expertise to influence others
- engage in entrepreneurial activity.

There are circumstances which are particularly favourable to charismatic leadership. Situations which are:

- stressful with considerable uncertainty, e.g. when there is rapid environmental change outside the organisation
- acknowledged as a crisis.

This is consistent with the observation that schools which are in trouble in some way are likely to rally to a leader who offers a clear solution to the problems and inspires confidence that the school can succeed. It is not clear if a sense of crisis leads to the attribution of charisma or whether in a crisis leaders come forward and exhibit the behaviour which leads to the attribution of charisma.

Bryman (1992) identifies the following circumstances as being inimical to charismatic leadership:

- mechanistic and rigidly bureaucratic organisations
- leaders with little autonomy
- environments with low performance expectations
- great restrictions on the leader's time.

Whilst the first three may be obvious the fourth may need a little explanation. For charismatic leaders to interact with followers, both in groups and singly, takes a great deal of time and so leaders who do not meet followers or don't have sufficient time to devote to face to face meetings are unlikely to be identified as charismatic.

It is worth considering these conditions as they apply to headteachers in schools. Headteachers who see themselves as carrying out government legislation and needing to fulfil the anticipated requirements of OFSTED inspections are likely to be viewed as having little autonomy and hence being unable to transform a school. On the other hand heads who are mindful of these requirements but stress the opportunities that their school can choose to take up could be seen as charismatic. Schools which are rule-driven are likely to have heads who are not seen as charismatic as are those with low expectations for pupils and staff. However, when performance must improve dramatically, as when a school is placed in special measures by OFSTED, the conditions may be far more conducive to the appearance of a charismatic leader.

Whilst most headteachers are likely to be under time pressures, there may be possibilities associated with how time is spent. Heads who spend time around school interacting with staff and pupils may be able to take maximum opportunity to influence compared to those who spend time alone dealing with paperwork, important though this may be.

Bryman (1992) identifies the particular contribution of charisma within transformational leadership as being associated with organisational change. He points out that transformational leadership per se was originally concerned with transforming *followers* not the *organisation*. Transformational leadership, it is claimed, 'ultimately becomes moral in that it raises the level of human conduct and ethical aspirations of both leader and led and thus has a transforming effect on both' (Burns 1978: 20). Organisational change is the contribution of charismatic aspects of leadership. Writers have increasingly brought both closer together (Yukl 2002).

Yukl offers the following advice on how to act as a transformational leader:

- Articulate a clear and appealing vision
  The vision should be communicated repeatedly at every opportunity and in a variety of different ways. The vision needs an ideological component and this is best communicated by imagery, symbols, stories and slogans. Metaphors and analogies are particularly effective as they challenge followers to search for the meaning within them. When speaking, conviction and intensity help to arouse emotions. People need to understand the purpose and priorities of the organisation. 'This gives the work meaning, serves as a source of self-esteem, and fosters a sense of common purpose' (p. 263).
- Explain how the vision can be attained
  The leader must convince followers that the vision is attainable. There needs to be a strategy. This should contain a few key themes that articulate values and principles which command acceptance. Followers should feel involved in the issues. The process of vision attainment should have some novel elements if it is to keep the confidence of followers.
- Act confidently and optimistically
  The leader should demonstrate self-confidence and conviction. Confidence and optimism should be exuded by word, action and expression so that they are contagious to followers.
- Express confidence in followers
  The leader needs to express high expectations of followers but also confidence that together they will achieve or exceed their expectations. Listing strengths and advantages compared to others who have succeeded helps give confidence to followers.

- Use dramatic, symbolic actions to emphasise key values

  The aim is to make an impact. This is to make an impression which creates stories which have a moral in the sense of illustrating a particular principle or value. Actions must be consistent with the rhetoric. Where two or more organisational values are in opposition, it must be clear which one has been upheld and why. Symbolic actions are likely to be particularly effective in both being talked about and having their meaning interpreted. An element of personal risk to the leader has particular impact.

- Lead by example

  Leading by example or role modelling, especially for tasks which are unpleasant or risky, will be particularly impressive. The actions and communications of leaders will be subjected to analysis by followers to interpret meaning whether the leader wishes it or not, so these need to be capable of withstanding this test.

- Empower people to achieve the vision

  Empowerment means delegating responsibility to followers about how to carry out their work. It involves asking followers to propose solutions to the problems that arise and for which previously they may have expected solutions from above. Empowering also means removing unnecessary bureaucratic constraints and providing resources to achieve the tasks. All of this implies trusting followers when the vision has been accepted and agreed.

An early band of followers who recognise the leader with charisma and who encourage others to follow is helpful. This is the role of opinion formers. A new headteacher may need to identify who are the opinion formers among the staff and parents and particularly strive to influence that group.

Bryman (1992) offers a critical evaluation of New Leadership. Amongst other issues he examines vision, empowerment, succession and the empirical support for the theory.

Vision

One of the more obvious signs of New Leadership is the need for a vision (Bryman 1992). This is concerned with higher values than a strategic aim. It needs to be specific to the organisation. As Bryman rather waspishly proclaims

> ... the more visions are just stylized blueprints for change which are translated with minor changes from company to company, the less appropriate it is to designate them as visions and the less appropriate it is to regard their promulgation as leadership rather than management.
>
> (Bryman 1992: 168)

So the content of the vision is vitally important and just having a vision is not enough.

This has implications for school leadership. As more training is provided before headship, this deals with many of the issues which headteachers need to be aware of. Thus candidates are made aware of the need to have a vision as headteacher but how to ensure that this is specific to the school that they are aiming for is more problematic (Fidler 2002a). When analyses of school aims have been carried out what is striking is how generic they are rather than differentiating one school from another. From what we have said previously, if the school is seen to have little autonomy to meet the specific needs of its pupils, this is not a situation which is conducive to charismatic transformational leadership.

Empowerment

The literature on transformational and charismatic leadership has tended to focus on the top executive and not others in the senior team. Are they followers or part of the leadership team? Where others are concerned it is assumed that they are empowered by the New Leadership. However, as Bryman points out 'For all the talk of empowering subordinates or converting followers into leaders, very little serious discussion seems to have arisen about how an organization would be pulled together if it had many leaders pursuing their personal visions' (p. 155).

Similar issues arise when distributed leadership in schools, teacher leadership and the many similar ideas are subjected to a little analysis. If leadership involves autonomy then this cannot be unlimited for middle-level and teacher leaders. If there is to be co-ordination of efforts then these need to be in line with the school's strategic plan. Such a plan may be drawn up in a participative way (Fidler 2002a) and involve all teachers, but after the plan has been agreed, those who had different ideas cannot pursue their own personal visions if organisational interests are also to be served.

Succession

As might be anticipated, there are problems in following a charismatic leader. The loyalty and emotion which is attached by followers to the leader makes it very difficult for the leadership succession. If it is at a time of crisis, which might be expected to be auspicious for a future charismatic leader, any solution will involve a change. Changing ideology is notoriously difficult. If the change of leadership is not at a time of crisis, the circumstances will not be auspicious for the new leader and he or she is likely to be compared unfavourably with the previous charismatic leader and any changes to the organisation will be difficult. Without a perceived crisis, the new leader will find pre-emptive change difficult because there isn't a felt need and he or she does not have a personal following to carry the case for change. Change is particularly difficult when everyone has become accustomed to the status quo and this is reinforced by strong organisational values and previous success (Fidler 1998). A charismatic leader may be a mixed blessing in the longer term (Bryman 1992).

Many new headteachers have experienced this effect when following a long established and much admired predecessor. A new primary head inherited a school which had a portrait of his predecessor proudly displayed in the staffroom. In such situations one solution may be to engineer a crisis so that there is an increased willingness from staff to change and a recognition that a different kind of leadership is required for these changed circumstances. In a very traditional grammar school a new headteacher engineered a number of crises so that long established staff would face up to the need for change.

Empirical support for the theory

The research and illustrations used to promulgate transformational and charismatic leadership has been largely qualitative. The identification of change with charisma is based on observations of the careers of some high profile leaders. Basing generalisation on exceptions is notoriously misleading. Quantitative studies examining leader behaviour and follower motivation and performance have yielded more mixed results. There have been some interesting laboratory experiments with actors playing the part of leaders (Bryman 1992; Yukl 2002). This raises the issue as to how deep-seated and authentic such leadership processes are.

Distinguishing leadership and management

It should be made clear that not all authors make such a distinction and that it is during the period of increasing interest in New Leadership that there has been a greater tendency to erect a distinction between leadership and management.

The early views of Zaleznik (1977) have been influential in conceptualising the differences between leaders and managers. He distinguishes between the two on the basis that not only is the work different but so are the people carrying it out.

He sees the differences in terms of

- orientation towards goals
- work
- human relations
- their selves (see Table 2.1).

He sees developments in early life as the beginning of these differences. Leaders also seem to need a mentor at a crucial stage in order to develop.

Kotter (1990) distinguishes leadership and management, the latter being concerned with 'consistency and order' and the former with 'constructive or adaptive change'.

There are contrasts illustrated in Table 2.2.

In the case of transformational leadership it is the effect of inspiring, energising and committing followers which is the key distinction whilst for charismatic

Table 2.1 Differences between managers and leaders (after Zaleznik 1977)

	Managers	*Leaders*
Orientation towards goals	'Managers tend to adopt impersonal, if not passive attitudes towards goals. Managerial goals arise out of necessities rather than desires ...' (p. 70).	Leaders are 'active rather than reactive, shaping ideas rather than responding to them ...' They influence and change the way people think about what is 'desirable, possible and necessary' (p. 71).
Their work	Managers view their work as an 'enabling process'.	Leaders 'develop fresh approaches to long-standing problems and ... open issues for new options' (p. 72).
Their human relations	Managers prefer to work with people and to maintain a low level of involvement in these relationships. Managers pay attention to *how* things get done.	Leaders who are more concerned with ideas relate in more intuitive and empathetic ways. Leaders pay attention to *what* the events and decisions mean to participants.
Their selves	Managers have had a straightforward life. They have a feeling of belonging.	Leaders have had continuous struggle. They have a feeling of separateness. They search out opportunities for change.

Table 2.2 Distinctions between managing and leading (after Kotter 1990)

Managing	*Leading*
Planning and budgeting (short- and medium-term targets)	Establishing direction (creating vision and strategies)
Organising and staffing (allocating tasks)	Aligning people (obtaining commitment)
Controlling and problem-solving (monitoring that results are in line with plan and fixing problems)	Motivating and inspiring (ensuring people are moving in line with vision despite obstacles)

leadership it is reducing resistance to change, seizing opportunities for radical change and exciting followers which are the hallmarks. A further effect of leadership is to inject a degree of intellectual stimulation into the work situation.

As Bolman and Deal point out both leadership and management are necessary:

> Leading and managing are different, but both are important. When organizations are over managed but under led, they eventually lose any sense of spirit

or purpose. Poorly managed organizations with strong charismatic leaders may soar briefly only to crash shortly thereafter.

(Bolman and Deal 1997: xii)

Most authors agree that management or transactional leadership is also required in addition to transformational or charismatic leadership (Bryman 1992). Indeed it has been noted that charismatic leaders do not relish more administrative functions, and that, as such leadership becomes routinised, the attribution of charisma is likely to wane. Thus it may need to be others who provide the more rational conventional management to produce plans and to staff and resource them so that they can be implemented.

In a recent study of 12 schools in England respondents indicated how they saw the differences (Day *et al.* 2000). Here are some of the responses:

> Leadership and management must coincide; leadership makes sure that the ship gets to the right place; management makes sure that the ship (crew and cargo) is well run. If it's just your vision you will not get to the right place – you must have a combined agreed vision with all the staff on board. You must have a strategy, therefore, for getting agreement.

[infants head]

> Leadership is about getting across to the staff where we are now and where we are going. It is not about the mechanisms by which that vision is achieved – that is management. Leadership is also about knowing what to do and being able to raise the morale of the staff.

[secondary head]
(Day *et al.* 2000: 38–9)

Day *et al.* summarised the views of teachers:

> For the teachers leadership consists of providing a role model, giving the school direction, having an overview, setting standards and making 'tough' decisions – all in all what could be described as a relatively traditional view of the role of a leader.

(Day *et al.* 2000: 75)

Although teachers expected a vision from the head

> what seemed to count more in terms of how they were judged as leaders was less the acceptability of their vision than how well they implemented it, how well they were able to build some form of common commitment, form cohesive groups within the school and bring them together.

(Day *et al.* 2000: 80)

Leadership in schools

It is worth recapping some of the findings on leadership in other organisations which have been built upon in education. Some of these are sometimes presented as if they depended on particular theories of leadership rather than being generally agreed findings.

- Leadership depends on circumstances
- Leadership is recognised by followers and not by appointing bodies
- Different styles of leadership can be successful
- Leadership does not come only from one person
- Leadership and management are not mutually exclusive.

A recent attempt to present approaches to educational leadership in the research literature is that by Leithwood and colleagues (1999). We first give a brief summary of their findings before we recast them into a form which we consider is more valuable and realistic to apply to practice.

They adopted a pragmatic, if rather arbitrary and atheoretical approach to identifying current leadership theories in education. They carried out a trawl for eight years of four journals: two US based, one Australian and one UK based. Twenty concepts of leadership were uncovered and were assigned to 'six broad categories, referred to subsequently as models' (p. 7).

- Instructional – this is concerned with influencing teachers' educational practice
- Transformational – this is concerned with change and empowering followers
- Moral – this is concerned with the 'rightness' of decisions and the ethics and values of leaders themselves
- Participative – this is concerned with involvement in decision-making – who and how
- Managerial – this is concerned with the tasks and functions that need to be carried out efficiently
- Contingent – this is concerned with the adaptation of style and substance to particular situations.

The intention here is to explain transformational leadership which the authors claim comes closest to an appropriate approach for current conditions and to develop what they term post-transformational leadership. They take the defining features of transformational leadership (Podsakoff *et al.* 1990) to be

- Identifying and articulating a vision
- Fostering acceptance of group goals
- Providing an appropriate model
- High-performance expectations
- Providing individual support

- Providing intellectual stimulation
- Contingent reward
- Management by exception.

Leithwood *et al.* (1999), after studying research findings, recognise that 'this body of evidence seems to provide only modest empirical support for using transformational approaches as a foundation on which to build a model of leadership for present and future schools' (p. 38). However, they point out that other searches for empirical evidence on the effects of the leader on school outcomes have been equally muted (Hallinger and Heck 1996).

Hierarchy of leadership theories for schools

Rather than propose one theory of leadership for schools we suggest that different theories are of value for different purposes. These form a hierarchy of approaches to leadership in schools. There are some general principles that should inform any approach to leadership. These are contingency, moral and educational considerations. We see these as considerations rather than theories of leadership in their own right.

Following these considerations we identify theories for particular levels of activity in schools. Thus transformational and transactional leadership cover the whole organisation whilst participative or collegial leadership cover the consensual aspects of internal working and political approaches cover conflict. Finally, instructional leadership deals with influence on teaching staff in classrooms and students (see Table 2.3).

Importance of a contingency dimension

Bryman (1992) points out that implicitly New Leadership including transformational leadership represents a retreat to the 'One Best Way' approach to

Table 2.3 Composite model of leadership in schools

Increasing specificity of action	General principles	Contingency principle	
		Moral leadership	Educative leadership
		Leading professional	
	Organisational level	Transformational leadership	Transactional leadership
	Internal working	Participative/ collegial leadership	Managerial/ political leadership
	Influencing classroom teaching	Instructional leadership	

management. He points out that contingency theory came in as a reaction to this. Further he points out that although the particular formulations of contingency theory that have been developed lacked appeal, the principle was never rejected and indeed the rejection of 'One Best Way' received broad support. Interestingly, Roberts and Bradley's (1988) study of a charismatic US school superintendent who became a commissioner but was unable to continue to function charismatically offers some evidence for the situational nature of leadership.

We believe that appropriate forms of leadership depend on the external context and the internal situation in a school. What is appropriate leadership for highly centralised bureaucratic school systems will not be appropriate for self-managing, market based schools. Equally, conditions inside a school will affect the choice of leadership approach. A school in crisis with poor student results and lack of parental confidence will require different leadership from one which is highly successful and has a highly competent and motivated staff.

Thus contingency implies making a choice from the lower level alternative theories in our hierarchy.

Moral and educational dimensions

Schools are organisations and in the UK school leadership means the leadership of the whole organisation including finance and staffing. Increasingly schools have become more like other organisations in the range of management functions which need to be discharged. They are, however, distinctive in a number of ways:

- Educational mission
- Moral nature of the enterprise
- Preparation for a democratic society
- Immature clients
- Professional workforce.

We take this to mean that

1 leaders should have educational principles and knowledge to lead an educational enterprise
2 there will be special considerations required for the moral education of the young and their preparation for a place in a democratic society which impose additional constraints.

These have implications for the 'what' of leadership and the 'how' of leadership which are different from most other organisations. Thus the unique features of schools are captured in the moral nature of the enterprise and their professional educational technology (in the organisational not technical sense). These need to pervade applications of transformational or other forms of leadership which are not specific to schools.

We have offered two alternative formulations of these dimensions. First there is educative leadership (Duignan and Macpherson 1992, 1993). This project took two important questions:

How should leaders in education decide what is important?

How will they know that they are morally right, when they act?

These subsume the educational and moral elements of leadership in schools.

An alternative is the work on moral leadership (Sergiovanni 1991; Bottery 1992; Hodgkinson 1991; Begley 1996) and the work on leading professionals (Hughes 1985). Moral leadership implies the need for moral principles and ethical conduct. However, this does not provide any easy prescriptions in terms of what to do in particular circumstances since it is the challenges when principles clash which require leadership: 'values constitute the essential problem of leadership … If there are no value conflicts then there is no need for leadership' (Hodgkinson 1991: 11). Thus there are some principles which will permeate all other leadership practices.

Hughes (1985) offers the following distinction between the leading professional and the chief executive roles in terms of discharging educational functions. The leading professional educator acts outside the school as the spokesperson for the school in educational matters and is involved in external professional educational activity. Inside the school the leading professional educator works with teachers to design the curriculum and ensure a high standard of teaching. He or she may engage in personal teaching and counsel pupils and parents on educational matters.

The chief executive on the other hand reports to the governing body and the LEA on the performance of the school and internally manages organisational functions such as staffing and finance. The headteacher, of course, operates in both roles.

Organisational level

The styles and functions of leadership will have much more in common with other organisations. Thus the appearance of transformational and transactional leadership at the level of the whole organisation as in other organisations. Transformational and transactional leadership together seem to offer suitable theories when they are informed by contingency, moral and educational considerations.

It should be noted that charisma is a key component in the leadership of change and improvement. Little has been heard of this in education perhaps because of its possible reminders of the 'Great Men and Women' of educational history. However, the modern version of charisma does not only depend upon personal attributes but it does require as a starting point some particular personal qualities. Some of these valuable skills can be developed and certain situations make it easier to be recognised as a charismatic leader. In other situations leaders may 'stage-manage' occasions where the attribution will be more likely to be made.

In a business context Bryman (1992) identifies the following as being likely to lead to the attribution of charisma by followers:

- Previous successes
- Personal talents
- Persuasive skills
- Unconventional behaviour
- Shared values.

All of these factors could apply to an educational context. This is intended as advice for would-be charismatic leaders and also a warning to followers.

Internal working

At the level of organisational working and decision-making there are two facets. For professional staff and to a lesser extent for other staff there are considerations of a participative or collegial style of involvement in some form or alternatively a more managerial or political mode of working.

Here we offer two alternate approaches. First, there is the participative and collegial approach for situations where consensus is the predominant decision-making style but we also offer political leadership for conditions where contestation and conflict are more prevalent.

Classroom teaching

At the level of influencing classroom teaching we offer instructional leadership (Bossert *et al.* 1982; Firestone and Wilson 1985; Fidler 1997; Southworth 2002) as a set of activities which can provide a mechanism for having impact on teachers and their teaching.

Part II

Learning and playing the game

Current headship practice

3 Learning about the job of headship and its contemporary demands

Introduction

This chapter and the next four deal with the route to headship. It begins with understanding and insights from a number of sources on leadership knowledge and how it is used and acquired. Professional knowledge is more than a series of facts and thus some understanding of its nature is necessary to appreciate why it is so difficult to acquire. Since the knowledge that is acquired depends upon individual perception and the nature of existing knowledge this will be different for each individual. This is the constructivist view of learning. To provide more systematic ways of viewing organisational events, we present four theoretical frameworks.

Professionals build on their knowledge acquired in training throughout their professional careers. Teachers first learn about teaching and as their career progresses they begin to learn about leadership and management. Much of this is subconscious and intuitive. However, there is a price to be paid for the lack of conscious thought. Learning may not be as effective as it might be and the knowledge base may be biased. Thus it is important for leaders and intending leaders to be reflective in a more explicit way. This section aims to provide information to enable readers to do this. One of our principal findings is that prospective headteachers need to learn about leadership throughout their career and not assume that this is acquired by a course before headship.

The chapter then examines the analyses which have been carried out into the job of headship and the different ways in which these have been viewed. This leads on to an examination of the skills and personal characteristics which appear to be associated with success as a headteacher.

To complement this formal analysis the following section begins to develop a picture of contemporary headship which comes closer to the job as practitioners experience it. This is developed further in the following two chapters. These are illustrated by many examples from schools of contemporary practice.

In succeeding chapters contemporary demands are examined in more detail and the process of headteachers' selection is studied. Chapter 7 then returns to preparation for senior leadership by considering career paths to headship and the opportunities to engage in the types of learning which are discussed in this chapter.

An overview of action, knowledge and learning in educational leadership and management

The purpose of this brief overview of how personal knowledge is used to guide actions is to highlight the importance of knowledge frameworks. When their significance is appreciated this focuses attention on how new knowledge is learned and added to the framework and how information is retrieved.

Knowledge is used to make decisions and to plan action. The decisions may be personal and intuitive or formal and shared but they have the same intention of affecting actions. Thus the quality of decisions and ultimately actions will depend upon the availability and use of appropriate knowledge.

Decision-making and action

Most routine actions do not require conscious thought. This is the case whether the actions are trivial or habitual and complex. For example, changing gear whilst driving or helping a child with a typical learning difficulty. This prevents overload of the conscious but the disadvantage is that we are not aware of how we think about these actions. This means that a further difficulty is how we can discuss them with other people. This has implications for how we learn how to carry out tasks, a point to which we shall return later.

Novel situations are different. Either the novelty is not recognised and habit operates until something goes wrong or there is a need for conscious thought. If there is sufficient time to react there may be conscious thought but more likely the following happens in the subconscious. We search our memory for events like this from the past so that we use this knowledge to plan action in the new situation.

A number of issues arise from such a sequence of mental events:

- How is the current situation perceived?
- How is past experience stored in memory?
- How is a plan of action formulated?

There are only partial answers to each of these questions; however, there are areas of scholarship which throw some light on each of them. In particular the value of theoretical frameworks for analysing situations and for influencing the storing of experience in memory should become clearer.

How is the current situation perceived?

Any situation is so complex that we have to simplify it in order to try to comprehend and interpret it. Again this simplification is not usually conscious. This raises the issue – how do we simplify? There are a number of clues. We use past experience to choose certain aspects to focus on, we notice differences from our expectations (based on past experience and perhaps our personal values) and aspects that almost literally catch our eye because they are extreme in some way. So it is almost certainly not usually a systematic appraisal and it may be under only partially conscious control.

There are two further areas of note:

- *Initial appraisals are crucial*
  We appear to appraise situations by a process of accretion. We take in some details and make sense of these before we are in a position to recognise what further information we need. When decision-making in preparation for action is rapid (as most interactions with people are), we may not have this further opportunity before we have to react. So the first appraisal has to capture the essence of the situation before we add more detail (if there is time).

  What are taken by an individual as the key facets of a situation are likely to be influenced by what we regard as important and right. They will also be influenced by how we feel about a situation. If we are unhappy about what we find the cues to action might be quite different from if we are satisfied with the state of affairs. Indeed such differences may be the initial cues that prioritise the search through past experience.

- *Reliance on mental schema*
  For most complex actions we do not think through a long causal chain connecting action and effect. From our past experience we have developed mental shortcuts or schema which connect in our mind a particular action with its likely result. These may cover relatively simple actions like reprimanding a child for being late to a lesson or really complex processes such as formulating a plan for improving a whole school. It is likely that we pay particular attention to what we regard as the critical elements in our mental schema.

How is past experience stored in memory?

There are two aspects to this question. The first concerns the process by which knowledge of all kinds including that acquired from experience is perceived and abstracted prior to storage. The second concerns how it is stored in memory.

We deal first with knowledge acquisition. *Propositional knowledge*, or that which is written down in books and publicly accessible, is personalised as we acquire it. We understand it in our own terms and this is crucially dependent on our current state of knowledge. We add this new knowledge to our current store. Similar processes must go on for *process knowledge* – the 'how to do' type of knowledge. This is more complex knowledge and must be personal. It is acquired personally by experience although it may be informed by propositional knowledge and discussion with others. We also acquire personal knowledge from others. However, this knowledge has more in common with public knowledge since it has to be passed on by others and only that which can be communicated in some way can be transmitted.

A basic problem with process knowledge, the practical knowledge about how to carry out some action, is that it is largely tacit. In other words we are not conscious that we have the knowledge or what it is. And indeed we are only able to demonstrate that we have the knowledge by our ability to perform the task, e.g. teaching a lesson or dealing with a difficult member of staff. This poses difficulties in terms of explaining how we acquire and store such knowledge. The process of reflection on experience almost certainly plays a major part in making aspects of this kind of knowledge more explicit. This in its turn raises issues about the process of reflection and what guides this process. Reflection may be both implicit and explicit.

We know little of how knowledge is stored in long-term memory. Clearly there must be some organising structure that influences both the storage and retrieval of information. A number of authors have likened this to storing data in a database on a computer. Whilst this is obviously an over-simplified description of a process which goes on outside conscious control, it may help to appreciate the issues involved.

In computer databases the criteria by which information is classified and stored have to be decided in advance. This requires a great deal of thought and needs to bear in mind how the data will be extracted from the database subsequently. It is very difficult afterwards to change the criteria. All this is involved in storing simple elements of data.

Long-term human memory stores knowledge of all kinds including process knowledge. It stores observations from experience as they happen (although they may be subsequently refined as a result of reflection). It stores whole episodes from the past. Thus storing knowledge in long-term memory is more akin to storing data in a multimedia database that has to evolve as new data and media become available.

We do not know what the organising principles in memory are but concepts appear to be major features. Work in the theory of personal constructs suggests that new knowledge is accreted into frameworks of existing knowledge and that inconsistencies are mentally noted. These are disquieting and start a mental search for ways of resolving them. They may trigger a search for new information which will help understand and resolve them. Occasionally, there is blinding new insight which causes some of the framework to change to better fit developing experience. People speak of 'seeing things differently'. Some process of illumination has occurred which has made connections or changed our mental framework which gives a new and more satisfying account of aspects of the world.

How is a plan of action formulated?

The way in which a decision is made or a plan of action devised does not appear to be under conscious control and does not appear to be an entirely rational process. It appears more intuitive, i.e. a complex set of criteria is used in ways which are not under conscious control. This suggests that very complex processes which subsume all that has been discussed in this section happen very rapidly and a solution emerges. This can then be subjected to rational critical appraisal but the way in which it is built up does not appear to be the logical way in which rational thought is said to operate. When individuals are asked to describe their thought processes as they happen it appears that they reach a decision and use rational thinking to support the decision they have reached rather than describe the actual decision-making process.

The value of theoretical perspectives

In the foregoing account there are a number of occasions where theoretical knowledge might play a part. The ones which we particularly want to highlight are those involved in analysing a situation, retrieving information from memory and predicting the likely consequences of actions. This latter use of theory is the rationale for acquiring and using most theoretical ideas. It is the more specific use of theoretical perspectives for the first two which is the purpose of this section.

For the reasons that we have previously cited, reality is so complex that we need to simplify in order for the task of perception to be manageable. This is particularly true of activity in organisations. Organisational life is simplified by taking particular perspectives or models which capture only certain features and ignore others. Bolman and Deal have proposed four perspectives with which to analyse actions in organisations. These perspectives or paradigms need to be self-consistent and to capture important aspects of organisational action.

> We need more people in managerial roles who can find simplicity and order amid organisational confusion and chaos.
>
> (Bolman and Deal 1997: xii)

Structural

Goals are assumed to be agreed and generally decided by top management on a rational basis. All parts of the organisation are assumed to play their part in goal attainment. Optimum structures and systems can be set up as a result of analysing the tasks to be completed. A bureaucracy is a highly developed structural approach to organisation. However, for organisations with a majority of professional workers a better description is a 'professional bureaucracy' (Mintzberg 1983). This is a structure which is basically hierarchical but has professional workers in managerial positions and a participative mode of operation.

Human relations

The human relations approach is rather like the 'concern for people' in the leadership grid (see Figure 2.1). A human relations approach recognises that organisations exist for human purposes rather than the other way round. It values staff members as individuals and concentrates on motivating and developing them – human resource management. A key idea is the fit between the individual and the organisation – individuals should find their work satisfying and the organisation should benefit from the human talent that is released. This approach focuses on individuals and groups and the behavioural aspects of organisational life.

Cultural

An approach to conceptualising organisations which has increased in popularity is to place great importance on the culture of the organisation or 'the way we do things around here' (Deal and Kennedy 1988). This is the habitual way in which organisation members go about their work and how they give meaning to their work. This generally reflects unacknowledged organisational values.

People need to believe in what they are doing if they are to work hard and with conviction. The organisational culture incorporates the principles and values that are highly regarded in a particular organisation. Practices have been developed over the years which reflect those values and which appear to meet with approval from the outside world. In the case of schools this would be parents and other stakeholders.

Political

The political view of organisations is the least used of the four perspectives and yet in many situations it may be the one to give greatest understanding and lead to the planning of action.

Hoyle (1986) gives the following definition of micropolitics:

> Micropolitics can be said to consist of the strategies by which individuals and groups in organisational contexts seek to use their resources of authority and influence to further their interests.
>
> (Hoyle 1986: 126)

There appears to be a general reluctance to recognise micropolitical effects in schools. Much writing about school leadership assumes consensus among staff and does not consider any dissension. We consider that this denies an important perspective that should be available to heads and potential headteachers to analyse and plan actions in schools.

> We cannot count the number of times managers have told us that they handled a particular problem the 'only way' it could be done. Such statements betray a failure of both imagination and courage.
>
> (Bolman and Deal 1997: 6)

Knowledge of the four perspectives on organisations is intended to be more than abstract propositional knowledge. It is intended to be used on a regular basis so that it becomes habitual. The value of knowing that Bolman and Deal have proposed four perspectives on organisations may be limited, but the value of analysing situations in a systematic way is immense. This involves recognising that there may be alternative perspectives which may give valuable insights into what is going on. This requires knowledge of alternative perspectives from which to choose.

Tacit leadership knowledge

A particular difficulty of acquiring process knowledge is that it is largely tacit.
   Three statements help bring out features of tacit knowledge:

- I don't know what I know until I say it.
- I know more than I know I know.
- I don't know what I know until I see what I do.

   The first statement brings out the difficulty of communicating tacit knowledge (Polanyi 1967). It cannot be readily verbalised and relies on metaphors, analogies, figures and diagrams to try to encapsulate facets of it. It is acquired through experience. The classic example is to try to tell someone how to ride a bicycle.
   The second statement points out that those who possess tacit knowledge are often unaware of the form of the knowledge that they possess and the extent of their knowledge (Spender 1998).
   The third emphasises that the acid test of much tacit knowledge is that its presence is indicated by a capacity to carry out some action or other (Weick 1990).
   Most if not all complex processes rely on tacit knowledge for their performance. Such knowledge is very difficult to track and has to be inferred. It is very difficult to pass on such knowledge in a formal way and yet it is at the heart of professional practice in education and in leadership.

The place of values and emotions

It is possible to discuss knowledge as if it were value free and attitudes to different knowledge were entirely rational. Begley (1996) is one of the few who has integrated a consideration of values into the use of knowledge frameworks. He recognises that individuals will have an attitude to particular aspects of knowledge and this will affect perception in terms of certain knowledge being seen as more desirable than some other.
   Feelings will affect how we analyse situations and how and what we learn from them. Whilst all of us will be affected by affect, some are more affected than others at particular times – to use a pun. This has implications for how we deal with others. Many differences of interpretation do not arise from differences which have an objective basis and which are capable of being clarified and agreed, they arise from different priorities and attitudes. This crucial distinction may often be overlooked in busy practice and will be difficult to deal with if it remains at the implicit level rather than being explicitly analysed.

Categories of management and leadership knowledge and how they are acquired

Eraut (1994) proposes six categories of knowledge which leaders and managers require:

- Knowledge of people
- Situational knowledge
- Knowledge of educational practice
- Conceptual knowledge
- Process knowledge
- Control knowledge.

Knowledge of people

This is important, acquired continuously and often informally. This means that evidence is gathered selectively, accessed in unrepresentative ways and stereotyped. This potential for bias needs to be recognised.

Situational knowledge

This is concerned with how people read situations: what they see as significant features and what they see as susceptible to change. Some of this is conscious and some subconscious. In terms of acquiring knowledge this is affected by perceptual frameworks and sampling bias. A further issue since much knowledge will be reported by others is that it will be filtered. This may involve distortion by the reporter – how it will reflect back on them, and perhaps what they think the leader wants to hear.

The process by which individuals understand the relationship between themselves and the organisation in which they work has been called 'sensemaking' (Weick 1995).

Knowledge of educational practice

This is the leading professional role.

> Thinking about educational practice involves not only situational knowledge, but also personal theories and values; and these in turn are likely to be informed by concepts and ideas from recognized educational theory, even though the thinker may not be aware of the influence.
>
> (Eraut 1994: 79–80)

Conceptual knowledge

Eraut (1994) defines this as 'that set of concepts, theories and ideas that a person has consciously stored in memory' (p. 80). The framework is largely implicit and 'filters and shapes' the acquisition of other knowledge. Because it is not subject to critical scrutiny he considers that this is a cause for concern. He also thinks that concepts discovered on courses are little used because of the 'iceberg' principle. Only when a concept is used does a true understanding develop.

The lack of explicit use of conceptual knowledge may be because of a concentration on action and insufficient explicit focus on personal analysis beforehand and evaluation and reflection afterwards using explicit conceptual frameworks. Training which uses experiential learning may neglect this intermediate stage of analysis. It may be as important to make the use of conceptual frameworks habitual as to make the practice, which experiential learning has tried to create, so.

Process knowledge

Although there may be theoretical knowledge which informs much process knowledge, the particular skills can probably only be learned by doing with feedback.

Control knowledge

This is the cybernetic interpretation of control of oneself – self-awareness, sensitivity and self-knowledge including knowing how to learn and control one's learning, reflection and self-evaluation.

Eraut (1994) discusses the particular value of longer courses. Trust develops, confidence is engendered, difficult problems can be tackled and entrenched attitudes can be surfaced. Such courses also allow more repetition of the application of theoretical and conceptual knowledge. Such repetition may further demonstrate the value of such knowledge and embed it in thinking.

Management learning in practice

Bullock *et al.* (1995b) identified seven opportunities for learning as a result of interviews with 13 recently appointed managers and 13 experienced managers in education. The sources of learning were often the same for the two groups. The most effective examples were often where two or more opportunities reinforced each other. There were two quite different approaches to learning – on the one hand there were those who expected to learn from reflecting on their own experience, whilst on the other there were those who expected to learn off the job, on courses, for example:

- Significant other colleagues
- Courses

- Texts
- Everyday experience
- Delegated responsibilities
- Management experience outside school
- Critical incidents.

Significant other colleagues

This was a very important learning source. It was the most likely source to be cited in a recent survey of leadership (Earley *et al*. 2002). The models could be either positive or negative and were not necessarily from school colleagues. The positive examples were generally more influential to their thinking than the negative ones. Often the influence was through observation of others at work and reflection on their actions. In some cases the examples were from teachers when the person was a pupil at school. Often it was a particular action and characteristic from an example which made its mark and hence a set of ideas about good practice was pieced together from many previous examples.

Courses

Courses provided a number of learning opportunities. First, there was the acquisition of new knowledge and ideas. Second, there was an opportunity to acquire a framework to restructure and reorder existing knowledge. Third, it was possible to receive reassurance and gain confidence in personal practice. This came either through theoretical knowledge or research findings about practice. Such reassurance also could come from talking to other course members. Finally, it was this discussion amongst course members which was recognised as an opportunity to learn from others and to hear about practice in other schools.

Texts

Texts of all kinds but particularly books were used by some of the respondents more than others. Those who found them valuable had been able to connect theoretical ideas in the reading to experience in schools. What were regarded as valuable texts was a very individual choice.

Everyday experience

Learning from everyday experience was regarded as important but few respondents could identify in precise terms what they had acquired. They were likely to express a view that indicated that observations accreted in their minds only in incidental ways unless there was a critical incident (see below) which highlighted the learning. Parallels were generally recognised between a teacher managing their class and teaching and the school manager managing other staff.

Delegated responsibilities (temporary)

This covers individuals who substitute or act in a position for a while to cover absence and also those who take on temporary tasks or take on tasks temporarily. As we point out later, when considering the value of acting headship, often such learning opportunities had come along accidentally in the sense that temporary arrangements had to be made to cover absence or illness rather than for personal development.

Management experience outside school

There are a range of opportunities for management learning outside schools. There are those who have had a previous career outside education who bring in experience from commercial organisations. They may have been managers or have been managed and they may bring either positive or negative experiences. In addition many teachers also play a part in voluntary organisations and may play a leading role in some or experience leadership by others. Both these experiences can be formative and may have much in common with life in schools particularly in dealing with the increasing number of volunteers who work in schools as parental helpers or industrial mentors.

A number of women identified learning from running a home and educating their own children.

Critical incidents

Critical incidents could arise from any of the previous opportunities but their distinguishing feature is that in retrospect they stand out as turning points in some way. They may be positive in the sense that at a point in time some incident was the catalyst which led to understanding or a feeling of confidence that a skill had been mastered. In some cases a negative experience, including the humiliation of an unsuccessful job interview, may cause a dawning revelation that preparation for management needs to be a more explicit learning process rather than to have served in the right posts and having practice to report.

The job of the headteacher

There have been a number of attempts to examine the job of a headteacher and the skills and abilities needed to be successful. There have also been similar examinations of managers outside education. Each of these offers some insights into the general work of a headteacher.

The types of study have covered:

- Roles played by managers and leaders
- Functions of senior managers and headteachers
- Competences, skills and personal characteristics needed to carry out the functions and roles.

Roles

An early look at the job roles of business executives suggested that the following were important (Mintzberg 1973):

- Interpersonal roles
  - Figurehead
  - Leader
  - Liaison
- Informational roles
  - Monitor
  - Disseminator
  - Spokesperson
- Decisional roles
  - Entrepreneur
  - Disturbance handler
  - Resource allocator
  - Negotiator.

Functions

A conceptual analysis of the job of the chief executive in business identified three types of task (Katz 1974):

- Technical (relating to the particular industry, e.g. educating children)
- Conceptual (general tasks involved in managing any organisation, e.g. planning, organising, staffing, leading, controlling, resourcing, evaluating)
- Human relations (all aspects of managing people).

This was adapted by Morgan *et al.* (1983) to provide an overview of the tasks of a secondary headteacher (see Tables 3.1–3.3). Although it wasn't intended for

Table 3.1 Headteacher technical functions (adapted from Morgan *et al.* 1983: 14–15)

Tasks	Examples
Goal identification	Identifying and determining in concert with all interested parties, overall school aims and objectives.
Academic curriculum	Determining a curriculum relevant to the academic abilities and needs of all pupils, allocating curricular responsibilities to departments and staff members to provide teaching, and grouping pupils for learning.
Pastoral curriculum	Determining a policy and organisation for pupils' pastoral care.
Ethos and culture	Determining the school rituals and norms of behaviour and discipline for pupils and staff.
Resources	Selection and appointment of staff, allocation of capitation allowances, determination of posts of responsibility and control of school funds and budget generally.

Table 3.2 Headteacher conceptual and operational functions of management (adapted from Morgan *et al.* 1983: 14–15)

Tasks	Examples
Planning, organisation, co-ordination and control	Determination of the rules, responsibilities and mechanisms for all internal school policy-making and management control, including the delegated responsibilities of the senior management team. Planning school development. Externally co-ordinating the school's provision with feeder schools and the needs of FE and HE colleges.
Resourcing	Ensuring adequate resources by maximising formula funding income, entrepreneurial activities and special purpose grants.
Staff deployment	Defining staff tasks and writing job descriptions.
Evaluation and record-keeping	Evaluating effective standards of teaching in the classroom and progress on all aspects of school policy generally by establishing measurement criteria and instruments. Compiling returns, monitoring the keeping of registers and statistical records.
Buildings, grounds and plant	Supervision, security and maintenance of the plant.

Table 3.3 Headteacher leadership and human relations aspects of management (adapted from Morgan *et al.* 1983: 14–15)

Tasks	Examples
Motivation	Motivating staff and pupils by personal influence, incentives, and concern for individual needs, health, safety and working conditions generally.
Staff development	Developing policy and mechanisms for the professional development, work enrichment and technical support of staff.
Interpersonal, group and inter-group conflict resolution	Solving problems and resolving conflict by applying chairmanship, negotiations, arbitration, and reconciliation skills.
Communication	Securing the effective dissemination of school policy, news of activities and events, and effective channels of two-way communication.

primary headships, it is generally thought to provide a useful starting point for them also. Morgan *et al.* found it necessary to add another category because the work of the headteacher involved relationships with the world outside the school so they added 'external management' (see Table 3.4).

Competences

Competences represent an attempt to analyse the skills needed in job performance and to assess whether these are being demonstrated in practice by job holders (Esp 1993). There are two different approaches to management competences:

Table 3.4 Headteacher external accountabilities and external relations aspects of management (adapted from Morgan *et al.* 1983: 14–15)

Tasks	Examples
Accountability to governors, LEA and OFSTED	Reporting to and advising governors' meetings. Preparing policy options for the consent of the governing body and working with the chair to mobilise the support of governors. Working in accordance with LEA policy and establishing mechanisms for curricular and other technical advice from LEA officers and advisers. Preparing for OFSTED inspections and any actions necessary afterwards.
Parents and the general community	Determining a policy to achieve the support and involvement of parents in the running of the school. Presenting news of the school to the local community and gauging community expectations for the school. Promoting the school and attracting pupil enrolments.
Employers and external agencies	Establishing communications with employers and employment opportunities; and linking the school with supporting external agencies.

- modelling superior performers (Boyatzsis 1982)
- skills needed to do the tasks within the job.

The superior performance approach identified superior performers, generally by receiving recommendations from superiors, and, on a battery of personality tests, identified those items which discriminated between superior and lesser performers. The assumption was that the tests identified characteristics which would help select and target the development of future superior performers. Whilst this approach was first used in the commercial sector by Hay-McBer, it was then taken up by the National Association of Secondary School Principals (NASSP) in the USA. They used this methodology to identify the characteristics of superior principals. Tests to discover these superior performers were then devised. This set of competences was adapted for use in England by the National Educational Assessment Centre at Oxford Brookes University.

These were:

Administrative competences
1 Problem analysis: ability to seek out relevant data and analyse information to determine the important elements of a problem situation; searching for information with a purpose.
2 Judgement: ability to reach logical conclusions and make high quality decisions based on available information; skill in identifying educational needs and setting priorities; ability to evaluate critically written communications.

3 Organisational ability: ability to plan, schedule and control the work of others; skill in using resources in an optimal fashion; ability to deal with a volume of paperwork and heavy demands on one's time.

4 Decisiveness: ability to recognise when a decision is required (disregarding the quality of the decision) and to act quickly.

Interpersonal competences

5 Leadership: ability to get others involved in solving problems; ability to recognise when a group requires direction, to interact with a group effectively and to guide them to the accomplishment of the task.

6 Sensitivity: ability to perceive the needs, concerns and personal problems of others; skill in resolving conflicts; tact in dealing with persons from different backgrounds; ability to deal effectively with people concerning emotional issues; knowing what information to communicate and to whom.

7 Stress tolerance: ability to perform under pressure and during opposition; the ability to think on one's feet.

Communicative competences

8 Oral communication: ability to make clear oral presentation of facts and ideas.

9 Written communication: ability to express ideas clearly in writing; to write appropriately for different audiences – students, teachers, parents, etc.

Personal breadth competences

10 Range of interest: ability to discuss a variety of subjects – educational, political, current events, economic, etc.; desire to actively take part in events.

11 Personal motivation: need to achieve in all activities attempted; evidence that work is important to personal satisfaction; ability to be self-evaluating.

12 Educational values: possession of a well-reasoned educational philosophy; receptiveness to new ideas and change.

(Esp 1993: 45–6)

An alternative to the identification of the characteristics of superior performers is to work from a functional analysis of the tasks to be done as part of the job and to identify the skills needed to be able to do them. This methodology was used by Jirasinghe and Lyons (1995, 1996) at the University of East London in the early 1990s. They carried out an extensive job analysis of the headteacher's work following the Education Reform Act in England and from this generated and validated management competences needed to carry out these tasks. Although their derivation involved a job analysis these competences were personal and transferable competences of individuals.

The first stage was an analysis of the tasks of headship (see Table 3.5).

The skills and attributes are formulated in the areas listed in Table 3.6. Their levels are compared with those of the general population. The ones in brackets

Table 3.5 A sample of the key job tasks obtained (Jirasinghe and Lyons 1996: 70)

Rank order	Task category	Overarching task areas from which response is drawn	Specific tasks	N = 99*
1	Planning	Managing tasks	Planning long-term objectives	(97)
			Setting up financial budget	(90)
			Planning short-term objectives	(97)
2	Motivating	Managing people	Creating a good team spirit	(87)
			Encouraging cooperation	(85)
			Gaining willing cooperation	(87)
3	Assisting/caring	Managing people	Looking after needs of children	(53)
			Looking after emotional needs	(46)
			Assisting in learning difficulty	(34)
4	Appraising Evaluating Developing people	Managing people	Assessing needs of people	(52)
			Creating confidence	(65)
			Appraising for promotion/ recruitment	(68)
5	Implementing Co-ordinating	Managing tasks	Organising resources	(55)
			Ensuring efficient coordination	(55)
			Allocating resources	(56)
6	Deciding	Working with information	Deciding action – with others	(58)
			Making decisions after evaluation	(58)
			Decisions affecting welfare, etc.	(58)
7	Controlling Directing	Managing tasks	Controlling people resources	(44)
			Directing implementation of policy	(38)
			Ensuring agreements are adhered to	(40)
8	PR/Developing relationships	Communicating	Getting on well – team/unit	(51)
			Maintaining good PR	(57)
			Establishing network of contacts	(48)
9	Counselling	Managing people	Advising on improving job performance	(49)
			Counselling on personal problems	(47)
			Advising on interpersonal behaviour	(44)
10	Influencing Advising	Communicating	Advising governors	(47)
			Making a spoken case for action	(49)
			Arguing a case in formal meetings	(48)
11	Learning Researching	Working with information	Keeping abreast of developments	(40)
			Learning new systems/methods, etc.	(38)
			Undertaking informal training	(39)
12	Assessing Evaluating	Working with information	Evaluating output of the system	(13)
			Making a logical evaluation	(39)
			Evaluating alternatives	(34)

Note:
* Number of raters per specific task is displayed in brackets.

Table 3.6 Skills and attributes of headteachers (adapted from Jirasinghe and Lyons 1996: 57–8)

Relationships with people

Persuasive	Enjoys selling, changes opinions of others, convincing with arguments, negotiates
Controlling	Takes charge, directs, manages, organizes, supervises others
Independent	Has strong views on things, difficult to manage, speaks up, argues, dislikes ties
Outgoing	Fun loving, humorous, sociable, vibrant, talkative, jovial
Affiliative	Has many friends, enjoys being in groups, likes companionship, shares things with friends
Socially confident	Puts people at ease, knows what to say, good with words
(Modest)	Reserved about achievements, avoids talking about self, accepts others, avoids trappings of status
Democratic	Encourages others to contribute, consults, listens and refers to others
Caring	Considerate to others, helps those in need, sympathetic, tolerant

Thinking styles

(Practical)	Down-to-earth, likes repairing and mending things, better with the concrete
Data rational	Good with data, operates on facts, enjoys assessing and measuring
Artistic	Appreciates culture, shows artistic flair, sensitive to visual arts and music
Behavioural	Analyses thoughts and behaviour, psychologically minded, likes to understand people
(Traditional)	Preserves well-proven methods, prefers the orthodox, disciplined, conventional
Change oriented	Enjoys doing new things, seeks variety, prefers novelty to routine
Conceptual	Theoretical, intellectually curious, enjoys the complex and abstract
Innovative	Generates ideas, shows ingenuity, thinks up solutions
Forward-planning	Prepares well in advance, enjoys target-setting, forecasts trends, plans projects
(Detail conscious)	Methodical, keeps things neat and tidy, precise, accurate
(Conscientious)	Sticks to deadlines, completes jobs, perseveres with routine, likes fixed schedules

Feelings and emotions

(Relaxed)	Calm, relaxed, cool under pressure, free from anxiety, can switch off
Worrying	Worry when things go wrong, keyed-up before important events, anxious to do well
(Tough minded)	Difficult to hurt or upset, can brush off insults, unaffected by unfair remarks

continued…

Table 3.6 continued

Relationships with people	
Emotional control	Restrained in showing emotions, keeps feelings back, avoids outbursts
Optimistic	Cheerful, happy, keeps spirits up despite setbacks
(Critical)	Good at probing the facts, sees the disadvantages, challenges assumptions
Active	Has energy, moves quickly, enjoys physical exercise, doesn't sit still
Competitive	Plays to win, determined to beat others, poor loser
Achieving	Ambitious, sets sights high, career centred, results orientated
Decisive	Quick at conclusions, weighs things up rapidly, may be hasty, takes risks
(Social desirability response)	Has tended to respond in a socially desirable way

are lower to some degree than the general population and the remainder are higher to some degree.

The Management Charter Initiative (MCI) (1995) devised competences for different groups of managers. This approach used functional analysis but assessed job-related skills by assessing job performance and added personal competences. Their competences for senior managers, which include strategic competences, are in four main groups:

1 Understanding and influencing the environment
    External trends
    Internal strengths and weaknesses
    Stakeholders
2 Setting the strategy and gaining commitment
3 Planning, implementing and monitoring
    Programmes, projects and plans
    Delegation and action
    Culture
    Monitoring
4 Evaluating and improving performance.
  The personal competences needed are:

- judgement
- self-confidence
- strategic perspective
- achievement focus
- communication
- information searching
- building teams
- influencing others.

Finally, in the mid-1990s the Teacher Training Agency in England produced standards for headteachers. These have been taken on by the National College for School Leadership in England. They were created to guide the development of the National Professional Qualification for Headship (NPQH). These are formulated in terms of

- core purpose of headship – to provide professional leadership for a school which secures its success and improvement, ensuring high quality education for all its pupils and improved standards of learning and achievement
- key outcomes for schools, pupils, teachers, parents and governors
- professional knowledge and understanding required of 16 specified areas
- skills and attributes –
  - leadership – the ability to lead and manage people to work towards common goals
  - decision-making skills – the ability to investigate, solve problems and make decisions
  - communication skills – the ability to make points clearly and understand the views of others
  - self-management skills – the ability to plan time effectively and to organise oneself
  - and 8 specified attributes
- key areas of headship – strategic direction and development of the school, teaching and learning, leading and managing staff, efficient and effective deployment of staff and resources, accountability. Full details are given at website: http://www.ncsl.org.uk/mediastore/htstandards.pdf.

Understanding the demands of contemporary headship

The formal analysis above resulted from research or discussion that was carried out some time ago. It is useful for many purposes but it doesn't really capture contemporary experience of headship. In this section and the two following chapters we try to convey a more impressionistic view that captures current realities as experienced by the headteachers we have spoken to.

When we first started researching this subject, it was because there seemed to be so many examples of headteachers giving up. It felt like there was a mass exodus because the job had become impossible to do successfully. Was it true? And if so, why? On further investigation we were relieved to find that the vast majority of heads are, generally, enjoying running their schools and taking pleasure in the same things that have always attracted people into teaching and then into education leadership. However, there is no doubt that headship today is extremely demanding; these demands do deter some potential heads from taking that step and some heads find the demands greater than they are able, or wish, to manage.

Our aim in writing this book is not to deter anyone from becoming a headteacher but to enable them to be as prepared as possible to succeed in the role. For every story we were told of difficulties, problems and failures there are hundreds of successes. We hope these accounts of problems will be thought-provoking and provide a handbook of experiences to help aspiring and incumbent heads deal effectively with whatever scenario presents itself to them.

A snapshot of advertisements for secondary heads

Although there is no doubt that many headteachers do decide to leave prematurely for all sorts of reasons which will be explored throughout this book, it is important not to paint too negative a picture: statistics suggest a turnover annually of one in seven, thus indicating an average tenure of seven years. This gives a very healthy impression but of course describing the average gives an impression of smoothness that is not a reality. For every head retiring after twenty years in post there must be three who leave in under the average time. On 22 February 2002 the *Times Educational Supplement* advertised eighteen secondary headships in England. These can be divided into clear groups:

- five where the head is retiring and being celebrated:
    - *Porthcawl: following the retirement of ... after 27 years of dedicated service, 14 of which have been as Headteacher.*
    - *Stafford: after 24 years of highly successful and committed leadership ... is retiring.*
    - *Colne: to replace the current Headteacher who is retiring after 15 years of excellent service to the school.*
    - *Haywards Heath: seeking to appoint a successor to ... who retires after 14 years of valued leadership.*
    - *Chesterfield: due to the retirement of the present head, whose strong leadership has created an environment in which staff and pupils thrive.*
- four where the head is retiring but the emphasis is on the appointment of the new head:
    - *Worcester: the retirement of the current head gives an opportunity ...*
    - *Sheffield: due to the retirement of the present headteacher ...*
    - *Wigan: the post of headteacher which becomes available on the retirement of the current head.*
    - *Keighley: the vacancy arises from the retirement of the current headteacher.*
- two whose heads are moving to prestigious new roles:
    - *Chester-le-Street: this vacancy has arisen due to the appointment of the Head-teacher as Principal of the first City Academy.*
    - *Norwich: to succeed ... who is moving to lead the first Business Academy of its kind in Europe.*
- three who make no comment about the current head
- two brand new schools
- one readvertisement with instructions to visit their website for details of the job, and
- one which leads with *We need more than a Superhead!*

It is very clear from the first five that length of time in post and the approach of retirement did not end in less successful headship and relationships. These do not sound like disillusioned people (either the heads or the governors). In the next group the wording could reflect more the style of whoever devised the advertisement than any comment on the success of the head, especially as all the schools in this group also seem to be successful, growing and popular. We cannot know whether the retirements are at full term. Four of the advertisements involve brand new posts – two moving to them and two seeking applicants. The only ones that immediately create questions in the reader's mind are the last two: why was the readvertisement not telling us anything about the school, and how could anyone be more than a superhead? This may have been an entirely atypical week's advertisements but it gives a picture of half of the heads completing a full and successful career, others potentially moving on to further success, other schools offering a new challenge and few where there might be questions about the success of the current or most recent incumbent.

Do governors have unrealistic expectations of their new headteacher when they advertise for 'an outstanding leader with exceptional creative talent' (Chester-le-Street) or 'a person of outstanding ability, enthusiasm and energy' (Norwich)? There seems to have been a change in emphasis since the time when most advertisements suggested that only superheroes would come near the person specification for the school's new head. Recognising perhaps that there are fewer applicants for headships, and that these will be choosing their school as much as the school will be choosing them, the priority in almost all the advertised headships is to market the school.

This was a useful week to choose as an example because decisions were being made at that point with effect from September. Interviews in early April work well because they give the successful candidate a full term to be involved in decisions for the following academic year. An added advantage is in the event of the governors not finding a suitable candidate, in which case they have time to readvertise and set up a second set of interviews before the resignation deadline and/or time to organise suitable interim arrangements if they do not appoint for September.

There has been a lot written about the extent to which delegating more authority to school level and increasing accountability have combined to transform the job of headteacher. From being the leading professional and therefore literally the head teacher, the role has more recently been described as being more akin to that of chief executive and the element related to teaching has become a comparatively small part of the job. A listing of some of the requirements of the job illustrates this and is further explored in the earlier section looking at the skills and attributes desirable in a headteacher. More important to this chapter is the demanding totality of running a school at the beginning of the twenty-first century.

So how has the role of headteacher changed in the last decade or so? As seen above, in chapter 1, the world of primary and secondary state funded education following the Education Reform Act in 1988 has been subjected to more changes than at any other period since compulsory education was introduced in 1870. Other Education Acts had extended the scope of education (to girls as well as boys, to age 14, 15 and then 16, academic, technical and vocational) but this was the first time that the whole curriculum was defined. This was quickly followed by financial delegation to schools. A new, regular and rigorous inspection structure was put in place to monitor and evaluate schools' success in implementing these changes. Now the government's stated intention to 'drive up standards' through performance management and hard-edged measurable targets for everyone in the system has added a further layer to the headteacher's role. To lead schools through all these changes requires headteachers to become more skilful across a wider range of areas than before and has seen the emphasis and perspective change as people have tried to adapt themselves and their expectations to this ever evolving role.

'Surely everyone knows why headteachers quit?'

This was the usual reaction to our question, whether the response was coming from a serving or ex-headteacher, an LEA or independent adviser, or almost any manager in a school. They would continue with a selection from the following list:

- initiatives to be implemented
- pressure for continued improvement in performance (staff and pupils)
- OFSTED inspections
- recruitment (staff and pupils)
- LEA
- governors
- leadership team (especially deputy heads)
- managing staffing changes
- pupils
- budgeting
- site management
- time and day-to-day management
- ICT.

It seems that any combination of these could be the reason for a headteacher deciding to leave. However, none of them is in itself a negative – they are all value free – and are in fact a list of the different areas comprising the totality of the contemporary head's job. It seems that managing them all without letting any become too prominent or any be lost from sight measures the skills of a successful head. Getting them out of proportion or perspective is likely to trigger problems. We therefore take a look at each one of these areas and explore potential difficulties and, where possible, look at preventive action or solutions.

In exploring further the demanding nature of headship today, it is useful to divide the issues into those which are driven by external decisions or events – new initiatives, pupil performance, inspections and recruitment of staff and pupils – and those which depend more on individual responses within schools – working with the different groups of people that make up the school community and managing the material resources particular to that school.

The next two chapters, therefore, explore separately the external demands and the internal demands of contemporary headship.

4 Understanding the external demands

Initiatives to be implemented

Initiative overload turned out to be a frequent explanation for poor performance in our earlier exploration of poorly performing staff in schools (Fidler and Atton 1999). Although mainly affecting teaching staff, the knock-on effect was also visible in support staff. How much more is it likely to be an issue for headteachers?

Role of classroom teacher in implementing new initiatives:

- acquire relevant skills
- integrate into current planning, etc.
- deliver
- assess
- evaluate impact and adjust planning accordingly
- restart cycle.

Role of headteacher in implementing new initiatives:

- be aware of initiatives being discussed
- acquire relevant information
- plan implementation and resources
- ensure staff acquire relevant skills
- monitor delivery and assessment
- evaluate impact and adjust whole-school planning accordingly
- ensure new staff receive appropriate training
- show enthusiasm for the initiative and positively support staff through it.

For classroom teachers who had seemed to be working satisfactorily using materials and planning they had developed over a long period, it was very destabilising to be required suddenly to deliver a new curriculum. It was even more difficult to have to learn new ways of teaching and, more demanding still, new ways of assessing what pupils had learnt. All this is equally true of a headteacher but across a wider spectrum. The leader has to assimilate at least the rationale and likely requirements of any new initiative. Having done this she then has to convince everybody else that they can implement it successfully. Responding to the constant expectation of enthusiastic leadership in the face of resistance and, possibly, cynicism is probably the most debilitating aspect of all this for a head. This is especially difficult when the head too is unconvinced of the value of a change imposed upon them, but they cannot afford to risk not moving accordingly. In a small school the head will have had to work through both sides of implementing whatever change it is.

There are cases where heads have not realised that they needed to keep alert and aware of changes, as illustrated in the following case study.

> The head of a small semi-rural comprehensive in the south midlands had been very satisfied with the outcome of the school's first OFSTED inspection in 1994. The inspectors, focusing on teaching and learning, as was usual for the first round of inspections, found all the teaching to be at least satisfactory. They were also complimentary about pupils' behaviour and relationships between staff and pupils. The points they made for action were mainly about developing schemes of work, policies and complying with the law regarding collective worship. As the head said at the time, hardly any school complied with that law and if the teaching and behaviour were all right, schemes of work and policies weren't really very important. He was proud of his stable staff, how well they knew the children and the happy atmosphere in the school.
>
> Four years later the school was deemed to have serious weaknesses and the quality of leadership and management unsatisfactory. The head was devastated. 'I can't understand it – they liked us last time and we're doing everything just the same now as we were then!'
>
> He had unwittingly pinpointed the problem exactly – what was accepted in the early 1990s was not at all the same as that expected by the end of the decade. Far from suffering from innovation fatigue, this head had failed to keep aware of likely changes. He had not been able to make active decisions about when and how to implement compulsory changes and had probably not been aware of voluntary initiatives (such as specialist school status) that might enhance the school's provision for its pupils and staff.
>
> Other factors including an equally unworldly and long serving board of governors and virtually no staff turnover had contributed to the school existing in a time warp that led to the head's resignation and a disappointing end to a seemingly successful career.

Issues of governors' training, LEA involvement and support for headteachers are all apparent in this small case study and are explored in more depth elsewhere.

The possibility of initiative overload was acknowledged by the government early in 2000, just before the introduction of performance management. At this point heads aged 55 or more who felt they were not going to be able to keep up with the next round of changes were invited to apply for early retirement. This was also a response to part of the problem caused by the decision to stop early retirement being readily available from age 55. When this latter change came into force in September 1997 there was a sudden rise in early retirements of teachers at all levels (as illustrated in chapter 6). Those who were not able to take that option and those reaching 55 in the next couple of years had therefore to revise their plans in terms of when their career would end. The extra five years would probably prove too long for anyone who had been contemplating completing a specific year, or project, etc., and then retiring. Furthermore a larger number than ever of teachers and headteachers were going on long-term sick leave and this extra option, however limited in its scope, would allow a substantial group to move out with dignity before their schools began to suffer from a lack of proactive leadership.

> Taking early retirement is not always a negative reaction: one head with over two years to go before his sixtieth birthday had just led his school through a second successful OFSTED inspection. After the inspection he decided to resign. In his case it was so that he could be sure of leaving with a feeling of having completed the job he set out to do. He also wanted a new head to take the school into its next stage of development without a period of treading water whilst he finished his time. He was fortunate that his personal financial position allowed him to do that and also that currently there are many opportunities for interesting paid employment for retired heads. As it turned out he was immediately sought out by the LEA to act as a mentor to new heads in difficult schools in the authority.

The following is a complete case study to illustrate the cumulative effect as a head gradually loses touch with the current needs of the role. The situation here was exacerbated because the governors at the time of Jim's appointment focused almost entirely on the skills associated with one aspect of the job.

> Jim had been head teacher for 12 years. He was appointed in 1987 and had been acting head twice before in his previous school, which was another local comprehensive. Jim believed he was appointed because he had skills that were required by the school at the time. He was an academic historian with interests in architecture and was very experienced as an acting head.
> Like many schools that had been founded generations ago, the school he moved to had started life in a historic mansion and the modern school had been gradually built around it. Unlike many similar establishments, the mansion had been allowed to fall into disrepair, but the governors and the LEA had plans for restoring the old building and moving some part of

the school back into it. Jim seemed to be the ideal person to lead them through this project.

He had never sought promotion: he had always thoroughly enjoyed teaching and only became a head of department when people persuaded him. Similarly he had been persuaded to apply for deputy headship and headship. He thought his skills and interests were just right for this particular school and really enjoyed the first few years of headship. Nineteen eighty-eight was the beginning of big changes to the role of headteacher. Jim did not enjoy what he perceived as the business marketing approach leading to competition between schools. He found that he did not have the skills to market the school in the way it seemed to be necessary. He was also tired of planning to use the mansion and telling prospective parents that the school would be moving back into it, then finding that the LEA would not finance the move. He felt he was telling lies to people.

He felt that his enjoyment of teaching, staff development and innovation was paralysed by the National Curriculum. He was frustrated by the endless meetings about the new curriculum coupled with the time wasted on planning to get back into the mansion.

An OFSTED inspection criticised lack of strategic planning. Jim's view was that constantly working on plans to move back into the mansion, followed by disappointment and then a new set of plans led to his losing faith in strategic planning. Jim felt that LEA advisers and the CEO were supportive of him but nervous of the chairman of governors. Jim felt strongly that the skills required of a headteacher in the 1990s were quite different from those required even in the late 1980s. The major thrust of change happened in the year immediately after his appointment. He also felt that the values of those chosen by the government of the time to lead the changes were not those of people who genuinely cared about pupil and staff development.

He had always planned to retire early; he had lots of interests and was already investing ready for this. He was particularly interested in photo-journalism and travelling. The changes about retirement during autumn 1997 made him think carefully about retiring. At the same time there were critical staffing problems at school. He made an appointment that caused uproar among the staff. This was the final straw. He felt that he could not continue once he had all this hostility among his staff as well as the difficulties of working with the very dominant chairman of governors. He completed his plans for retiring and left the term after the OFSTED inspection.

The following term an experienced local head was brought in to set up systems and repair relationships so that the school would be in a good position to start afresh with a new head.

Another sad end to a successful career, and one that is replicated all over the country, is typified by the head of an inner London junior school in the following case study.

He had worked for the same local authority for most of his career, had received a 25 year service medal and still had two or three years to go before retirement. He had been very effective for most of the first ten years of his headship. Although everyone respected him for his kindness and support of his colleagues, they became increasingly frustrated by his inability to focus on raising standards, his poor knowledge of the National Curriculum and his seeming lack of capacity to develop the skills needed. When the literacy and numeracy strategies were introduced he felt totally overwhelmed and resigned soon after an otherwise good OFSTED report criticised his management of new initiatives. The governors and LEA agreed to pay him until the end of term but he did not return to the school after resigning. Afterwards he returned to the classroom as a supply teacher.

Some heads in this predicament might coast the last couple of years – the governors do not wish to embark on capability procedures that, in the worst case scenario, would take over a year to complete and cause more problems for the school in terms of turbulence, uncertainty and low morale than would the temporary dip in pupil performance resulting from the head's poor leadership. But the recent pattern of four-yearly OFSTED inspections gave governors no choice about taking action: leadership and management were likely to be criticised if they did not deal with the problem.

One primary head was 58 and nine years in post when the school had its second inspection. The first OFSTED inspection was barely satisfactory and the second put the school in special measures. The head felt he no longer had the energy to move the school forward, although he tried and accepted that he needed lots of support. ICT in particular was beyond him. His experience before headship had been very limited as he had been promoted from the post of deputy in the same small village school. There had been poor SAT results but the pupils were well-behaved children, in a safe and happy environment, so no one had felt any anxiety about him. The inspection team found that moral and social education in the school was very good. So to be judged to be requiring special measures was a real shock to everyone concerned with the school. He had been warned after the previous inspection that there were concerns but had seemed to refuse to accept this. Perhaps he did not know how to address the problems. Now nearly 40 per cent of lessons were deemed unsatisfactory. He felt he lacked management training and should have had more support at an earlier stage. Until the second OFSTED inspection governors had protected him (or not realised the extent of the problem) but a new body took over after the second inspection to construct and drive through the action plan. Everyone felt this was a very sad case as he was well-respected but he hadn't changed to meet the new requirements. His place was taken for a term by a retired head who agreed to be acting head in the school for three days a week whilst the deputy head developed the necessary skills to run the school.

The new pattern of inspections and more emphasis on school self-review will put the onus back on the governors to be proactive if the head seems to be losing the motivation or the energy to keep the school moving forward. Performance management arrangements now in place for setting targets for headteachers and an annual review will be useful in giving governors the opportunity to monitor the head's performance and look at support from an early stage if necessary. There should be fewer occasions where either the head or the governors are caught unawares by such problems.

Pressure for continued improvement in performance (staff and pupils)

The government's stated intention of 'driving up standards' has affected head-teachers in different ways. Some have used the impetus to develop strategies that have impacted on whole-school effectiveness. Others have targeted specific curriculum areas and/or specific ability groups and/or age groups of pupils in the school. Whatever their response, it will have set the scene for a more or less stressful time as the improvements become more difficult to maintain.

Unsatisfactory teaching may have hampered some improvements. How has the headteacher solved that problem? As we found in our research for our book on this subject, managing poor performance requires determination but also an ability to keep people on your side. Even though colleagues are sometimes the first to complain when they are trying to compensate for a team member who cannot control a class, or whose subject knowledge is inadequate, they may also be the first to protect that person when the latter is put under pressure to improve.

Jean took up her post as head of a large primary school in January 1998 three months after an OFSTED inspection. The previous head having left at the end of the previous term, the deputy had been acting head for the autumn term. Jean's appointment took place just before the inspection so she was able to work with the deputy and governors immediately to see the implications of their findings and to devise an action plan.

The inspection report was not enthusiastic about the levels of achievement in the school and particularly questioned the quality of teaching and learning in the classes of three of the very experienced teachers on her staff, two of whom decided to take early retirement at the end of that year. The third had been absent during much of the week of the inspection.

On the surface there were no problems. The school staff was very stable and experienced – five teachers had been in the school some twenty-five years each, two had been there about seven years and the five new teachers had been appointed as staff retired and numbers of classes increased as the roll grew. Many of the parents had been pupils themselves at the school, had been taught by the same teachers and had an understandable loyalty and affection for them. There were no discipline problems; pupils were polite and biddable. The atmosphere in the school was warm and friendly.

The OFSTED inspection, however, showed up inconsistencies of expectations between classes and a general lack of teamwork and co-ordination leading to signs of considerable underachievement in some curriculum areas across the school and in most areas in this particular teacher's class. Jean's first priority would be to clarify the roles of subject co-ordinators and set up systems to enable teams to work on schemes of work, etc. Graham, the teacher causing concern, was science co-ordinator as well as head of Years 3 and 4, and as such was a member of the senior management team. He had not produced any schemes of work, nor any materials to promote science in the school. Along with the other older members of staff he had been used to working autonomously, using his experience to decide which bits of the syllabus he would cover and how. After the inspection the other older teachers understood the need for collaboration and planning: one decided she did not want the workload this required, so retired. Another made a great effort to take on the new way of working, was delighted with the positive effects of sharing ideas and so found a new enthusiasm for her work.

It soon became apparent that there had been previous undercurrents of discontent about Graham's work. The chair of governors' children had passed through his class and she embarrassedly confessed to Jean that she was glad when the children moved on to the next teacher, even though the children themselves had been very happy in Graham's class. The deputy head had been uneasy about the poor quality of display work in the classroom but had not felt confident to comment, thinking that this was just an area where the teacher was not talented. Some parents were unsure about the progress their children had made but lacked the confidence to ask questions; after all, Graham had so much experience.

In order to raise standards generally and to ensure that the pupils in Graham's class received the same curriculum as in other classes, Jean decided to prioritise English and the classroom environment. The English co-ordinator was very competent so would set a good standard for other co-ordinators to follow as their subject became the priority. All would be very open and shared.

It soon became clear that, for whatever reason, Graham was not taking his share in the work. His planning consisted of descriptions of tasks rather than learning objectives or evaluation. Jean provided INSET and worked individually with him to build up these skills. Graham eventually conceded that he was finding it all too much and began to take time off with stress-related illnesses. The post-OFSTED inspection check carried out by advisers found deficiencies in Graham's paperwork and commented on low expectations of standards of work in his class. They also criticised the science documentation. Graham said he had not wanted the co-ordinator role; it was too much along with all the other work he was expected to do.

Then began a regular series of meetings where Jean and Graham looked at possible ways out of this problem. He asked for a year off to gain different experiences. The governors refused this. He asked to drop the SMT role. Governors agreed. He asked to co-ordinate a different year group. Governors refused. A different subject area? It was eventually agreed that he should take over the co-ordination of PE. This raised issues regarding Graham's salary – he was no longer a member of senior management and was now responsible for a less significant curriculum area in terms of planning and assessment. Historical anomalies in the pay structure in the school still prevented implementation of a clearly formulated pay policy, so Graham was not the only member of staff seeming to be paid at a higher rate than his actual role might merit. Jean and her governors were looking to improve Graham's performance, not to demotivate him. Furthermore Jean had not yet been able to put clearly defined job descriptions in place, so there were no benchmarks in existence linking roles with salaries in any way. It would therefore probably have been impossible to argue that Graham should take a pay cut in line with the cut in responsibilities.

The new year began with the change of roles. Jean allowed time for Graham to settle into his new situation but by half term there was still no proper planning for PE and the work in English in his class was still at an unacceptable standard. The English co-ordinator complained that the reading corner was not being properly used, reading records were perfunctory and not developmental, and children with learning difficulties in English were not being identified.

At this point (the end of October) Jean decided she could accept the situation no longer and began the informal stage of the capability procedures. All previous meetings and requirements had been documented so she was able to show Graham that her expectations had been clear and that he had not met them. At the meeting precise targets were set (e.g. reading records to be completed in line with school policy, planned use of the reading corner to be documented and implemented) and the English co-ordinator was enlisted to work with Graham to meet the targets by the end of term.

This is the current position. Jean is confident about the route she is now on but she is very concerned about the likely outcomes. Graham is himself the NUT representative in an area where the professional associations have been investigating accusations of bullying of teachers by their heads. Parents will support him through loyalty and through genuine fondness for someone who has always been in their lives. Children are fond of the avuncular teacher who always has chocolate bars in his desk drawer. Colleagues, although exasperated by his failure to carry his share of the workload, are not keen to see a long-term peer dismissed, especially as he only recently married another local teacher.

Although it was strongly resisted when first proposed, the link between pupil progress and the ability of individual teachers has now been formalised in evidence in the portfolios of those teachers applying to pass the threshold for performance-related pay. The link is also made when schools' pupil progress targets and actual performance are measured: if the children in one class have exceeded their targets and those in a parallel class have barely met theirs it may be deemed a fluke the first year but, if it proves to be a trend, then it is more likely attributable to the teacher's ability. As schools become more data rich and more skilful in interpreting these data, it becomes more possible to track the quality of a teacher's input and therefore more possible to target professional development needs. It does, however, put increasing pressure on teachers as their work is monitored and the output measured. This is a new aspect of a headteacher's role, and one which some have found difficult to come to terms with.

Other improvements may have needed a change in the priorities within the curriculum. This has happened in secondary schools at each stage in the development of the National Curriculum, and more recently in the new post-16 curriculum. How was this to be staffed? At the early stages in implementing the National Curriculum many schools had to manage redundancies – the new curriculum required more science, technology and modern language teachers and fewer historians and geographers. Some teachers retrained or brushed up their second subjects but this was not always possible. Obviously school staffing should depend on curriculum decisions, but the head has then to manage the ensuing staffing changes and the effects these have on the morale of all concerned from the individuals to the school community at large. The recent increasing difficulties in recruiting teachers have further exacerbated this dilemma – should the curriculum balance be abandoned because of the impossibility of recruiting a teacher with the required subject specialism? Is it better to have an acceptable teacher even if they cannot teach the needed subject and to skew the timetable to accommodate this? What about the next year? This area is further explored under the section on budgeting in chapter 5.

OFSTED inspections

We all know of heads who are feeling elated and delighted for their staff after an OFSTED inspection that has observed and acknowledged the excellent work going on in the school under their leadership. But, rightly or wrongly, an OFSTED inspection seems to have been the nemesis for more headteachers than any other single aspect of the job. It is also important to note the change in style of inspection more recently: we must not assume that the problems encountered in the past will continue to exist under the new OFSTED framework. Lighter touch inspections and a greater emphasis on school self-review will undoubtedly take away a lot of the pressure and stress that accompanied the inspection regime until very recently.

It is clear that a poor OFSTED report has been a major factor in schools having a change of headteacher. What is less easy to establish is a correlation between the two in terms of the headteacher's performance. The HMI briefly interviewed as part of the initial feasibility project on the subject of headship today, was clear in his view that poorly performing schools suffer from poor leadership and that a change of leader is necessary if a school is to move out of a cycle of poor performance. Whatever her qualities the head may become the victim of the necessary public relations exercise in the aftermath of a poor OFSTED inspection. In order to retain the confidence of other stakeholders, changes must be seen to be made and the most obvious sign of changes is a change of headteacher. This in itself is not evidence that the headteacher is incapable of performing satisfactorily: there are other reasons for a school's weaknesses that may be beyond the headteacher's control.

It is not necessary for a school to have had a poor inspection report for a headteacher to be vulnerable. There is evidence that parents and governors are not satisfied with a report that deems the school's leadership to be 'satisfactory'. They want their school to be described as 'good' and 'well led'. Anything less than this suggests that the current leadership is mediocre and they want to change that perception. A diocesan adviser commented particularly on the number of OFSTED feedbacks he had been to recently, where he had seen the head criticised for weaknesses of leadership and management. It may only have been for certain aspects within an otherwise satisfactory report but he felt that in the eyes of governors there is no excuse for any weaknesses on the part of the headteacher.

Our other informants gave views and examples which included the following:

- OFSTED inspections were sometimes valuable in that they exposed weaknesses that had long existed but were hidden. These could be weaknesses across the school because no one in the school knew what current expectations were or they could be weaknesses in leadership and management that a competent but loyal staff colluded, either consciously or unconsciously, to cover. In both cases it was likely that the head was not capable of managing the necessary changes. This could be because of a lack of awareness of recent developments. It could need a change of management style or a culture change to enable staff who would also be encountering the same problems to make progress. This would equally apply to the pupils in the schools and their expectations of achievement and behaviour. This would be a very challenging scenario for a new head to take over: initiating and managing change would require very skilful handling.

Could this situation have been avoided? Yes, provided that someone with influence had kept the head aware of expectations – this could have been the link adviser from the LEA, the chair of governors or a deputy head. This is much less likely to happen under current performance management arrangements because an effective external adviser will ensure that, at the annual review with the head, suitable advice is given. Even if this advice is not taken directly, it will at least have raised questions for the governors and head to reflect on.

- Similarly OFSTED exposed weakness in implementing new initiatives, especially ICT, which long-term headteachers sometimes felt incapable of getting to grips with. One headteacher whose school had had a good inspection report pre-empted possible criticism in that area by deciding to take early retirement whilst he still felt that he and the school were successful. In this way he enabled someone confident about implementing the latest batch of new initiatives to take over before a decline could start.

- In the view of one adviser, the headteacher 'stands out like a sore thumb'. When there are public comments about leadership and management there is no hiding place for the headteacher. Criticism of middle management, separate departments or implementation of policy can be shared among a group and, although the group is very likely to know the source of any weakness, individuals are not usually pinpointed. This is not true of any criticism of leadership, management (of people or of material resources) or standards. Headteachers, and prospective or potential headteachers, are genuinely wary of receiving such criticism, especially when they have seen the effect it has had on colleague heads.

- In one particularly difficult case described to us (and by no means typical), a poor OFSTED inspection specifically criticised the quality of leadership and management and the Registered Inspector gave inaccurate feedback to the SMT, telling them that the school would be under special measures (in fact it was serious weaknesses). The head was so shocked by this that he went to his doctor immediately after the meeting and rang the LEA who agreed his retirement at the end of the month. The speed with which the decision was made and implemented suggests that there may have been more to the background of this case than the adviser knew but it does highlight the impact of criticism of management on the individual who leads the management team.

- Another scenario involved a very high profile headteacher who retired officially at the end of that term but who went off on sick leave and was unlikely to be able to do any teaching again. The school had a bad OFSTED report that specified that the school had 'serious weaknesses in the areas of leadership and management'. That head had been very highly regarded by colleagues, had been lecturing internationally on management issues and suddenly she seemed to lose everything. In the adviser's view there is no scope in the way OFSTED inspections work for heads to survive and recover their standing as leaders when the quality of leadership and management in the school is criticised.

Could this have been avoided? Yes, if the head had ensured that the rest of the leadership team had the skills to lead positively in her absence. Yes, if the local authority had been monitoring the school's performance. There was clearly an imbalance between the head's interpretation of her role inside and outside the school. Some LEAs have been proactive in trying to avoid this type of scenario by working more closely with heads in schools where problems seem to be developing. They hope to provide the right kind of support for the head to develop the necessary skills to manage the situation. LEAs already involved rightly see this as good management of their resources; others are joining in to avoid headships becoming vacant and difficult to fill.

- In one adviser's experience, many of the schools where OFSTED judged there to be weaknesses were ones where the relationship between the governing body and the headteacher and staff was not as successful as it ought to have been for whatever reason. It is obviously very important, if not crucial, that all concerned are working to the same principles with the same set of aims and objectives. The headteacher and chair of governors need to have a good professional relationship in order to ensure this: a clash of personalities here can lead to many serious problems for the school. The power of the personality of the chair of governors is a factor in the success of the headteacher's leadership of the school (see section on working with governors).

- Different styles of inspection team and interpretation of data in the final report can give different impressions of the same findings. This can not only give the impression that one school is functioning less satisfactorily than another but also that a school that was functioning well at the first inspection is less successful at the second because the report after the subsequent inspection does not seem so enthusiastic about the quality of the school.

Schools in special measures

- An important issue was that of the position of the headteacher when a school was put under special measures. One of the LEA advisers interviewed had special responsibility for schools causing concern. The following scenarios were those he was involved with at the time of the interview. In this LEA five heads were leaving after the school had been under special measures. In the adviser's view they had been very well supported but had not been able to make improvements and capability procedures had begun. Of the five, two older headteachers recognised the need to get out of the situation before formal procedures were instigated, so agreed to take early retirement; another left in spite of having no entitlement to a financial package; another was dismissed after formal proceedings; and the fifth took early retirement on medical grounds. Sometimes heads try to stay with schools under special measures – often this has been for financial reasons if there was no likelihood of being granted early retirement or a financial package which would enable them to fulfil their financial commitments. Unfortunately this would not ensure that they were capable of raising standards and we found few examples of cases where the head in post when the school went into special measures had successfully led it out again.

- Heads were equally vulnerable in schools where there was cause for concern. There were six schools in this category in the same local authority as above. In all cases the governors set targets for the heads and in all these cases the head decided to resign or retire, depending on their age and financial situation.

Second or subsequent OFSTED inspection

A second or subsequent inspection during a head's time at one school can be reassuring as it confirms the head's continuing success in developing the school but it is no less stressful: this time the pressure is on everyone in the system to show that they continue to work at least at the same high standard as before; they cannot risk being perceived to be less successful. This is often very difficult; as we see in the chapters on the life cycle of a head, most sharp and visible improvements are made during the first years of headship. If a previous inspection had revealed areas for development or unsatisfactory aspects of the school, the new head will have addressed these. Where possible, underperforming staff will have been supported or replaced and a system will have been established to identify and support underachieving pupils. By the time of the next inspection there are unlikely still to be major areas for development and visible improvements will be much smaller.

Furthermore, sometimes a successful first OFSTED inspection is followed by problems at a second inspection for another reason: the first round of inspections was focused very strongly on the quality of teaching and learning in a school. More recently there has been a stronger emphasis on the quality of leadership and management. A headteacher must keep up with the current focus. In one scenario a school had had a very successful first OFSTED inspection and the head was devastated after the second inspection when the school was deemed to have serious weaknesses. The head's bewildered question was 'What's changed in the system? The school runs just the same as it did then!'

She had failed to notice the change in emphasis but, even more seriously, had relaxed her vigilance generally – there are always new expectations and a successful head must keep an awareness of trends in order to use what is appropriate for the furtherance of her vision for the school's future.

Staff recruitment

An article in *Headship Matters*, 12, is mainly concerned with the fact that many headteachers say they do not have time to take a break during the school holidays. There are many demands on heads' and teachers' time during the periods of school closure but the current reason for much of this 'holiday' time being used on school matters is the staff recruitment crisis in the south of England. Difficulties over finding staff are adding to the head's workload in the following ways:

- Advertising, interviewing – if anyone shows an interest the interview has to be set up at short notice before the prospective candidate finds a job somewhere else.
- Less suitable candidates are being appointed so need more support.
- Supply teachers are taking up longer contracts so are no longer available to stand in for absent teachers, whether on courses or off sick.
- The head is the only person available to take the class – this may be to cover at short notice or to teach a class or a subject semi-permanently. In the three schools built together on one campus in one town in the south-east, the infant school head had to take the reception class from January to July, the junior school head could not find a replacement to cover a maternity leave through the summer term and the secondary head, an economist, had to take over an upper sixth Business Studies class. This then removes the head from being round the school and able to deal with problems before they can escalate.
- Monitoring performance becomes impossible because of lack of available time.
- Staffing policies have to be ignored in favour of ensuring a teacher is in place, thus risking damaging morale among the rest of the staff.
- Expenditure on extra points for recruitment or finders' fees for agencies result in financial planning being readjusted and previous priorities may have to be postponed.
- Parents are unhappy with the provision made: lack of class control, pupil progress, or continuity are all likely to cause concern and will require the head's time and patience reassuring parents.
- It is an endless damage limitation exercise! This is all made even worse by the constant gap-filling, induction of short-term staff and evident lack of progress resulting from it.

This is a problem that is not going to be solved in the short term. There are two career points at which the situation is at its worst – recruitment of Newly Qualified Teachers and recruitment of headteachers – and there are geographical points where the situation is exacerbated – most noticeably London and the south east of England. More places on training courses and the development of more flexible entry routes into teaching (which may themselves have extra costs in terms of support time and training) may begin to address some of the problems but external factors such as the cost of living, particularly housing, in the south-east will continue to prevent young graduates being able to afford to become teachers in these high cost areas.

At the other end of the teaching spectrum there are two major issues regarding recruitment:

- the age profile of the profession. In the next few years a large number of teachers (and headteachers) will reach retirement age, leaving serious difficulties in recruiting to senior posts.
- the lack of applicants to headship posts. Already there are posts that are attracting no applicants at all; some attract one or two and these may not be suitable for the context of the school; often it takes several advertisements before a post is filled.

It is obvious that these two issues overlap – there will be more headships available and even fewer people with the skills and the desire to apply for them. If the same proportion of senior staff as at present choose not to apply to become heads, then the number of posts attracting few or no applicants will be substantially greater. To avoid a major crisis in recruiting headteachers the reasons for the problem need to be addressed. Much of the material on which this book is based provides evidence and examples of these reasons. Solutions lie elsewhere.

Pupil recruitment

Some schools do not have any concerns about the number of pupils the next new intake will include. This might be because they are selective and take the 150 highest achievers in their selection tests. It might instead be because they serve a rural community and there is no other school within reasonable commuting distance. For most other schools, however, this is not the case, especially since more open enrolment.

> The head of a Roman Catholic comprehensive situated on the edge of four outer London boroughs has no natural intake cohorts for his school. Two of the neighbouring boroughs retain grammar schools (some mixed, some single sex); the other two are non-selective but do have some single sex secondary schools. Some of these schools are also specialist schools of various sorts. In fact this particular small area represents exactly what the present government says it wants to offer parents – a wide range of choice. In practice there is a hierarchy of choices available: if your child is academically able and your family is Roman Catholic you can choose from the full range of schools and probably succeed in obtaining a place for your child in the school of your choice. If your child is less able and you have no religious affiliations the choices begin to be more limited and injudicious choices on the application form could result in your child being offered a place at a school you would not have chosen.
>
> Seen from the schools' perspective there is a similar problem: the grammar schools can select whichever pupils they choose from those who have applied to them. For fear of not getting places in the grammar schools a substantial number of parents also put their child's name down for some comprehensives

– a school with church connections is likely to be higher on the list than others – and since the grammar schools are not in the same local authority as the comprehensives no one can tell until places are accepted which pupils have applied for places at more than one school.

Recent OFSTED reports, league tables and articles in local newspapers and the local grapevine all affect parents' views of the schools in their locality and, if they have no natural loyalty to a particular school, their interpretation of any of these will affect their choices when they apply for secondary school places for their children.

Therefore, for most of the schools in this patchwork area, the actual intake numbers cannot be planned for properly until very late in the school year. For the RC school in the centre of it the problem is most affected by their being in the middle of the range of choices – a substantial number of potential pupils will be waiting on the outcome of applications to grammar schools, yet the total number available to apply is limited by their church connections (Roman Catholic children can go to any other school but it is less likely that non-Catholics will make the school their first choice) and it is exacerbated by the number of migrant families passing through the area – typically Irish, Hispanic or Italian.

A small number of Roman Catholic primary schools have a loyalty to the secondary schools, but even numbers from them depend on grammar school selection decisions.

The case study above may be extreme but it illustrates the difficulties heads have in planning ahead in terms of pupil numbers. Marketing the school is not just a shiny up-to-date prospectus. It is everything that everyone associated with the school does. Even the behaviour of pupils who have long left can be reflected back into the public perception of the school. Heads obviously have no power over ex-pupils' social lives, but they do have to ensure that the school is always seen in the best possible light. It is now quite usual for parents of pupils even two years younger than the entry age for the school to ask to be shown round and they usually feel more positive about the school if the head has spent time with them. Often heads like to take charge of these visits entirely so they know exactly what the message is that the parents are receiving, but this is yet another very time-consuming activity.

It is very important to keep up to date with social, demographic and economic trends in the locality. Surging house prices will affect the age group of new purchasers, new housing developments may bring young families into the area, and a change of use of older properties will change the social groups that live in them.

Several army and air force garrisons have recently been disbanded. Where the accommodation was in barracks for single occupation, these have been demolished or sold off for office, or even hospital use. Family units have been upgraded and sold to private buyers. In several Berkshire, Hampshire and Surrey locations this has been the perfect opportunity to solve some of the housing demands without using green field sites.

This has affected local schools both positively and negatively. In an Aldershot school the movement of a whole garrison created a substantial budget deficit. More than thirty children left the school within a few weeks. These were obviously spread throughout the school so classes could not be contracted as the numbers fell but the effect was to have 1.5 teachers too many for the budget. On the other hand, as new families move into the newly created private estates, schools are seeing their numbers creep up and will have a few years needing extra classrooms whilst the families grow up.

Sometimes the pattern of the school intake changes significantly because of the change in designation of some properties in the school's locality. The following school came up with an innovative solution to an increasingly common problem.

In one school's area, some older properties have been turned into council funded accommodation for single parents. At first the staff were unsure how best to work with the challenging behaviour of some of the children who were already having to cope with turbulence and uncertainty. The head soon realised that she needed to work with the parents too. There was nowhere on the estate where the mums (in practice it was nearly all very young, single women) could meet socially, so she got together with the governors and they agreed to turn a spare classroom into a social space for them. Here they could make coffee, chat and allow their children to settle more calmly into the school. Problems could be dealt with in a calmer atmosphere and more quickly if the parents were at the school too. Soon this developed into a self-help group and the mums began to help the children with their reading and so on. They also asked for help with parenting issues and with developing their own education. Working so proactively turned a potential problem into a positive development for the school as parents now feel a strong loyalty to it and promote a positive feeling about it. The project eventually attracted funding both towards the practicalities of maintaining the centre and towards paying for time for the teachers in the school to work with the parents as well.

This vignette highlights the value of creative thinking – a skill that cannot be taught on leadership courses – in foreseeing a problem before it becomes difficult to solve and turning it into a strength.

Finally there is the financial dilemma facing schools with expanding pupil rolls: what do you do when a few too many pupils want to join the school and at what point is it viable to increase the number of forms of entry? An intake of 174 can be comfortably, and economically, divided into six classes of 29 pupils, leaving space for pupils moving into the area later. An intake of 185 cannot be divided comfortably – six classes of over 30 leave no flexibility for different sized sets, no room for extra pupils later, and problems over the number of groups required for laboratory and workshop work. If it is divided instead into seven classes, the extra staffing required would cost much more than the amount brought in by the extra pupils.

The current trend for micro-management of school finances by government, with special purpose budgets, prevents the flexible deployment possible with a single line budget. Although it ensures expenditure in certain preferred areas, it may not ensure the best possible use of the money in the individual school's context. However, if the head has a clear vision of the intended strategic development of the school, these issues will be easier to solve – a short-term loss may be a crucial step in ensuring pupil numbers in future years.

LEA

The role of local education authorities has changed considerably since the political decision to devolve financial responsibility and, eventually, over 90 per cent of the education budget to schools. Before then LEAs held the purse strings and were therefore the main decision-makers in the implementation of education policy. Some were seen as benevolent despots, with good reputations for positive and proactive management. Others, however, had less successful relationships with the headteachers of the schools under their authority so in these areas more heads and governors took up the option of becoming a grant-maintained school, which gave schools complete freedom from any LEA. Sometimes these decisions were made where heads felt their local authorities were seriously underfunding schools, but, whatever the reason, after 1988 LEAs' powers were considerably diminished: heads and governors could choose to buy in their services or to look elsewhere. The break-up of some counties and larger towns into unitary authorities further weakened some smaller education authorities who could no longer afford to employ experts across the range of education services. For many secondary schools this was all seen as an opportunity to develop their own initiatives and make the most of the freedom afforded. For smaller schools, however, this was less appropriate and not welcomed: budgets were too small for it to be possible to buy in services, particularly curriculum expertise and financial advice.

Rebuilding LEAs

Now there is a movement towards rebuilding the responsibilities of LEAs. They already have a major role in monitoring the performance of those schools whose leadership and management is deemed to need improvement. The government's expectation is that the LEA takes responsibility for schools' performance, finding ways to help schools deal with serious weaknesses or special measures – this usually involves diverting a substantial amount of money to that school, to pay for a change of image and probably a change of head. They will have a major role in implementing, for example, the new initiative to deal with underperforming teachers at all levels, including heads. How they manage that will, to a large extent, depend on the size of the local authority: large ones like Hampshire and Nottinghamshire will have a range of experts on their staff ready to deal with any contingency.

In the new, small unitary authorities there is no question of covering all areas internally: the senior officials we talked to seemed to feel that their new role is to work symbiotically with schools, helping each other with expertise and acting as brokers to match service providers with the schools needing the service. How each head will choose to work with the local authority will obviously depend on their personal experience and on the local history. Some local authorities have a good reputation for supporting aspiring and actual heads; they use their knowledge and experience to be proactive in pre-empting problems, aiming at a collaborative approach to school improvement. Others, often because of lack of personnel with the necessary skills to highlight and diagnose potential problems before they escalate, only become actively involved in a school when deteriorating SAT results or a critical OFSTED inspection triggers their involvement. In general the current rule seems to be for intervention in inverse proportion to the success of the school.

As for supporting heads, as opposed to schools, most LEAs feel they have a major role in developing new heads – induction and support whilst they feel their way into the role. As well as genuinely offering a service, this is also a preventive strategy; the shortage of candidates for headship results in potentially weaker candidates being appointed. If at all possible the LEA must avoid schools being less successful than before.

Not all LEAs work closely with their schools: in response to a request for references for schools applying to be involved in a recent initiative, one LEA returned the request uncompleted but with the comment that they did not feel they were in a position to make a judgement on the schools in question.

5 Understanding the internal demands

Governors

To some extent governors represent the interface between the external and internal facets of the head's job. The board of governors is composed of people from inside the school and those whose value lies particularly in the outside breadth of their expertise.

An understanding board of governors can be a huge source of support to a headteacher. Members of the board bring expertise in areas that are probably less familiar to someone whose career has been entirely in education. They can act as sounding boards for ideas, critical friends and someone to offload problems onto. When they have the time to get to know the school well, they can be the only people who fully understand the role of the headteacher and have knowledge of all the issues filling the head's in-tray.

The head of a small rural primary school has no deputy head and a substantial teaching commitment. She therefore has limited opportunities either for discussing management issues or for professional debate. She does not want to use more of her teaching staff's time than she needs to in meetings so looks to her governors to fill the role of professional think-tank. She says that she looks forward to governors' meetings when they can get past the paperwork and into real debate about teaching, learning and school improvement. To help her move forward with pupil target setting, two governors have taken on the task of learning to use Assessment Manager on the school's ICT system, inputting all the data and then providing her with whatever outputs she needs to set targets and track progress. The governors have helped her manage her workload and agree priorities. Because she knows that they all have the same vision for the school she feels able to move forward with confidence. (It comes as no surprise that this school has just been reported as very good after its recent OFSTED inspection.)

In another quite similar school two governors have put the library catalogue on computer and set up a system so the children can use the library independently, thus cutting down staff time doing library administration and freeing them up to work with the children. In this school a problem with a poorly performing teacher has been the cause of a lot of speculation between parents at the school gate. In a small community this has the potential to cause a great deal of ill feeling and negativity about the school, or, more specifically, the headteacher. The governors made sure that they all took the same approach in countering potential problems out in the wider community and minimising the friction inevitable in such cases. The head feels that she would have been less confident about embarking on capability procedures if she had not been so sure of the governors' support for her actions within the constraints imposed by the required procedures and confidentiality.

Not every head feels as confident of governors' support and some are taken unawares by the extra dimension governors bring to school leadership and management. Chapter 12 tries to model relationships between head, governors and school. In some ways the governors are like the board of directors of a company but, because they represent such diverse and disparate aspects of the community, they can behave like pressure groups with very different priorities: those who are chosen by the local authority may want to implement policies that do not correspond with those favoured by parent or teacher governors. They are also volunteers and as such cannot be compelled to act in any particular way or follow any particular line. Since they are not paid to be governors they must have another compelling reason for being there – this may or may not be for the good of the school, or in line with the head's thinking. A final point not to be overlooked is the timing of governors' meetings. They are meetings where the head needs to be well prepared and alert but they usually have to take place in the evening after what may have been a long and demanding day. We were told of three headteachers who were on long-term sick leave because they had been involved in road accidents on the way home late in the evening after governors' meetings.

The relationship between the head and the school's governors, especially the chair of governors, is a delicate one and it is often difficult for the individuals to establish clearly the differences between the two roles. At its most simple, the governors' role is to establish policies. The head's role is to put these into practice. There is a continuum from those who leave everything to the head, through the many governing bodies who rely heavily on the head to guide them, to those who have a clear view of how they want to proceed and hardly involve the head in the process.

Those who leave everything to the head, take no active part in the school's development and simply turn up at a minimum number of meetings are probably being school governors for political reasons only. A wise head will be very aware of this and tread carefully: if something goes wrong, these governors will not be sharing the responsibility. Some long-standing governors who have been working for several years with a headteacher leave everything to the head because they are confident in the way that head is leading the school. These governors will still be keeping up with developments and will be there to support the head when there are problems. Others leave everything to the head because they lack confidence in their own ability to carry out their role effectively. In this case it is important that the head and the LEA ensure that support and training are available. There is a huge turnover of governors and many schools have difficulty filling vacancies, especially for parent governors. It would seem preferable to support and train new governors so that they can feel valuable in their role – and keep on fulfilling it – than to be constantly trying to fill vacancies.

As well as politically motivated governors, there are those who seek election because they wish to put pressure on the school to act in a particular way: they may have a child with specific needs that they think the school is not fulfilling, or they may feel that a member of staff does not perform satisfactorily and they want to force something to be done about it. There are a multitude of agendas that any individual may bring to their interpretation of the role of school governor. The skill is to use these people constructively.

Others may seek to become governors because they have some free time and genuinely want to contribute this to something worthwhile. There are two distinct groups from whom these are drawn: the first group may be retired people whose experience of being in school dates back forty to fifty years and they will need some time to adjust to the changes that have taken place. In spite of that they are likely to have a lot to offer and could be among the head's most useful allies once they have understood their role. The second group are young parents who want to be more involved in their children's school. These people have an understanding of current terminology and know from the pupil's perspective the pressures in school nowadays. These too can be a valuable resource for the head as they can give instant feedback about current issues and early warning of other issues that may be developing.

The type of area the school draws its pupils from will also affect both the types of people who offer themselves as governors and their attitude to the head. The composition of the board of governors of the secondary school situated near a long-established university is quite different from that of the primary school built in the 1950s to cater for the children of families moving into the terraced houses near the town's largest industrial estate. The governors of a rural comprehensive in the north of England think the head is very well paid compared to them and expect him (it is still more likely to be 'him' the further north the authority) to justify receiving his salary. Yet at the same time the highly paid executive governors of one comprehensive school in a very affluent area wanted their headteacher to receive a pay rise well beyond what she felt the budget could justify.

Where the governors work together well as a team the head can feel relatively confident in the responses he can expect and can proceed accordingly. Problems arise when the governors are divided in their feelings about a major issue and change their minds when action is already being taken. This tends to happen when dealing with pupil exclusions. Governors hear people in the community complaining about young people's behaviour and parents suggesting that the school is not firm enough in dealing with disruptive pupils. Their response is to insist at meetings that discipline should be firm and pupils dealt with in a manner that leaves no doubt that poor behaviour is unacceptable. Then a pupil is permanently excluded after a series of serious incidents of inappropriate behaviour to both staff and other pupils. At the exclusion hearing governors hear of the difficult family situation and other mitigating circumstances and overturn the head's decision. The pupil then returns to school in the knowledge that it is against the wish of the head and the staff, and even possibly a substantial number of other pupils. The internal school community then feels that the head has let them down and there is an understandable nervousness about taking firm action in the future. This is not to say that the head's decision must be automatically rubber stamped by the governors but that all concerned must understand the likely outcomes of such a policy decision.

The following scenario explores many issues but is included here because the key to the ultimate departure of the headteacher lay in the governors' change of mind:

Simon was delighted to be appointed to the headship of an 11–18 Catholic comprehensive situated on the corner where three northern LEAs joined. He had previously been unsuccessful in several headship interviews and had not been optimistic that he would be successful at this interview either. There had only been three people interviewed, none from local schools, but he knew that there were comparatively few people suitably qualified for headship of specific faith schools and did not worry particularly about this.

The previous head had been there for 15 years and was a well-known local personality who was a personal friend of most of the longer-standing governors by the time he retired. They had very much left him to manage as he wished and this was storing up problems for the next head to deal with: there were many long-term middle managers, several of whom were heads of department, but there was no logical staffing structure; a typical anomaly was that the head of history was on a higher salary than the head of maths. This lack of structure had led to overstaffing in some departments, who had plenty of non-contact time, and pressure on some departments who lacked sufficient specialists to cover all elements of the National Curriculum. Therefore Simon inherited a substantial overspend on the staffing budget. Student numbers had recently been increasing so Simon's view was that it was better to hold staffing levels as they were and wait for pupil numbers to meet them, thus achieving a year on year percentage decrease in the teacher/pupil ratio.

It was not a happy school. The previous head had worked his way up from a junior post so had little external experience and seemed to have behaved like a benign uncle. Those who pleased him received presents (promotion) on an ad hoc basis that led to dissatisfaction and ill-feeling elsewhere.

The change in pupil numbers came about because there had originally been two separate, single sex schools on the same site. With the retirement of the head of the girls' school at a time when numbers on roll had been dwindling the diocese had decided to amalgamate the two schools. Some parts of the buildings were in need of refurbishment. Maintaining specialist teaching rooms in both buildings would be expensive and inconvenient so there was to be an extensive building programme to rationalise and improve the school's resources. With this came a projected rise in pupil numbers. A firm of education consultants had been employed for the building project so governors asked them also to look at management effectiveness throughout the school (including the senior management team). Some of the governors had been against the idea of external advisers, so there was likely to be some disagreement with their findings. The consultants recommended middle management training, support of individuals and changes to the management structure, including the redundancy of a senior teacher post.

As there seemed to be a consensus among the governors that the recommendations should be accepted, Simon set about the restructuring process including the redundancy. As the school was grant-maintained he did not have the automatic involvement of an LEA so took personnel advice from one of the headteachers' professional associations and a neighbouring LEA. He reported back to governors as he received this advice but it seemed to be conflicting and unhelpful in dealing with the two situations at once. Simon felt that the lack of secure advice undermined the governors' confidence in him. Also, he felt that the chair of the staffing committee was not really in support of the redundancy. Furthermore the partner of one of the governors was from the personnel department in another LEA and gave further advice that differed again from what he had already been advised. Simon felt that the 'rug was being pulled from under' him.

Restructuring procedures rolled on to the point where professional representatives were involved. Simon was unnerved by their professional confidence and wide experience of dealing with these matters in contrast to his own lack of experience and knowledge. They also seemed to him to make the issues far more complicated than they actually were. Simon found it very wearing dealing with such a large number of different interested parties – governors, staff members, union representatives (both in school and from the regional office), and personnel. Eventually the governors decided not to go through with the redundancy. They gave the conflicting advice as their reason, saying that they would lose at an industrial tribunal because they had not followed the correct timescales for action. Two governors had had experience of tribunals and did not wish to repeat the experience.

Six months later, after a meeting where the finance committee reported their anxiety about the continuing budget deficit, they decided to restart the redundancy procedures – and then changed their minds again.

Whilst all this had been going on Simon had not had any problems with the teaching staff as they knew the senior teacher had not been pulling his weight and they saw the advantages of the restructuring – more effective management and better budgeting. All the same, they too began to be concerned by the lack of consistency in the governors', and therefore Simon's, behaviour.

Then the school had its second OFSTED inspection. The supportive chair of governors resigned just before the inspection. The chair of the staffing committee became chair of the main governing body. She was an ex-primary teacher with no management experience. She felt she knew and understood teachers and she had always encouraged staff to go directly to her with their concerns. One of the teacher governors did this a lot. Simon felt there were a lot of 'loose cannons' in a very unprofessional situation.

The previous OFSTED inspection had been just before Simon took up the post. It had been critical but rather vague and had not made it clear where the weaknesses were. Simon felt that a lot of work had taken place on improving teaching and learning but the inspection focused on examination results. Incomplete initial information on pupils and assumptions made by the inspectors about the 'average' intake of the schools in an area where there were several grammar schools made their findings seem very bad.

Immediately after the inspection an adviser from the Funding Agency suggested that Simon did not tell staff that the school was likely to receive a very critical report until they actually saw the report. He felt greatly undermined by this as staff obviously wanted feedback, and became suspicious about his reluctance to talk to them about it. Then he found the chair of governors discussing it with staff. The situation was exacerbated when the reporting inspector did not keep to the expected timescale, so the report was late.

Simon was obviously concerned about his own position but could get no response about it at first from governors. But after he had completed the post-OFSTED inspection action plan the governors sent him a letter stating that they had no confidence in him. The Funding Agency adviser who had helped with the action plan was also helpful in giving Simon advice about possible ways forward for himself professionally. He also had advice from the head of personnel for the diocese; this person seemed to be appalled at the letter that Simon had been sent and thought he would have had a good case against the governors. His professional association had been very supportive but could only confirm that this was not unusual behaviour for governors. Simon was summoned to a meeting with the diocesan commissioner the following week. He decided not to fight the case for his own and for the school's benefit, and so agreed to resign if an acceptable package was offered. It was.

At one point Simon was asked not to go into school any more but he persevered until the action plan was finished. He finally left towards the end of June. For a while he could not decide on his professional way forward; he tried, for example, several schemes involving selling computer software to schools but eventually realised that he most enjoyed working with pupils in school. In the autumn he returned to school as a supply teacher, was soon offered a permanent contract and has since returned to a management role as a head of year.

There are several issues to be explored in this case:

- Having the confidence to deal with personnel issues. Simon found this very stressful indeed. He had many sleepless nights and felt very unsure about the rightness of his actions, both for the individual and for the school – was it really a Christian way of dealing with people? His situation was made worse by the difficulty in obtaining correct information and consistent advice.
- Grant-maintained status. He wished it had not been a grant-maintained school, then he would have benefited from LEA support and the governors would have been under less pressure if they had not had the anxiety of being employers. This is an interesting point of view considering how very unwilling heads and governors have been to return from grant-maintained status to the LEA. Perhaps it reflects his own lack of confidence more than the status of the school, but inexperienced heads need to bear this in mind when they take on headships in schools which are controlled by business/education partnerships, or are funded by private enterprise, or in any other stand-alone educational establishment.
- Preparation for school culture. He felt ill-prepared for the type of school – it had a very different culture than any school in his previous experience. This is particularly important in preparation for a headship – it is important for the aspiring head to choose a school that will suit his experience, personality and skills. As has become clear from earlier scenarios, the correct choice of school is more important than the acceptance of whatever headship is offered.

Leadership team

A head's ability to succeed depends on her relationship with the leadership team and one of the aspects of being a head that many comment on with the most pleasure is having the opportunity to appoint a new deputy head. The same year that the head of one of the country's largest comprehensives retired, one of her deputies also reached retirement age and a second moved to a headship. At a conference where she was being asked about the advertised deputy headships her comments about getting people in place before the new head came met with strong opposition. Her view was that she ought to leave the school with as many staffing 'problems' solved as possible so that the new head would be able to get on with the main task of running the school without worrying about appointing new staff. Her listeners felt that most new heads would consider the disadvantages of spending a term without key senior staff more than compensated for by the rare opportunity to recruit new deputies to fit his or her vision for the future of the school.

More often than not, a new head will 'inherit' a leadership team appointed by her predecessor. How this team reacts to having a new leader will depend much on their personal agendas, as discussed in chapter 10. A wise new head will have found out as much as possible about these people before taking up the appointment so that she is able to work sensitively on developing a working relationship with them. Several new heads we talked to commented on the pleasant surprise they had on finding how willing the senior staff were to be supportive and prepared to make changes. Where this did not happen it was usually only one member of the team who obviously found it difficult; in this case the head tried to find a different way of using skills to give the person a new focus. In one comprehensive where one deputy was appointed to the headship of the school, he found an opportunity for the other to lead the school's bid for specialist status and the ensuing developments. There are cases where all attempts fail to integrate a disappointed deputy into the team and the best way forward is for this person to find a job elsewhere, but it is not easy for someone who has held a senior post in a school for a long time to find another satisfying post. We found a substantial number of heads who had learnt eventually to work round a deputy or senior teacher whose style or attitude was not sympathetic to the way they wanted the school to progress. If this was the position with more than one senior member of staff the situation could be impossible.

The head of an inner London primary school resigned after leadership and management of the school were criticised by OFSTED inspectors. This was a situation we had come across in all the LEAs where we talked to advisers, but the background of events that led to this outcome was different: OFSTED had exposed weaknesses that had been there for a long time. It seems that, for the five years since the head's appointment, a core of powerful teachers had been 'running the school for their own convenience and refused to respond to the head's attempts to initiate change'. The LEA had been monitoring and trying to support the head but he had been unable to make any progress. This group of teachers, including the deputy head and other senior staff, had devised a strategy of seeming compliance with the head's wishes but then failure to put them into practice. The previous head had been well-known in the authority for his unwillingness to involve himself and his school in developments; the senior staff in the school had been appointed and led by him in the view (endorsed by the evidence that he was in no way taken to task about his attitude) that they could safely ignore directives for change. With such a powerful group working against him the new head had no chance of success, especially as they were all able practitioners in the classroom.

Ensuring consistency

In primary schools the head has very little flexibility: there may not be a deputy head and all members of staff may have management roles as key stage or subject leaders.

In this case the issues are to do with ensuring a consistent standard through managing the individuals in the team.

One rural primary head met with a great deal of passive opposition from one key stage leader who seemed to be refusing to carry out much of her role. At first it was clear that she did not really know the full extent of the job and the head responded by putting clear job descriptions in place after consultation with the relevant advisers and other key stage leaders. This did not have the desired effect, probably because the teacher now felt she lacked the skills to carry out the role properly but was fearful of admitting this. Eventually the teacher agreed to relinquish the management role to concentrate on classroom teaching. The head could then redistribute the management responsibility and re-establish a leadership team.

It is very hard to minimise the negative effects of dealing with issues like these. They drain the new head's energy, create anxiety and insecurity amongst the rest of the staff and can even spread out into the wider school community. If mismanaged, this can be interpreted as bullying or harassment or lead to accusations of constructive dismissal. It is equally clear, however, that the problem has to be tackled if the new head is to ensure that the pupils receive their entitlement and the school continues to improve.

Managing staffing changes

When a new head is appointed other changes in staffing are sometimes necessary. A previous head may have been aware of underperforming staff but was unwilling to embark on capability procedures in the run up to her retirement. On the other hand she may have become less acutely aware of the teachers' performance as the years had gone by and did not realise that standards were no longer as high as they ought to be. Further staffing changes would be triggered by the need to bring the school up to date with current management needs: clear lines of management in response to performance management requirements or the development of the roles of SENCO (Special Educational Needs Co-ordinator) or assessment co-ordinator have been recent aspects of staff restructuring. Other staff changes could be expected in order to straighten up the school's finances or release part of the staffing budget to give more flexibility – perhaps away from senior management into recruitment and retention.

An experienced head was appointed from a difficult London school to a large comprehensive in a shire county with a mandate to restructure staffing, especially senior management: the old structure had three deputy heads and part of the restructuring would entail the redundancy of one of these posts. Her previous experience suggested that she had the skills to make tough decisions but, although both the LEA and the governors supported her, she was eventually forced to resign. The staff unanimously signed a petition to the governors confirming that they had no confidence in her. For several months prior to this the senior management team had excluded her from meetings and had been managing the day-to-day running of the school without involving her. Their main objection seems to have been to her autocratic management style and lack of consultation and communication. After her resignation another experienced, but local, head was brought in for two terms to re-establish professional relationships and to help ensure that the next head would not encounter the same problems. It seems that the reason for the intended redundancy was to remove a powerful and dissident personality from the senior management team rather than because of financial constraints. An additional problem was that the school had no tradition of effective financial management – the bursar responded to management decisions about staffing, etc. on a yearly basis without any forward planning or recognition that curriculum and staffing decisions should be costed before implementation. The failing headteacher had not taken a lead in moving towards proper financial planning and was not therefore in a position to carry out redundancies in the proper manner; the proposed redundancy seemed arbitrary. When a new head was appointed the governors chose someone whose interpersonal skills were very strong. No management restructuring has yet taken place.

Isabel had been in post for two years at the beginning of our contact with her. She had been appointed from deputy headship in another junior school in the same authority with a mandate from the governors and the LEA to make staffing changes. The school's league table performance was not good in comparison with other schools in the authority and they wanted her to improve performance by dealing with any poorly performing teachers, but she succeeded in uniting a powerful group of the staff against her, including the deputy head.

She took up the post a few weeks before an OFSTED inspection. The inspection team found the teaching generally satisfactory. In fact the overall picture was generally satisfactory. This was not the view of the LEA advisers. They felt the school was in difficulties because of weak management and poor teaching over an extended period. There had been a big staff turnover because of this and relationships were somewhat tense. The staff Isabel took over seemed well mixed in terms of ages and length of experience. However, the longest-serving member of staff who had been in post eight years, was perceived by the link adviser to be the weakest.

In the school Year 5 and Year 6 pupils were taught in mixed age range classes. This teacher (Sheila) had been part of this teaching team for many years, along with the deputy head and a teacher who had become a close personal friend of Sheila. This group had formed a clique who did not mix with other colleagues, partly because they were the only smokers on the staff and usually went off site at lunchtime. They had developed their own working style and shared very little with other staff. Because she already knew the school and had the opportunity to work with the governors beforehand, Isabel decided on some changes to take effect immediately. One of these was to break up the existing staff teams, ostensibly to enable experienced teachers to work with newer members of staff. She brought in from another local school an experienced and strong teacher to work alongside Sheila. She did not discuss it beforehand with the staff, but did take time at her first staff meeting to explain her reasons for doing it.

Sheila was not happy with this change and was soon taking time off for what seemed to Isabel to be very trivial reasons (e.g. having an electrical appliance repaired). After several absences she complained to Isabel that her class had been allowed to get out of control during her absence and then interpreted Isabel's response as a criticism of her own classroom control. Every discussion between Isabel and Sheila seemed to turn into a confrontation.

Isabel felt that other staff encouraged Sheila's attitude. Since the LEA had made it clear they felt the school was underperforming there was a general atmosphere of insecurity and defensiveness. The fact that the OFSTED inspectors did not entirely agree with the LEA encouraged staff to resist LEA intervention. Any attempt on Isabel's part to insist on particular courses of action, especially by Sheila, was seen as intimidation and the rest of the staff seemed to join ranks against Isabel. Her relationship with the deputy head was particularly strained.

Two years into headship Isabel was feeling utterly frustrated. She had not succeeded in making any of the changes she wanted to happen and felt that she had no possibility of success now that staff had seen her inability to make changes. A further difficulty, from Isabel's point of view, was the first round of applications to pass the threshold for performance-related pay. Sheila was one of the staff eligible to apply. Isabel could have used this evidence-based application process to prove Sheila's capability: either she had evidence of success in all the required areas, or Isabel was right in trying to find ways of improving her performance. Unfortunately this too seemed to work against Isabel: pupil progress could not be directly attributed to Sheila's own work because of staff turnover the previous year and a substantial amount of team teaching (or at least teaching covering Sheila's absences) with the newly appointed year co-ordinator who Isabel had brought in to support Sheila in particular.

Isabel agreed that there was a problem with the quality of Sheila's performance but she was not backed up by the OFSTED findings, threshold applications and the views of her deputy head. She felt that she had been told what to do on being appointed but had not taken the opportunity to check it out for herself and to work out her own strategies for dealing with the problem. To manage change effectively you need to start off with some others wanting the same changes as you and a substantial number of those involved having some dissatisfaction with the status quo. When Isabel started to try and change the school no one on the inside was on her side and few were unhappy with the way things were. It is not surprising therefore that she failed to make the changes asked for.

Isabel has now a good understanding of the principles of managing change and has moved on to the headship of a school in a very different area.

Pupils – behaviour

The staff and pupils (boys) of a failing comprehensive in a London borough were taken by surprise by the new, young, small, female head who bounced in with a smiling assumption that everyone could achieve good things. Initial wariness subsided as they realised not only that her belief was genuine but also she would give endless time discovering the sources of problems and working with parents and pupils to solve them. She backed up all this with clear expectations that unacceptable responses would be dealt with firmly. It seems clear from all studies of successful heads that their starting point is a passionate belief in all pupils' potential to succeed – how they manage this is less easy to define.

It seems to be the normal perception of each adult generation as it becomes older that young people are less hard-working, less motivated and generally more difficult than those they encountered at an earlier stage in their professional lives. These views are usually countered by quotations from classical writers complaining about the very same thing, so suggesting that the perception is more to do with adults growing older than any changes in younger people's behaviour. However, there does seem to be evidence that lifestyle changes are resulting in more children reaching school age with underdeveloped social skills and with more potential behavioural problems. A lot of children can cope with sophisticated computer games but have never learnt to communicate and play games with other children. More children experience family breakdowns than ever before and nowadays they are more likely to be without the support of an extended family. Pressures from home inevitably accompany children to school and can show themselves in challenging behaviour from an early age. Because of this and because of the pressure on schools to improve pupil performance outcomes, the numbers of infant age pupils being excluded from school have risen exponentially over the last decade. Further pressure on schools, exerted through financial sanctions, encourages heads to keep very difficult children in the classroom. Thus a tension is created between a genuine commitment to provide the best support available for these needy pupils and an equally strong commitment to the education of the rest of the children in the school.

When teachers are under great pressure to show progress in pupil achievement and pupils are struggling to deal with problems that do not allow them to focus on learning in school there is likely to be a great deal of friction and the headteacher is the person who ultimately has to deal with the outcomes of this. In the simplest scenario the head might be brought in to remove a disruptive child from the classroom, give her space to calm down, deliver a homily on acceptable and unacceptable behaviour, decide on an appropriate punishment and return her to the classroom. More often it is more complicated and further investigation is needed. It is likely to involve parents or carers and there is likely to be a stressed and unhappy teacher involved too. Parents now expect detailed written information about this and are more likely to complain about how the incident is handled.

Where at all possible a headteacher will establish a positive culture that builds on rewards rather than using a deficit model relying on sanctions to keep order. But it is difficult and exhausting setting a positive agenda in a school where there has been a lot of challenging behaviour and where tired teachers find it hard to keep looking for the positive rather than reprimanding pupils all the time.

An experienced headteacher working as an adviser with his local authority was asked to take over an outer London primary school in the middle of the autumn term. The school was in special measures and the previous head had been asked to leave. He did so immediately. The first month the new head spent in the hall, corridors and classrooms dealing firmly with the most difficult children and taking every opportunity to praise positive behaviour. During this time he made no attempt to look at forward planning and he did any necessary paperwork at home. He set up systems for dealing with challenging behaviour and made it clear to staff that they must follow procedures consistently. If they did that, then he would ensure that he dealt swiftly with the problem. In this way he got the staff working properly together and pupils soon discovered that unacceptable behaviour was dealt with consistently, that they could not get away with poor behaviour in some classes and not in others.

The next step was to begin to celebrate pupils' success through displays, certificates and other tangible and very visible strategies. Teachers began to find time and energy to improve classroom displays and develop a positive ethos in their classrooms. By the following Easter the school had a totally different atmosphere and had been taken out of special measures. The headteacher is pleased with the success of his strategies but still feels it is necessary to be visible around the school most of the time. Staff turnover has been quite extensive and he feels that the systems he has implemented are still not embedded into the school culture. Because of this he is not sure how much longer he is willing to stay at the school. He is very tired and admits that whilst the physical demands he made on himself to be actively around the school were fuelled by strong motivation to see changes in the school, now that it requires the same physical input to maintain the status quo he lacks the motivation and energy to do it.

Budgeting

Money problems lead to people problems

Some heads and advisers have a negative view of the effects of the decision to delegate financial management to schools, especially because of the lack of flexibility small schools actually have in making financially dependent decisions. An adviser told of a small, rural secondary school where, in his view, managing the budget has destroyed one headteacher. It was very much a community issue. The school had a budget deficit so she was appointed with a mandate to make a redundancy straightaway. As soon as she tackled that, which she did very professionally, the wider community of the school actively turned against her. They did not want somebody coming in and doing what they described as a hatchet job on one of their long-established teachers, so they really made her life impossible. She resigned with nothing to go to. The same adviser went on to describe another head who had just had to go through another redundancy situation and was having serious health problems. He felt that these problems are particularly difficult in small schools where everything is so high profile and very public.

An ex-headteacher who had been working as an adviser in church schools felt that

> one of the greatest factors which has made life in small primary schools difficult has been the advent of LMS. It was a secondary scheme and an idea which was bolted on at primary level. I think LMS continues to be a mismatched system. In a large school, yes, it makes a difference if there are one or two fewer pupils but in a small school it can result in a redundancy, which leads to a lack of confidence, which is enough to start the downward spiral. But it doesn't work the other way – a couple of extra children and it makes life easier but it doesn't mean you can take on extra staff. So LMS has had a purely negative effect on the small school. It is not being tackled because politically it has been seen as positive. Heads like the freedom but not the inability to cope with fluctuation. To move things forward in terms of headship I think they would have to reassess LMS.

This is a particular view that is not necessarily widespread, but it is true that talk about financial planning seems to have little interest to the head of a small school whose budget is almost entirely committed to paying for the teaching staff necessary to cover the curriculum in teaching groups of an acceptable size.

The class size conundrum

There are also issues emanating from mismatches in Planned Admission Numbers and the basic demands on the school budget. The number of pupils a school is allowed to have on roll is decided by a strange formula allocating a specified amount of floor space per pupil. The division of this floor space into areas deemed appropriate for teaching creates one set of issues and the totals arrived at create another. An infant school in Reading has an admission number of 67 pupils per year. This means that a possible total school roll is 201 pupils. Teachers' salary scales are the same for whatever age range they teach in, but the amount of money allocated per pupil in the infant age range is much smaller than that allocated for older pupils and infants are not supposed to be taught in groups bigger than thirty. The head and governors have an insoluble puzzle: they cannot afford to run three classes of about 23 pupils in each year group, but they are not allowed to have two classes of about 34. However they do the calculations, an admission number of 67 creates an untenable financial situation. Their current petition to reduce the number to 60 will lower the total income but create a much less expensive school.

Recognising the importance of managing the finances

There are comparatively few heads in post now who were appointed before Local Management of Schools (originally Local Financial Management) was developed in the late 1980s and ensuring that the school's budget is properly managed is one of the most important aspects of the contemporary head's role. She might have the most charismatic personality with a vision for the school that all are eager to fulfil but nothing can happen without the funds to pay for it. The huge diversity in schools' incomes is dependent on decisions made by a range of other indirect stakeholders. Legally the governors are responsible for setting the budget but how the money is actually spent is ultimately the responsibility of the head-teacher. At the time of writing we were aware of four headteachers suspended pending an enquiry into their schools' financial situation. Yet we are not aware of any governors being investigated because of their handling of a school's finances. The difference is that the governors act as a body and are volunteers so none of them can be made responsible for corporate decisions.

All the above is about handling the money that has come into the school's account. Knowing the processes that decide the school's income is important for forward planning. There are many aspiring heads, however, who really have no idea about how these decisions are made. When they do find out how it all happens, it is less surprising that some react by querying the value of budgeting exercises when they have so little influence over their schools' future incomes. After government priorities are stated and the chancellor allocates the global figure for the next year to education, this department decides its priorities and allocates accordingly. In the meantime local authorities decide their own priorities for their allocation to education and their education departments further reallocate depending on their priorities. Most of this allocation is divided by the number of different aged children in the area and distributed to schools as annual age-weighted pupil units. The rest is earmarked for special needs, special projects, major building maintenance, etc. The individual school has no influence over any of this but has to accept the amount delegated to it depending on the information returned to the LEA after the detailed pupil census in January each year. The generosity or otherwise of each authority's spending per pupil is debated annually when the newspapers produce league tables of highest to lowest spending authorities. Schools situated on the edge of a low spending authority are constantly fighting to keep standards high on a low income when parents can easily choose to send their children to more generously funded schools nearby. It is essential to know the current formula and to maximise income – pupils' entitlement to free school meals is an issue both financially and for league tables (since comparative data is based on percentages of pupils entitled to free school meals).

The school has to accept the formula on which its funding is decided. It also has to accept, and fully fund, any pay rises agreed for staff. (Pay rises for teaching staff are subject to different negotiations and conditions from clerical or technical staff, and there are usually different start dates for the different types of contract.) Neither of these can be accurately planned for in advance. It is, however, essential that a head is fully aware of the direction governmental policies are going, and of any likely changes, politically or economically, in the local council. Then planning can at least be based on the likely impact of such changes.

Generating an income

The school's budget is not simply built on the formula funded income. Schools with specialist status of all types, single faith schools, Education Action Zones, Excellence in Cities and so on, all attract extra funds. And, wherever possible, a school will generate an income specific to itself:

- Probably the highest earner of all is the school which has created and marketed its ICT-based GNVQ. This is the equivalent of four GCSEs and enables pupils to achieve much greater success than in the traditional GCSE subjects.
- A Hampshire school has the enviable geographical position of being opposite Farnborough Aerodrome. For the fortnight of the Air Show it rents out its extensive playing fields for car parking for a substantial fee.
- A similar situation brings a good income into the schools bordering Old Trafford football and cricket grounds.
- Other schools run courses for adults alongside the children, especially computer-based and vocational courses, but also literacy and numeracy.
- A school built round a three-storey tower block was one of the first to rent out roof space to a telecommunications company.
- A newly built Hillingdon school has generated a regular income by letting out its restaurant facilities for wedding receptions (not a vision most schools could realistically have for their canteen!).
- Another outer London infant school decided when building provision for nursery children to create a crèche as well. This not only brings in money, it also develops parental loyalty to the school and therefore stable pupil numbers.
- Several specialist Technology Colleges provide teaching and resources for employees in local small businesses to keep their computer skills up to date.
- Similarly, Language Colleges provide the expertise and state of the art language teaching technology for adults to learn a range of languages, both for business and pleasure.

Other ideas do not necessarily create a big income but they solve or prevent other problems:

- A multi-ethnic Southwark primary school has for many years provided space for parents to have English lessons or advice on filling forms for governmental departments.
- Parenting classes are held in a primary school which takes in a lot of children from disadvantaged backgrounds.

Outcomes cannot always be foreseen

Some ideas that seem perfect for generating a regular income can have a different effect from that which was expected.

As a particularly large cohort of pupils moved out of school into further education it seemed a perfect solution for an 11–16 Hampshire school with redundant classrooms to let them to the local tertiary college which was now having to accommodate the extra numbers of students. However, once the older teenagers were on site the idea proved to be very far from perfect. They did not wear uniform, they were allowed to smoke and they no longer had any loyalty to the school whose campus they were on. Their example was not what the school wanted for its pupils. It became more difficult to monitor the behaviour of the school pupils mingling with the college students and parents were unhappy about the influence the older students were having on the younger children. It took some time to find another venue for the college courses and even longer to undo the problems the idea had caused.

The value of a good bursar

It is very important that a head understands how the school's finances work, but she should not be responsible for producing the paperwork! The role, and therefore the cost, of financial assistants in school has changed more than any other. The financial administrator, or bursar, is there to handle the paperwork, deal with contracts and contractors, produce statements and keep the head and governors fully informed about the state of the school's finances. The head should be able to rely on all this being done effectively so that she and the governors can devote their time to the strategic deployment of the school's resources.

The governors' budget

It is also an area where governors often play a very important role – either for good or bad in terms of the head's success. Governors in general do not have a background in education other than as pupils and often lack confidence in discussions about the curriculum and pastoral care, but many of them are, or have been, involved in business and feel much more confident when talking about budgets and finance. In a positive relationship between the head and the governors, the business skills of the latter are exploited for the benefit of all concerned, leaving the head to be the expert on educational matters. Where the relationship is less successful, the governors may wish to control the school through their handling of financial affairs, or the head may prioritise finances with the governors to the detriment of wider school improvement, and perceived financial mismanagement is often the reason given for lack of confidence (or worse) in the head.

Sometimes governors take insufficient interest in the school's finances. Legally they are responsible for the school's budget but either through lack of confidence or lack of interest they leave all budget decisions to the head and do not even monitor expenditure through the year. It is then that something like an OFSTED inspection exposes problems.

> The head of a rural comprehensive had been in post for seven years. The governors had left everything to him, only expecting to be given a report from time to time. He had been very happy with this although he knew his financial paperwork was not always as complete as it ought to be. No one minded as long as the school seemed to be running smoothly and everyone was happy. Then a question arose through the annual audit about improper financial proceedings. The governors panicked and reacted immediately by suspending the head pending an investigation of financial misconduct. Eventually he was dismissed. He was only in his mid-forties and was effectively rendered unemployable in any managerial role.

There are issues here about the role of the LEA in monitoring schools' financial planning and ensuring that governors are carrying out their responsibilities with regard to setting and monitoring school budgets. The head should not have been left in such a vulnerable position, even though he had unwittingly set up the situation for himself. The role of LEAs is discussed further in chapter 4 and that of governors at the beginning of this chapter.

> In 1991 the head of a notoriously underachieving boys' school left the school at the end of the Friday prior to an inspection and never came back. His departure was only realised on the Monday morning when the deputy head found a note in his pigeonhole. The OFSTED inspectors not only found that the school had serious weaknesses in teaching and learning but also that there was a budget deficit of nearly £100,000 that the governors did not seem to know about!
>
> Unusually knowledgeable (for the time) in ICT, the head had been encouraged by the few governors who were active in their role to take as a priority a lead in developing computerised systems in the school. They had also felt that these were the right skills to enable the school to start off well in the new Local Management of Schools initiative. During his first year in post he spent a great deal of money redesigning and refurbishing his office and the administrative area of the school (effectively sealing it off from teachers and pupils) and installing computer hardware. He then dedicated himself to developing the systems and training the administrative staff. He bought software for records of achievement and school reports based on optical mark readers and comment banks and tried to implement these without consultation or staff training. At this stage these were very unsubtle, difficult to adapt to suit the school's needs, and they met with a great deal of resistance from the staff.

In the meantime the deputy head was running the school to the best of his ability. The already low status of the school led to recruitment problems and staff shortages; lack of leadership further undermined those who were trying to achieve satisfactory standards of performance and behaviour in the school.

Notification of the school's first OFSTED inspection must have galvanised the governors into action. They must have realised that they needed to know much more about the school and started asking questions about important things they had left with the head until then: the budget and pupils' achievement. This in turn must have made the head start looking at how he would be responding to questions from governors and inspectors. He evidently decided that he did not have satisfactory answers and left.

A very unstable period followed during which first the deputy ran the school until he obtained another headship and then the senior teacher became acting head. This resulted in the school being put under special measures at its next inspection. Finally the LEA agreed to underwrite the school's debts and encourage an experienced local head to take over.

Although it is unlikely that such an extreme scenario could exist a decade and two rounds of OFSTED inspections later it stands as a reminder of the possibilities for problems where proper accountability is lacking. All the same, the combination of a lack of up to date financial records and falling pupil numbers could quickly create a deficit of hundreds of thousands of pounds in a big secondary school.

The fact that the budget remains the governors' responsibility should ensure checks and balances when, as is usual, they take this responsibility seriously.

In 1999 a group of headteachers from Africa came to a British university to study for a degree that had been created specifically for them. The course covered all aspects of leadership and management and was designed to give them a comprehensive overview of education leadership so that they could become advisers to other heads on their return. One module of the course was on financial management. In some ways this was rather forward-looking as they would not be managing budgets on their return and did not have responsibility for appointing staff and resourcing the curriculum. It did, however, provide them with an opportunity to look at how they would make decisions about their priorities, and they were asked to plan for developing, marketing and implementing an appropriate project. The project they chose was a residential conference for headteachers in their region and their planning included deciding on venue, number of days, subjects for seminars, and numbers of speakers/trainers required. Having decided all the elements necessary to the project they then had to present a proposal bidding for funds for the project.

During the course the group had explored the various aspects of financial planning – being clear about priorities, fixed versus variable costs, essential versus desirable elements, human and material resources and so on. The project was the opportunity to put these notions into practice. Without exception, every member of the group decided that the essential elements of the project were cooks and transport. Apparently there was no point in them even beginning to plan any kind of input into the conference unless they had made sure there would be vehicles and drivers available to go and fetch the headteachers from their villages and that there would be plenty of food for them on arrival. If the funding for the project were to cover all they wanted, then they would have several trainers and would run workshops. If, however, and this seemed the more likely scenario, the funding turned out to be rather more limited, then they would have one trainer to do everything.

They were adamant that, whatever the funding, the number of cooks and drivers would remain the same. There was no point in having the most famous trainers in the world waiting for the headteachers if there was no transport to bring them from their villages and they certainly would not stay if there was not enough food. Priorities for the group on the course were very clear. Their issues were very straightforward and they did not have to weigh up the pros and cons of each decision as headteachers do here.

Until the advent of the NPQH there was no expectation that headteachers should have any formal expertise in managing budgets. Masters degrees in education management may have had a module devoted to school finances but students on these courses would probably not be able to explore this in any great depth as they may not have had access to information back at school. Unless it is specifically their role, most secondary deputy heads do not have a brief that includes finances, and primary schools often do not have anyone other than the head in a position to deal with the budget, so there is comparatively little opportunity for learning before taking up a headship.

Site management

Managing aspects of the school environment has always been a part of a head's role, even before Local Management of Schools. Although buildings were, and still are, the local authority's responsibility, there has never been enough money for all that is needed and heads lobby to keep their school's buildings high on relevant lists. Even though there is now an allocation of resources to help bring school buildings up to an acceptable standard (though we are not clear about whose standards this refers to) it can depend on political decisions and seem very arbitrary as well as likely to be inadequate to cover a school's total needs. The quality of a school's teaching does not depend on the buildings – many OFSTED reports confirm this – but no one can deny that new buildings and fresh resources encourage higher morale and better performance. Every Fresh Start school has an injection of money for improved buildings and new computer suites. A fresh, graffiti-free environment can be more easily maintained in that condition when all stakeholders take a pride in keeping it that way.

> One deputy head decided finally that headship itself was not for her when she found herself, whilst on interview, discussing with the chair of governors the problems of cleaning contracts and flat roofs. During an extended period of acting headship she had spent time every single day checking whether the cleaning had been done satisfactorily when a newly contracted company had found it impossible to meet the requirements of their contract. This company had tendered for the work based on their experience of working in office buildings and had not appreciated the difficulties they would experience in attracting people prepared to work as cleaners in a school. This resulted in an inadequate and unreliable work force, some employees failing to turn up for work (when they found better paid and more congenial jobs elsewhere), no one being available to cover for them and the school being too dirty for pupils and teachers to work in.

It is very difficult indeed to attract staff to cleaning jobs in schools in affluent areas, especially if these schools are not served by public transport, because there are usually plenty of more pleasant jobs available with easier access. Failing to find any other solution to the problem, some schools have become cleaning companies themselves and appointed sixth formers to the cleaning jobs under the supervision of the site manager. This of course adds to the head's responsibilities but is felt to be preferable to endless confrontations with cleaning company managers who move on to different jobs once they realise that staff recruitment is beyond them.

Where it is possible to appoint a site manager at a genuinely managerial level this will relieve the head of some of the time consuming problems described above. As with all financial decisions this is more likely to be a possibility the larger the school.

Teachers in general do not work in the most luxurious environments but are themselves not always the tidiest and most organised people. Several heads commented on how wearing it was to be always receiving complaints from staff about their working conditions and from cleaners, builders, engineers and so on about inaccessibility of areas to clean or repair because they were covered with what seemed to them to be rubbish. Similar complaints about the heating (too much or too little) and the food in the cafeteria – both of which are beyond the head's control – further added to the irritation felt by these heads. Even if deputies or site managers dealt directly with the complaints they were obviously referred on to the schools' heads, who felt even more that they were blamed for all ills. It was often issues such as these which turned out to be the final straw for heads in difficulties because they felt totally helpless to find any way of solving the problems.

Timing of building programmes

The timing of building programmes can be another pressure. If a school has increasing numbers of pupils coming in, there is the possible excitement of planning new buildings and being part of the physical development of the school. Managing this development requires a different set of skills from those normally needed by a head: this time the head is dealing with people who do not see life in terms of school terms and holidays. These people are also used to completing their input to one project and then moving on to the next. It is therefore often very difficult to synchronise the building programme with the school's needs. One head was put under great pressure by staff, parents and pupils when the building of a new creative arts complex next to the school's hall coincided with the main examination period. Workmen were constantly having to stop work whilst examinations were on, their managers were worried about costs escalating whilst the work was held up and pupils complained at home about the noise when they were trying to concentrate. All schools want contracts to be carried out in holiday periods. Unfortunately it is not always possible to arrange this, and even when it seems to have been carefully worked out, a few days' bad weather or a key person's illness can upset the schedule and move the work back into school time. Furthermore, unexpected school closures because of building work (no water or heating because the water or electricity supplies have to be turned off for a short period) always cause public relations problems – parents have to take time off work, arrange emergency child care and so on – but now the possibility of pupils missing targets in tests adds the extra pressure of longer-term concerns.

For most heads the prospect of new, or refurbished, buildings is an exciting and revitalising one. It is a rare opportunity to influence the working environment and possibly involve staff in making decisions about at least the cosmetic elements of the programme. A newly built school whose first Year 9 pupils have just completed their SATs is oversubscribed even though parents have no examination or test results to base their choice upon. It is crucial not to lose the focus on the real reason for the building programme – to improve the education opportunities of current and future pupils in the school. In that sentence the key words are 'current pupils': future pupils will reap the benefits but those currently in the system are experiencing their education in a building site, in temporary classrooms, without workshops or laboratories, with reduced playing areas and with extra noise and disturbance.

Time and day-to-day management, and ICT

All the aspects of the role discussed above have to be fitted into the time available to the person doing the job. There are no contractual hours in the contracts of those on the leadership salary scales but a stated expectation that the head will carry out all that is necessary for the smooth running of the school and the others in the leadership team will carry out the functions delegated to them by the head. There are therefore no suggested time parameters within which the head should be working. Our e-mail inboxes provide many examples of heads working late nights, early mornings and at any time during the weekend. Most of these contacts are negotiations for in-service training, developmental or evaluative aspects of the role, and further discussion with heads shows that it is only away from school in the evening or at weekends that they have the opportunity to think out and begin to put into practice anything proactive.

A long day's fragmented activity

It has been for many years a prerequisite for delegates on management courses, at whatever level, to write a detailed diary of how they have spent their time over, for example, the week or month leading up to the course. Even a superficial look at these diaries reveals a long working day broken into a large number of different activities that are usually interrupted and uncompleted. This becomes more typical of a head's working day in a smaller school, as the head is more likely to be the only person able to deal with whatever may crop up. Most heads start work early, finding that the hour or two before school starts is the best time for organising the day and completing some tasks without interruption and when their brains are alert and functioning. It is also the time for site meetings, dealing with problems of cleaning, vandalism, etc. In many schools the head is on duty during lunchtime and, in spite of legislation that states they must take at least half an hour's break for lunch themselves, few seem to do this. At the end of the school day the meetings schedule starts up: those involving teaching staff are usually immediately after school and would typically include a weekly leadership team meeting. It is also the time for individual meetings with staff. Then there are the evening meetings – governors (main and subcommittees), parent associations, open evenings, community groups, consultation evenings, school productions and meetings for prospective parents.

In between times the head has to keep up with paperwork from the DfES, the LEA and, since managing the budget, companies trying to sell any goods or services a school could possibly want to buy. There will also be all the individual letters and phone calls from parents and other members of the local community. Obviously a good personal assistant will relieve the head of the need to deal with the initial sift of these but the heads of small schools do not have exclusive use of administrative services; the secretary may also be the receptionist and may be only part-time. There are times in the day when the head is the only person available to answer the phone or let a visitor in. However unacceptable this may seem as use of the time of the most expensive member of the school staff, it is often an unavoidable fact. The call has to be answered – the health or safety of a pupil could otherwise be put at risk. The result of all this is that in the majority of schools the head is not at liberty during the typical school day to work uninterrupted on strategic thinking or to give serious thought to the implications of the most recent initiative. The time for this has to be found elsewhere.

In both the paragraphs above there are comments about the extra difficulties in managing time for heads of small schools. The budget, dependent on the number and age of pupils, has to be committed almost entirely to teachers in the classroom, so the head has to be part of the teaching team, with little non-contact time and very little administrative assistance. Several letters in the TES have highlighted this particular problem and in the case quoted below it led to illness and a decision to leave teaching altogether (TES 31 May 2002: 20).

> The writer had just resigned his headship of a small rural primary school after six months absence through stress-related illness and an OFSTED report critical of the leadership and management of the school. He had been head for eleven years and had become 'ground down' by the pressures of being both a class teacher and a head. He had regularly asked the LEA to provide money to enable him to have more non-contact time but none was available and he had to carry out his job as head on one day a week. He found it impossible and made a plea for all heads of small schools to have a minimum of two days per week non-contact time so that they did not need to sacrifice themselves and their families and become failures. He no longer wanted to teach but was hoping to find something to do which allowed him to 'have a life' as well.

Delegation

Why not delegate meetings to other senior staff or governors? Many heads, particularly of larger schools, successfully delegate attendance at governors subcommittee meetings to relevant deputies, cross-phase liaison meetings to heads of key stages, and so on, but for many the amount of delegation possible is quite limited. Many of the meetings described above may not formally require the head's presence but she may be the only person able to agree a course of action, may be the only member of the group who has the complete picture, or may be required to give the meeting status or reassurance that its function is valued. Several very experienced heads we talked to had concluded that work could generally be saved in the long run if they attended as many meetings as possible. They had found that, especially at governors and parents meetings, issues were brought up that did not appear on agendas. Sometimes these were simple questions that the head could respond to immediately; sometimes they were the first indication of some underlying problem. Being there on the spot enabled the head to hear everything first hand, explore and respond appropriately. Another person may not have picked up on the problem, may not have been able to respond immediately, or may have misunderstood and answered inappropriately – in all these cases the head would eventually have work to do that could have been simplified if she had been there herself.

Using your computers

The development of computer technology has had a great effect on the work of many teachers and headteachers. Like almost every other heading in the list of the demands of the job, headteachers see its impact as potentially very positive or very negative. On the positive side, some have relished the accumulation of data as they have seen the possibilities of accurate tracking of pupils' progress and teachers' performance. Others have been overwhelmed by the abundance of data input required, unsure of their own competence with the software and unable to delegate the input and manipulation of data to anyone else – whose time should be paid for to do this activity rather than some other, possibly more important and certainly more urgent, task?

There is no doubt that there are many benefits for those who are at ease with computers. In large schools where all staff have easy access to a computer communications are quicker and more reliable – such items as agendas, memos and pupil information can be circulated with the confidence that information is received and is secure. Registers can be completed electronically, pupil data can be stored and manipulated to create targets, assessments and reports can be generated and planning can be adapted as needed. Even contacts with parents and carers can be made electronically, from access to pupils' timetables on the website, to discussions about individual educational needs. State of the art specialist technology schools and colleges can even expect the bulk of pupils' work to be created and stored on computer. The reality for most schools, however, may contain only some part of the description above, depending on the skills and enthusiasm of key members of staff. The challenge for the head is to have sufficient knowledge of ICT resources to be able to make decisions about their use and sufficient knowledge of her staff to know who could use them to the most benefit for the school.

It is not the head's job to spend hours typing figures onto spreadsheets – but she does need to know how to interpret them. The secretary/personal assistant/bursar should be inputting data and providing the head with the figures she needs. As it is easy to be persuaded by sophisticated presentation that the contents of a pupil's essay is of good quality, so a head can convince herself that time spent at a computer keyboard is time well spent. We heard of several heads who allowed themselves to be so seduced by their computers that they failed to carry out their role as managers and were surprised when their schools began to fail, as already illustrated in the vignette in the budgeting section. However, and most fortunately, most heads are far more interested in finding out what their pupils are learning and how well they are being taught to want to spend any more time than necessary at their newly provided laptop computers.

6 Selecting and supporting headteachers

Introduction

This chapter examines the selection of headteachers. First it examines trends in headteacher appointments in England over the last few years. Trends are apparent from a study of national statistics, which show, for instance, a rise in appointments of female heads. Further statistics from a survey of headship appointments give an indication of the extent to which those appointed were internal or external appointments.

The next section deals with the selection process viewed from the perspective of selectors. This involves deciding on the qualities and experience which the new headteacher requires and then deciding how to assemble evidence to assess these. Candidates need to consider how they can provide this evidence.

Following appointment there should be arrangements for induction of the new headteacher. There is evidence that mentoring by a suitable experienced headteacher can be of great benefit both to the new head and also the mentor.

The number of headship promotions

Statistics of Education 2002 (DfES 2003) gives the number of classroom teachers promoted to headships in England and Wales each year (31 March deadline) (actual numbers from the Database of Teacher Records with rounding errors), as shown in Tables 6.1 and 6.2.

The statistics show the following trends:

- A peak of promotions between 1996 and 1998
- About 80 per cent of the promotions are from the post of deputy head
- Primary headships have a rising proportion of females
- Secondary headships show a similar trend.

The gender balance of all headteachers in 2001 is shown in Tables 6.3 and 6.4.

A study has shown how there is a tendency for the proportion of male heads to rise with distance from London. This may be difficult to change despite efforts to do so.

Table 6.1 Primary headship appointments by gender 1995/6 to 2000/1

Primary	95/6	96/7	97/8	98/9	99/00	00/1
Male	510 (30%)	500 (27%)	570 (27%)	320 (23%)	550 (30%)	380 (25%)
Female	1,200 (70%)	1,360 (73%)	1,550 (73%)	1,100 (77%)	1,260 (70%)	1,140 (75%)
Total	1,710	1,860	2,120	1,420	1,810	1,520

Table 6.2 Secondary headship appointments by gender 1995/6 to 2000/1

Secondary	95/6	96/7	97/8	98/9	99/00	00/1
Male	270 (69%)	300 (65%)	320 (60%)	230 (58%)	230 (61%)	260 (58%)
Female	120 (31%)	160 (35%)	210 (40%)	170 (43%)	150 (39%)	190 (42%)
Total	390	460	530	400	380	450

Table 6.3 Gender of primary headteachers and deputies in 2001

Primary	Heads	Deputies	Assistant heads	All teachers
Male	6,900 (39%)	3,400 (26%)	500 (23%)	26,900 (16%)
Female	10,600 (61%)	9,900 (74%)	1,700 (77%)	142,700 (84%)
Total	17,500	13,300	2,200	169,600

Table 6.4 Gender of secondary headteachers and deputies in 2001

Secondary	Heads	Deputies	Assistant heads	All teachers
Male	2,600 (68%)	4,400 (64%)	3,100 (61%)	82,700 (46%)
Female	1,200 (32%)	2,500 (36%)	2,000 (39%)	98,100 (54%)
Total	3,800	6,900	5,100	180,800

A colleague deputy head was preparing to apply for secondary headships. Her mentor advised her to send for details of any reasonably suitable school advertising the next week so that they could look at what was required and prepare a 'practice' application. A school in Doncaster was advertising for a new head so she sent off for the details. Having used the information as a tutorial tool she forgot about the school until she received a telephone call several weeks later. It was the current head of the school inquiring why she had decided not to apply for the job. They had had twenty requests for information, five of these had been from women but no women had sent in a completed application. The school was taking part in a project to find out why so few women applied for headships in the authority. They seemed to be locked into a cycle of having no women heads but no opportunity to appoint any. Unfortunately, this colleague's reason for not applying did not help them solve the problem!

The following statistics have been compiled from data collected on behalf of NAHT and kindly made available by John Howson of Education Data Services. These were based on a survey of headteacher appointments in the school year 1998/9. The returns covered about half of all appointments.

Primary headship internal and external appointments

For primary schools in 1998/9 27 per cent of new heads were internal appointments and 73 per cent were external. There were more applications (10) for externally filled posts than for internally filled posts (8).

Table 6.5 shows that deputies are more likely to be promoted in their own school. Of external appointments it is probably heads who take the larger schools and teachers who take the small schools. The category of teacher covers all posts other than head or deputy. The appointment of heads internally is likely to involve mergers of schools.

Secondary headship internal and external appointments

For secondary schools 24 per cent of new heads were internal appointments and 76 per cent were external. There were 19 applications where an internal appointment was made and 25 for an external one. Table 6.6 shows the sources of these internal and external appointments.

Selection

As so many cases of poor performance demonstrate, mistakes at the selection stage are very costly. Although the importance of the process is appreciated by those who are carrying out the selection process, this does not necessarily carry over into a realisation that it is worth investing financial resources in the process as well as a great deal of time. A consideration of the head's salary over a five-year period will give some idea of the scale of the investment which is being made. If any costs of selection are balanced against a small improvement in the

Table 6.5 Source of primary headteacher internal and external appointments 1998/9

	Head %	DH %	Teacher %	Other %	Total
Internal	8	58	29	5	100
External	39	5	47	9	100

Table 6.6 Source of secondary headteacher internal and external appointments 1998/9

	Head %	DH %	Teacher %	Other %	Total
Internal	7	42	51	0	100
External	32	3	57	8	100

return from this investment, the case for investigating the selection process becomes more compelling.

The Peter Principle (Peter and Hull 1969) suggests that there is more to selecting for more senior positions than being good at the current job (see chapter 3).

Whilst a pre-qualification before headship is a clear step forward, selection panels for headteacher appointments to particular schools will still need to ensure that the candidates are matched to the particular school and its current state and future direction. They will also need to choose a candidate with whom they feel comfortable and with whom they can work. As we see later (chapter 12) the relationship between the headteacher and the governing body can be a source of great tension and can ultimately lead the headteacher to be unsuccessful in that school and to leave.

Assessment centres

Assessment centres are arrangements for assessing the skills and competences of candidates for particular posts. Although the term centre suggests a location, the concept is of a process rather than a physical centre. They can be used as part of selection procedures or they can be used to identify development needs of candidates at any time. Assessment centres use a variety of means to assess candidates – inventories, interviews, simulated tasks. Candidates are often observed and assessed whilst performing simulated tasks. These tasks are chosen to cover the range of competences which successful job holders will need. Small groups of candidates are also assessed whilst they interact on some of these simulated tasks. The research on assessment centres suggests that they can give a valid assessment of the capabilities of candidates. The competences on which assessment centres are predicated will be those of job holders in general, thus even an assessment from such a centre may not give an accurate picture of the ability of a candidate to perform in a particular school if its context and situation are not typical.

In principle, assessment centres for particular contexts and situations could be created. This would require an analysis of the characteristics which make job holders successful in those specific conditions. Then exercises would need to be created and validated to assess those competences. The closer the match between the analysis of context and situation and its replication through simulations, the better the predictive value of the assessment for specific schools.

An account of the assessment centre set up at Oxford Brookes University in 1990 is given by Esp (1993) and was briefly described in chapter 3. Although this process received good feedback, it was quite expensive since a number of trained observers were required to assess candidates over a number of days and provide feedback and debriefing.

The simulations which may be incorporated into the selection process for headteachers use similar principles to those on which an assessment centre works but the simulations are unlikely to have been validated against the skills measured and the observers have not been trained.

Research findings

For research on headteacher selection we have to go back to that of Morgan *et al.*
(1983) on secondary headteachers. This was at a time when LEAs controlled the
process. Much has changed in the job of the headteacher since then and there
have been advances in selection for senior executives which might be
incorporated. The research of Morgan *et al.* led to improvements in the selection
process but we do not know how far those operate 20 years later. We offer the
following based on their findings, what we know of selection processes outside
education and the increased power of governing bodies.

Using consultants in the selection process

Although the chief education officer of the LEA has a duty to give advice to the
school's governing body on their choice of headteacher, the selection process
and the choice is the responsibility of the governing body. Many governing bodies
have taken the opportunity to employ an educational selection consultant to
guide and advise them.

A number of organisations have appeared which offer consultancy services to
advise governors who wish to appoint a new headteacher. Experienced consultants
can be of enormous value. They can

- Advise on all stages of the selection process
- Provide simulations and other activities as means of generating evidence
- Help to publicise the post and solicit candidates to apply
- Provide professional advice on the quality of applicants.

They can be of particular value when they have experience of a great many
similar appointments. They will know of common pitfalls in the process and be
able to facilitate the group dynamics of the selection panel. It is important that
they assist governors to reach their own conclusions on the kind of headteacher
that they wish to appoint. Since many of the ideas of governors will be tacit, the
role of the consultant is to help governors to make their wishes more explicit and
to help them to appreciate the likely consequences of different courses of action.

Principles

One of us has suggested (Fidler 1992) that the task of selecting a new headteacher
by the governing body should be seen in two stages:

1   Identifying the field of candidates who *could* do the job
2   Selecting from this group the one who the governing body feel that they can
    best work with.

This gets away from a search for the best headteacher. That suggests that there
is some objective view of best and this makes all those not selected appear second

best. The issue should be – who is an appropriate headteacher in the particular circumstances? The circumstances here refer to the state of the school, the aspirations of the governing body and the satisfaction of parents with whom the new headteacher will have to work. One should note here that this implies that as circumstances change the 'fit' between the headteacher and the situation might change.

The guiding principle in appointing a headteacher is to think in terms of a fit between the needs of the school and the characteristics of the applicants. This involves analysis of the present state of the school and a recognition of the personal characteristics and skills which a potential headteacher will need to bring to this particular job.

Process

At the point where a vacancy for a new headteacher arises there will be decisions about whether there is time to appoint a new headteacher to provide continuity with the one who is leaving. This will depend upon whether this is a planned departure such as retirement or promotion or whether the vacancy has arisen without warning. If there has been no warning there will have to be an acting headteacher; in other cases there may be a choice to be made. Contingency plans will need to include the possibility that the post of headteacher has to be readvertised if a suitable group of applicants is not attracted the first time. This delay will almost certainly mean that an acting head will have to be appointed. As we shall see later in chapter 7, a period of acting headship for a deputy is very developmental and provides very good insight into what it means to be a headteacher. Thus, if possible, this should be borne in mind if an acting head has to be appointed. Where there is more than one deputy head and for these developmental reasons the most senior is not to be appointed as acting head, this will need very sensitive handling.

It is probably appropriate to have a general discussion in the governing body about the choice of a new head and to encourage all governors to give their views so that these can be taken into account in the selection process. A smaller panel of governors will need to be selected to carry through the selection process and recommend a choice to the full governing body for ratification. The smaller group of five or six should be broadly representative of the interests in the governing body but will be conditioned by which governors can give up the substantial amount of time involved. It is important that all members of the panel take part in all stages of the process and particularly where candidates are providing evidence which will influence the selection process. All candidates should receive equitable treatment. The commitment needs to be clear so that some of the panel do not have to drop out as the process proceeds.

The stages are:

- Formulating requirements
- Drafting the advertisement and further particulars

- Long-listing
- Short-listing
- Selection activities
- Making the choice
- Debriefing unsuccessful candidates.

Formulating requirements

Governors have access to much more information on the performance of their school than has been the case in the past. In particular there are two sets of documents which will be invaluable to governors in assessing the needs of their school.

- PANDA reports
- OFSTED inspection reports.

These two documents will provide evidence about the current performance of the school compared to schools with a comparable intake. The Performance and Data (PANDA) report provides evidence of the extent to which the school helps children make progress from one key stage to the next. Studying these documents over a number of years can also indicate any overall trend in performance. A school with increasing progress is a very different one from one with a falling pattern. This has obvious implications for the skills of the headteacher. A rising profile needs someone who can reinforce existing practice whilst a school with worsening progress needs someone who will hold an inquest and bring about change.

Such external sources of information will be supplemented by governors' direct knowledge of the school and any data that has been collected for marketing and promotional purposes. Many schools conduct satisfaction surveys of parents and increasingly of children in the school. These may give pointers to changes that are needed. An analysis of the intake numbers to the school and recent changes may indicate trends which need to be reversed (Fidler 2002a).

Governors who have known the school for some time may feel that they have a good idea of the future progress which they hope the school will make. The issue then becomes how to decide on the characteristics which a headteacher will need to be able to deliver this progress. A related question to which thought also has to be given is 'how will we tell if each of the candidates has these characteristics?'

In *Poorly Performing Staff in Schools and How to Manage Them* (Fidler and Atton 1999) we formulated the job of headteacher in five areas:

- Teaching
- Educational vision
- Management
- Relationships
- Leadership.

This framework provides a means of analysing the skill areas which a headteacher will need. The earlier analysis of the current state of the school will indicate which of these areas have particular priority. For all except teaching heads in very small schools, it will be the final four which are most important.

The degree to which candidates possess these skills is for the selection process to assess. A selection process can have a number of components, each of which assesses skills with some degree of certainty. This approach suggests that skills are fixed and the problem is largely one of accurate assessment. However, it is generally held that individuals operate differently in different circumstances and so skills are to some degree context-dependent. Thus the problem becomes one of predicting how a potential headteacher will operate in a particular school and the selection process becomes one of assembling a variety of evidence on which to base this prediction.

We have already referred to the transition which almost all candidates would need to make to operate in the post of headteacher of a particular school. Their previous practice will have been in another post and probably in another school. Thus the relevance of that experience will require an assessment of the degree to which the previous situation was similar to that likely to be encountered in the post on offer. Where an assessment is provided by others, for example in the form of a reference, there will be a further task of assessing the competence and motives of the reference writer. More objective accounts of past practice may be available by consulting the latest OFSTED inspection report of the previous school.

HOW TO ASSESS CANDIDATES

What we know of other people is dependent on

- What they say
- What they write
- What they do.

With this in mind it is clear that to form a rounded picture of candidates a number of forms of collecting evidence need to be used (Fidler 2002b). This also has implications for candidates as they can also make assessments of their opportunities to present evidence of differing kinds to selectors. Such evidence falls into two broad groupings:

- General evidence on candidates' knowledge, principles, values and personality (see Table 6.7)
- Specific evidence on practice related to particular contexts (see Table 6.8).

Drafting the advertisement and further particulars

In view of the general difficulty of attracting a good field of candidates for many headships, the advertisement needs to be eye-catching and 'sell' the school and

Table 6.7 Sources of general evidence on headship candidates

Evidence	Sources
Personal characteristics Educational knowledge and leadership principles and values	Personality tests • Written submissions • Interviews exploring knowledge, principles and values

Table 6.8 Sources of specific evidence on headship candidates

Evidence	Sources
What a candidate *has done* in previous situations (either as self-report or as reported by others)	• Application form • References • Written submissions on previous practice • Interviews dealing with previous practice • Observation of practice, e.g. teaching
What a candidate says he or she *would do* in a hypothetical situation	• Written submissions addressing a particular scenario • Interview based on a scenario
What a candidate *does* in a simulated situation intended to be like the post in question	Analogous test, e.g. discussion group, in-tray exercise, role play
What a candidate *does* in an actual situation	Simulated activity in a real situation, e.g. giving feedback to a teacher after observation of their teaching in the school in question

its needs. See the examples of headship advertisements in chapter 3. Thought needs to be given to an application form, where it will be returned along with any responses and information requested in the further particulars.

The further particulars need to be available for candidates as they request them following the advert. It is very frustrating if there is a long delay before they are sent. Consideration will be needed about what information is sent to give an adequate background to the school and on which candidates can base any response. The dates for likely interviews should if possible be contained in the further particulars so that potential candidates who cannot meet these dates do not waste their time applying.

It will be clear from the analysis of how to obtain pertinent information, that the application stage is the point at which candidates can be asked for some specific responses. These will help in the long-listing process otherwise this will have to be done on the basis of their experience and what is volunteered in a letter of application. This is the stage at which the decision-making is least informed by evidence. This suggests that the application process needs to generate valid evidence on which to select potential candidates for the next stage.

Internal candidates

As the earlier statistics show there are a large number of appointments of internal candidates (about 25 per cent). Where there is a strong internal candidate it is clear that they should apply and be considered alongside other candidates. There may be issues concerned with convincing other candidates that the selection process is open and fair irrespective of whether it is so. The harder issues may concern considerations of continuity and change. This may be easier to deal with if the selection process is seen as selecting the best fit for the particular job rather than selecting the person with the best headship skills. It may be that an internal candidate would make an excellent headteacher of another school but this one needs a change of style and fresh ideas. Such delicate issues will need sensitive discussion and offers to assist career progression. Here, providing a period of acting headship can be an invaluable asset to an internal candidate who wishes to gain a headship in another school.

In many ways the more difficult issues are where there are unsuitable potential internal applicants. We mean here candidates who the selectors have no intention of appointing. This is very different to the case above where there is a real chance that the internal candidate might be appointed. There are different opinions on how this should be handled but our advice is that such potential candidates should be 'counselled out' if at all possible. Certainly taking them through to short-listing as a moral obligation is, we consider, highly undesirable. They will make the selection process more protracted because of the time for one or more extra candidates and if they have a negative attitude this may disturb other candidates.

It is important that deputy heads and others on the senior management team who will work with the new headteacher, and others who will work with them have an opportunity to meet and discuss the school and its future. The present senior management team may be a material aspect of the fit between the new headteacher and the job. As a number of our and other examples show, a headteacher who either is not supported by their deputies or is undermined by them has a very difficult time. Whilst this may be sorted out successfully, it can be a very painful process. And this may prevent the headteacher being successful and lead to their removal.

Long-listing

This is an optional stage. It is used to include those candidates who might be worth inviting to the face-to-face stage of the selection process but when more information is required to make that decision. These people will be included in the group whose references are obtained as further information to help decide whether they should be short-listed. To reach the long-listing and subsequent stages there should be a systematic assessment of each candidate using criteria which have been agreed when the school's requirements were formulated. This means some kind of grid which each selector can use to grade each candidate so that there can be systematic discussion of each one with each selector able to contribute.

One or more professional advisers will be required at this stage to give an educationalist's perspective. This may be the consultant, an LEA adviser or both. In planning a schedule of meetings to run through the whole process, the difficulty of finding times and dates as more people are involved, increases far faster than the number of people involved.

Morgan *et al.* (1983) found three uses of references: substantive, problematic and corroborative. The first was to establish 'minimum credibility' (p. 49) or differentiate between those who should be considered further and those who shouldn't. The second and third are where they are used to detect problems and eliminate candidates or to confirm that they should be included. Similar use should be made of references for all candidates.

When the process was operated by the LEA there were clear opinions about the value of references and what weight should be placed on different types and sources of references. That these varied from LEA to LEA should indicate that these were only conventions that had been adopted but at least they were consistent. It is now for individual governing bodies to judge the references. However, there is rather more public information about the schools from which candidates come including the latest inspection report. This can be expected to make an explicit comment on the leadership of a serving headteacher and may give clues about the leadership of other senior managers. Whilst any judgement expressed in the inspection report should not be taken as accurate (Fidler *et al.* 1998), it adds the perspective of disinterested professional observers, to be added to the other information volunteered by candidates.

Short-listing

This is the stage at which those applicants who are to appear at the final stages of the selection process are to be chosen. The number will depend on the format of the final stage. If it involves a preliminary assessment of a number of candidates before a smaller number are invited to stay for the final stages, the number may be higher than if all are to be retained for longer. In order to decide on numbers (assuming that the field of candidates permits) the final stages should be planned so that time schedules for the process are manageable. If more than 5 or 6 are to be invited the schedules need particular scrutiny to ensure that with the inevitable small hitches they are still workable and do not involve late night sessions unless everyone is prepared for that.

Selection activities and making the choice

Following the research of Morgan *et al.* (1983) it became obvious that there were advantages to taking more time and involving more activities in the final stage rather than relying on a formal interview only. Morgan *et al.* drew attention to the value of analogous tests or simulations of management practice. Since then some of these, such as in-tray exercises, have become a little hackneyed but the value of seeing candidates in simulated situations should not be underestimated.

As the analysis of evidence gathering above indicates, interviews only involve the candidate talking about what they have done or would do. A simulation adds an extra dimension. Thus any of the exercises which would form part of an assessment centre could be used.

Since the work of Morgan *et al.* a selection aid which has appeared is the personality test. There are a range of tests and the results need interpretation. As we have seen earlier, if leadership is more than a set of behaviours which can be developed, then there is a case for probing the personal characteristics of would-be leaders. Whilst any assessment of these will not be definitive it will provide further evidence to probe and weigh in the final assessment.

The literature on personnel selection has increasingly offered personality tests as a valuable aid to selection decisions. In the 1980s attempts to set up a taxonomy for describing personality began to achieve acceptance from scholars and in the 1990s occupational psychologists made progress by examining which characteristics contributed to occupational success. The 'big five' personality dimensions which have been investigated are:

- extraversion (ambition and sociability)
- emotional stability (anxiety and security)
- agreeableness (co-operation and tolerance)
- conscientiousness (will to achieve and dependability)
- openness to experience (curiosity, imagination and intelligence).

Meta-analysis of research in the USA was compiled to examine the correlation of these factors with job performance (Barrick and Mount 1991). Teachers were one of seven professions investigated and managers in commercial organisations were another group investigated. The results suggest that conscientiousness is an important correlate with occupational success in a wide range of jobs. Extraversion was a valid predictor for managers. A further finding was that openness to experience and extraversion were predictors of training readiness and training success. Whilst the correlations for the meta-analysis were small, the methodology used was conservative and designed to set a lower bound on the possible correlation. This suggests that there is more potential for the use of personality tests in personnel selection decisions in schools.

A further source of selection evidence which some schools have tried is visiting the schools of short-listed candidates. In the case of teaching heads this may involve seeing the candidate teach. Such information for headship candidates will need to be gathered by the professional consultant and needs to provide comparable evidence for all candidates. This provides evidence on actual performance but is still in a different context and situation from the appointing school.

Where teaching performance is a critical aspect of the appointment, some schools have arranged for candidates to teach a specimen lesson to children in the appointing school as part of the selection process. Although this is a sample of actual performance the results are comparable with other simulation evidence since the situation is an artificial one as candidates are meeting the group of children for the first time. A suitable process for headteacher appointments which has been trialled is to ask each candidate to observe and comment on a teacher's lesson in the appointing school. This can bring out a range of evidence not only on the candidate's views of effective teaching but also how they establish rapport with teachers and how sensitively they are able to give authentic feedback to the teacher.

Finding opportunities as part of the selection process for staff and pupils to meet and react to candidates is a valuable if again a rather artificial exercise. Selectors can observe the candidates' reaction to the encounter in addition to hearing of the reaction of teachers and children.

A range of analogous tests or simulations includes:

- In-tray exercise
- Demonstration lesson
- Observing and giving feedback on teaching of a staff member
- Dealing with children individually and in groups
- Simulated discussion of management activities.

There can also be a range of interviews – small group, specialist panel, one-to-one – before the final formal selection interview. These interviews can be planned to probe the candidates' experience, their views on a variety of school matters and what they say they would do in hypothetical circumstances.

We believe that the final stage of headship interviews and selection should take at least two days. The candidates must be given the time and opportunity to get to know the school so that they can make a decision on whether they would like to take the job. And selectors need to acquire and assimilate as much information about candidates as possible in order to make an informed decision. This means that the selection process must build in time for selectors to assimilate and discuss the large amount of evidence on each candidate. And then there may be a discussion negotiating salary.

Debriefing unsuccessful candidates

One of the least enviable tasks in selection procedures is to debrief unsuccessful candidates. This is particularly the case if the process has been envisaged as the search for the one with the best headteacher skills. The problem is lessened a little if it is seen as finding the most appropriate headteacher for the particular post. In that case those candidates who have been assessed as competent can be given the reassurance that it was a matter of fit that led to the final decision.

What irritates many candidates is to be given reasons for their being unsuitable for the post which should have been obvious from the application form. This really indicates that the selection process has not been conducted efficiently or that the feedback is not authentic. Where facts have only been clarified during the final selection there should be lessons on both sides about how to bring matters to light earlier. Genuine feedback on presentation or skills to be developed can be of enormous help to candidates but it should be remembered that these are only judgements and other selectors might make quite different judgements. This means that any comments should be weighed up by candidates rather than acted upon as authoritative feedback.

Induction and mentoring

As we emphasised in *Poorly Performing Staff in Schools and How to Manage Them* (Fidler and Atton 1999), induction is a very important part of staff management for all staff. We saw this as having two aspects:

- detailed factual introduction to the new job and the new organisation
- induction into the culture of the new organisation and its expectations.

However, there are particular issues for headteachers. Who is to induct them? The culture they might be inducted into may need changing. How do they pick up the culture? As we see later in chapter 8, new heads are simultaneously learning what it means to be a headteacher (professional socialisation) and learning about their new organisation (organisational socialisation) and with much less help and guidance than other new members of staff who will have superordinate established staff to turn to.

As small scale research from Scotland (Draper and McMichael 1998a) showed, as the preparation of candidates before headship improves so the focus moves on to induction in the first post. As the paragraph above and the study by Parkay and Hall (1992) demonstrate this is inevitable. Prior training can prepare for professional socialisation into headship, and can alert candidates to expect that learning about the new organisation quickly will be a challenge. But the sense-making required in a short space of time in the first few days and weeks in the job will be full of surprises. We suggest that a range of organisational perspectives (see chapter 3) and the learning from previous moves of school can provide some preparation for the task.

Whilst LEAs can provide an induction programme for entry into the LEA, induction into the school is a self-help project. However, mentoring by another headteacher in the early period of headship has been found to be of great benefit. What is also clear from the literature is that mentoring can have benefits for the mentor as well as the mentee.

Mentoring

A number of studies have examined the concept of mentoring and practice in other countries (Daresh and Playko 1992; Stott and Walker 1992) and there is also an evaluation of an English pilot scheme of mentoring for headteachers (Pocklington and Weindling 1996). A definition of mentorship (Ashburn *et al.* 1987: 1) 'the establishment of a personal relationship for the purpose of professional instruction and guidance' doesn't really bring out the non-directive and non-critical role that distinguishes a mentoring relationship from a managerial one (Stott and Walker 1992). A mentor should act as a guide and offer support but should also challenge established views to ensure they are securely founded.

A mentor for a new headteacher needs to have other characteristics in addition to being an effective headteacher him or herself. They need to

- Ask the right questions and not just supply answers
- Accept other ways of doing things and not tell mentees 'the right way' in their opinion
- Encourage mentees to aim for higher performance however good it is already
- Model principles of 'continuous learning and reflection' themselves (Daresh and Playko 1992: 149).

A further thought in setting up a mentor system and choosing mentors is to consider the impact on school leadership. The chosen mentors will be seen as role models and so the effect of this style of leadership on new heads should be anticipated. Mentoring presents an opportunity to influence the leadership of schools. Partly this will depend on whether these heads are also successful as mentors rather than instructors, since there may be a reaction of new heads against prescription.

Mentors also need training and development for the role. In addition to any technical skills of mentoring they also need their interpersonal skills developed (Daresh and Playko 1992). The development of mentors needs to be continuous so that they can deal with common issues that are found to arise.

In addition to care in selecting mentors, further thought needs to be given to the fit between individual mentor and individual mentee. Experience in Singapore suggests that mentors, mentees and the organisers of mentoring should be able to express a preference for the matches and that based on these the organising body should attempt to set up pairs. Mentors were given the opportunity to reject the match they were given.

The English advice to mentors about how to approach new heads (Pocklington and Weindling 1996) was to 'build up an understanding of the nature of the management task, its impact on the school and his/her reasons for the chosen line of action' (p. 178). The authors comment that 'Implicitly, it was about encouraging the novice headteacher to reflect on aspects of school management and thereby become more aware of what was entailed in managing effectively' (p. 178).

The new heads listed very pressing issues they discussed with mentors, with most mentioning members of staff and relations with the governing body. These included what to do about staff, sometimes key members of the SMT. There was more variety of governor issues – content of annual report, relationships and boundaries, and countering unrealistic expectations from governors.

From a large group of new heads the most frequent mentions of topics for discussion with mentors were:

- Managing time and priorities (67 per cent)
- Legacy of previous head (64 per cent)
- Improving teaching and learning (63 per cent)
- Staffing structure (57 per cent)
- School development plan (SDP) (56 per cent)
- Creating good public image (55 per cent)
- Improving consultation and communication (54 per cent)
- Getting staff to accept new ideas (47 per cent)
- Getting staff to work together (46 per cent)
- Getting post holders to assume school-wide responsibility (45 per cent)
- Dealing with a weak member of senior management (43 per cent)
- Working with governors (43 per cent)
- Deciding how much to delegate (42 per cent).

It is interesting to note that the legacy of the previous head loomed large in the first six months of the new head's experience.

A number of examples from case studies illustrate the value of mentoring. The first is of the head of a secondary school in an area of urban deprivation who inherited powerful deputies.

> The head of a secondary school was having difficulties with the two deputies who had virtually run the school under the previous head and who had been passed over when the new appointment was made. The mentor gave counselling sessions in which the head talked out the issues and helped focus on past experiences which would be helpful. The new head found this helpful as it made her feel more in control and put things in perspective. The mentor saw the task as helping the head sort out those issues on which she could do something and make progress compared to those on which she could not.

The second example is of the head of a small rural primary school.

> The head's perception was that the school had been allowed to stagnate even though it ran smoothly and was popular with parents. The staff did not share the perception of ossification. The new head and mentor considered various options but spent much time exchanging accounts of their dealings with their respective staffs. From this analysis new insights emerged. In particular the mentor was able to identify and analyse the actions which the new head had taken to work out whether they had been successful. The mentor gave advice and cautioned against doing too much too soon.

A third is of a deputy promoted in the same school.

> The new head was enabled to make a transition:
>
> Previously, I was the main mechanic, the nuts and bolts man ... That's not my role any more. Now I'm driving the train, not shovelling the coal ... *That* was the big step I had to take.
>
> (Pocklington and Weindling 1996: 184)

The fourth illustrates increasing self-confidence by receiving reassurance about actions or praise for achievements.

> The new headteacher ... found herself confronted by a very knowledgeable and powerful vice-chair of governors, to whom others invariably would defer. Her mentor counselled and encouraged the head against allowing herself to be intimidated.
>
> She said, 'Don't let the governors ride roughshod over you, take a stand'. So, at the end of last term I said 'No' to the vice-chair, and it worked. Afterwards he came up and said 'Thank you for putting me in my place – you needed to show you are in control'.
>
> (Pocklington and Weindling 1996: 185)

The advantages for heads who were being mentored

These emerged as:

- Emotional support
- Increased self-confidence by receiving reassurance about actions or praise for achievements
- Opportunities to raise issues and discuss in a non-threatening way without fear of repercussions
- Justify action, talk things through and use as sounding board
- Develop reflective abilities.

The advantages for mentors

These emerged as:

- Hearing about practice elsewhere sometimes produced good ideas to take on themselves
- The opportunity and incentive to think about their own practice

- After a while the mentor could raise problems in their own school for discussion in order to get help
- It provided a form of networking.

The final one is particularly worth noting. Taking part in an organised arrangement for mentoring brings experienced heads into contact both with new heads and also with other experienced heads who are mentoring. This helps to reduce the feelings of isolation which have been noted particularly since the ERA, with more competition between schools and less LEA support (Mercer 1996).

A recent review of LEA arrangements for the induction of new headteachers noted that only a minority had good programmes which included appropriate guidance materials, training and the pairing of new heads with more experienced colleagues (OFSTED/Audit Commission 2001).

Performance management

Headteachers do not easily fit into schemes of staff appraisal or performance management because they do not have any direct superordinate (Fidler and Cooper 1992). They share this with other chief executives.

Performance management is set up for situations where a manager can give feedback on performance to a subordinate, set targets, organise development and remove obstacles. The headteacher is expected to do this for senior staff in his or her school and set up schemes to ensure that this happens for other teaching staff. But the lack of a direct line manager complicates arrangements for the performance management of the headteacher.

In the statutory scheme of staff appraisal introduced in 1991, the appraisal of the headteacher was carried out by an official of the LEA and a peer headteacher. Although this arrangement was very time consuming there is evidence that headteachers welcomed this form of support (Hellawell 1997; Gunter 2002) and that it was developmental for peer headteachers to carry out such appraisals. Within five years the staff appraisal scheme was being subjected to criticism and fell into disuse until a new statutory scheme was put into place.

In the mid-1990s there was pressure from DfES and the School Teacher Review Body to implement performance-related pay for headteachers, and governing bodies were required to set targets annually for their headteachers. Any progress up the salary scale was expected to be dependent on satisfactory meeting of pre-set targets.

In the late 1990s a new scheme of performance management for teachers which included a leadership spine for senior staff was implemented. A sub-group of the governing body was to review the previous year's progress of their headteacher and set targets for the coming year. A consultant from Cambridge Education Associates was to be appointed to provide professional advice to the sub-group in that task. The consultant was to study performance statistics on the school and to advise the governors' sub-group on the targets which would be appropriate for the headteacher for the following year. Following this advice it was for the sub-group to agree their targets with their headteacher. This group was to recommend any progress of the headteacher up the leadership spine on the basis of this performance review. We are not aware of any research on the working of this new system of headteacher review.

7 Achieving headship

Introduction

Preparation for headship should be of interest not only to prospective headteachers but also to existing heads. A theme which we have been stressing is the complex nature of headship and the difficulty of acquiring the skills to be successful. Much of this learning will be experiential and can be greatly facilitated by existing headteachers. This can range from the provision of opportunities to lead activities and broaden experience to the more proactive mentoring and coaching of deputies and other staff by the headteacher.

This chapter deals with the career path of prospective headteachers and the value of acting headship and study as a preparation for headship. The final section examines the process of applying for headships and the selection process from the candidate's point of view.

Preparation before headship

Not all teachers wish to become headteachers and not all those who wish to become heads would make good heads. Thus selective mentoring and coaching is required. Some of those who might not have the skills and characteristics to become good heads may begin to appreciate their limitations if they are given responsibility and are helped to reflect upon their successes and failures.

The more interesting and difficult cases are those who have never thought of aspiring to headship but who might become good heads if they took this as a possibility and began to develop their potential. What are the indicators which senior staff should use to help identify those who have potential but are either not in leadership positions or their position does not allow them to demonstrate their potential? The concept of potential does not mean merely that such people are good at their current job although being a failure is hardly a recommendation.

Different leadership positions in schools require different talents and it does not follow that those who are competent at a lower level will be successful at the next level. The Peter Principle was formulated in 1969 and succinctly expresses the point 'in a hierarchically structured administration, people tend to be promoted up to their "level of incompetence"' (Peter and Hull 1969).

This was propounded from the observation that those who are good at their job get promoted into more senior and different jobs until they are no longer successful.

Career paths before headship

There is little in the literature about career paths before headship. We have assembled the following which we think from our experience are typical patterns. There may be many exceptions but we think these are helpful as points of departure to consider issues concerned with preparation for headship. We have considered primary headship and secondary headship separately and we have also considered whether there may be differences between appointments to small or large schools.

Generalising about progression to headship and appointments to headship is more difficult now than it was in the past because much more decision-making about appointments takes place at school level. For appointments up to deputy level, the influence of the headteacher is likely to be paramount but for more senior appointments governors are likely to be involved and for headships the decisions are made by governing bodies. The influence of the 150 LEAs in England is much more limited than in the past. There may be adviser input into appointments up to deputy head level or there may not. For headships the chief education officer has a duty to give advice but this may be only one input of professional advice into such appointments and whilst governors have a duty to consider the advice from the CEO they are not bound by it. Provided they do not act irresponsibly they will not be legally liable for any repercussions from their decisions.

It is remarked in both the business literature and that examining progress towards headship that at various stages a mentoring relationship from a more senior and experienced colleague is invaluable. This may arise in the course of formal performance management but the combination of temperament and willingness to act in this kind of role by a senior colleague may arise more spontaneously. A consideration of the value of a mentoring relationship within schools indicates that this can be extremely valuable to the mentee but can also be a stimulating learning experience for the mentor. We think that this should be more widely practised in schools.

Small primary schools

We have considered progression to the headship of a small primary school from either another small school or from a larger primary school (see Figure 7.1). We have used the term 'promoted post' to indicate the possession of a responsibility allowance since all primary teachers are likely to have some whole-school responsibility in addition to class teaching. In a small school there may not be salary points to reward the responsibility.

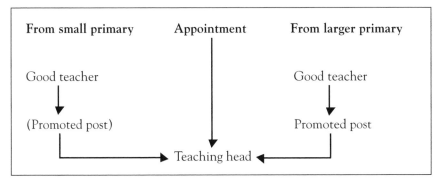

Figure 7.1 Career paths to the headship of a small primary school (stage in () is optional)

Large primary schools

We have considered progression to the headship of a large primary school (see Figure 7.2). This may be from the teaching head of a small school or after promotion in a larger school.

Although we think that progression in similarly sized schools is probably the more frequent path we have considered how those from small or large schools might aim for headship. Where teachers have moved post earlier in their career they may have experience in other sized schools which would make the transition easier.

Issues arising

We have identified a number of issues involved in moving to primary headship.

• The salary of deputy head of a large school makes headship of a small school unattractive.
• Too much promotion in one school makes a move to headship more difficult because of a lack of experience in different schools. We have seen increasing cases of sideways moves at deputy level or lower in order to increase experience in different schools.

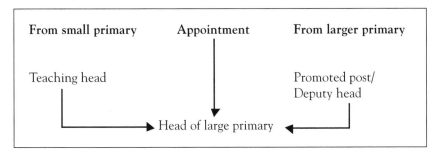

Figure 7.2 Career paths to the headship of a large primary school

- Those who have experienced teaching headships, where a substantial proportion of teaching is required each week, report that this can be very energy-sapping. Those who take the headship of a small school in the expectation of gaining headship experience and moving on to the headship of a larger school need to be aware of the pressures on teaching heads since these may prevent them moving on to a larger school.

Small secondary/11–16 secondary

Although Figure 7.3 shows a progression entirely down one route most candidates will have added to their experience by deputising or taking some responsibility in the other route at some point on their progression through to deputy head.

Issues arising

There are a number of issues arising:

- Often the first responsibility undertaken is voluntary and unpaid in order to gain experience. This may also be the case where additional responsibilities are undertaken in order to broaden experience across the two routes we have shown.
- The transition to senior management is a difficult one. The number of potential middle managers who might wish to progress to senior management is very large and there is likely to be stiff competition. Also middle managers often struggle to get a whole-school view before senior management; thus

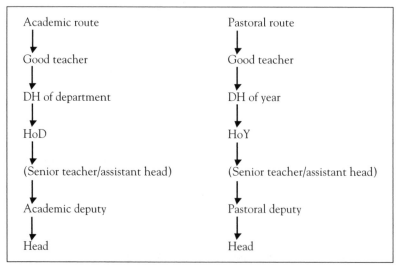

Figure 7.3 Career paths to the headship of a small secondary school (stage in brackets is optional)

working parties and initiatives which operate across the school provide particularly valuable experience.

- There are a number of combinations of deputy head and assistant headteacher which may cover the curriculum and academic responsibilities in the senior team. All are likely to involve a specialist function in addition to whole-school roles.
- Some schools may rotate the duties of deputies which can be helpful in rounding the experience of deputies in preparation for headship but this has to be balanced by the needs of the school in terms of expertise in each post and skills and experience of post holders. This may make rotation difficult if candidates with fairly rounded experience have not been selected for senior staff appointments. For example if timetabling or specialist skills and knowledge are involved with a particular post this may mean the pool of individuals who can move into this post is limited.

Large secondary

The progression to the headship of larger secondary schools may be from the headship of a smaller secondary school or from the deputy headship of a large secondary school. There may be issues about moving from a school without a sixth form to a school with one. Governors may consider such experience essential and thus candidates may need to ensure that they have recent sixth form experience or other credentials. We have detected an increasing trend to take more than one post at assistant head/deputy head level in order to increase experience but also more strategically to ensure that the profile of experience appears rounded to selectors.

Posts in denominational and independent schools

There appears to be movement between sectors up to middle manager level but it is rarer at more senior levels. In the case of the denominational sector there may be specific faith requirements for more senior positions. This narrows the pool of potential candidates and, in view of the generally reported difficulty of attracting a field of appropriate applicants for headships, it is increasingly important that this pool is well qualified and experienced if school leadership in this sector is not to suffer.

There is increasing interest in leadership development in the independent sector and an increasingly clear career structure for progression to headship. In the senior team there is increasing recognition that the post of deputy head or director of studies is a route to headship whilst senior master or mistress represents a senior appointment to a particular school. Appointments to boarding schools require particular senior experience in that sector.

Recent developments/trends

We have observed a number of trends which we think will probably be continued in the future:

- Formal preparation through NPQH will create more evenness in expectations of progression across the country.
- Careers for women have achieved greater recognition and time off for child rearing has achieved greater acceptance as an alternative to further experience in schools.
- There is less movement between schools in the progression to deputy head than was previously the case and we suspect that partly this is because the salary increases for movement do not compensate for the upheaval and costs involved if moving house is required.
- Increased recognition of the responsibility of middle managers to lead and manage will contribute to preparation for headship.
- The recently introduced 'fast track' promotion through the teaching career could provide good experience before headship if it involves a structured series of posts each of which involves graded challenging opportunities.
- There are an increasing number of people who take more than one post as assistant/deputy before applying for headship.
- Rotation of deputy responsibilities is less common than in the past.
- There are a number of people who take posts as heads of challenging/recovery schools who specialise in that task and move on when the recovery is well under way.
- Moving to a second headship is now more common than in the past.
- There are more opportunities for portfolio careers after headship.

Acting headship

The developmental value of acting headship has long been appreciated by those who have had the opportunity but it has been little studied. A recent national leadership survey (Earley *et al.* 2002) discovered that 30 per cent of heads had spent time as an acting head at some stage in their career and 10 per cent had been acting heads immediately before being appointed to headship. Of course acting headship is not the same as substantive head but it probably provides the most realistic precursor to the actual position itself. It also does not follow that those who experience acting headship then wish to go on to headship.

Types

Little is known about acting headship in England; however, a recent study in Scotland (Draper and McMichael 2002) has provided a useful framework for analysis and also produced data on the situation in Scotland. It should be borne in mind that the situation in Scotland is somewhat different to that in England.

Local authorities still have far more control over schools and their appointments so that many decisions about acting heads are taken by LEA officers. In England these decisions would be taken by school governors but there is no reason why local authorities couldn't draw up guidelines which schools could be recommended to follow if they were based on researched good practice.

Acting headship can be analysed by three criteria. This helps explain a number of features of acting headship.

Reason

The first distinction is between those posts which come about because the permanent head is unavailable and those which are motivated by a school need (see Figure 7.4).

The substantive head may be unavailable for a number of reasons. Most of these will be temporary such as illness or secondment but some may be longer-term when there is difficulty in appointing a new permanent headteacher.

A feature which has recently expanded in number is the case where the school's circumstances require a particular function to be discharged by an acting head-teacher. A frequent case is where a school has failed an inspection or there is some other kind of acute issue which requires a change of leadership. This type of acting headship usually involves a temporary appointment from outside the school rather than an internal appointment of someone 'acting up'.

Degree of planning

Another distinction is between posts which are unexpected and planned.

The most common expectation of acting headship is that the need comes up at very short notice and a very quick response is required. This would typically involve unanticipated illness where the need appears quickly and the period of acting headship is likely to be uncertain and depend on the health of the head.

On reflection, however, there are many examples where the need for an acting head could have been foreseen which allows more time for planning. Examples of planned temporary replacements for a headteacher are where the head goes on maternity leave, or on a planned secondment to another post. In this case there

		Type of need	
		Head unavailable	School need
Type of vacancy	Unexpected	Illness	Inspection failure
	Planned	Secondment or external special assignment	Long-standing head or school performance deteriorating

Figure 7.4 Type of vacancy and type of need for acting headships

is time both to consider the needs of the school and also the developmental potential of the post and who should benefit.

There are probably examples that are between the two types above in that they can be planned but only on a contingency basis. For example, when appointing a new headteacher, there is a possibility that the planned appointment will not be made if a suitable candidate does not apply and that an acting head will be required until a permanent appointment is made. A slightly more subtle example is when a school has problems or an unwell headteacher struggles on. In such cases the precise timing of an intervention may be difficult to plan, but there is a high probability that action will be required. This permits some contingency planning and also the possibility of choosing the timing of any intervention.

Length of time

The final distinction is between posts which are fixed term and those which are open-ended. Each of these can be of different lengths; each may be short or long.

There are three parties who are affected by the length of the acting appointment:

- School
- Individual
- Temporary holder of previous post.

Fixed term appointments permit planning by all three. All those connected with the school know when the acting headship will end; the individual is able to plan their work to some conclusion or transfer point and those who are concerned with the previous post of the acting person can plan resumption of their normal work. All of this focuses attention on the disruptive nature of open-ended acting posts. These might best be thought of as a series of fixed term appointments which might be repeated for a fixed number of times before alternative arrangements are made.

All of this analysis has tried to focus attention on the possibility of a greater degree of planning of acting posts such that they benefit the school but also are used for the planned development of individuals as far as possible. Some LEAs are attempting to operate in this way but it is possible that many others view acting headship as a crisis reaction that cannot be planned.

Although the discussion has been of acting headship, acting posts can occur at any level in schools and as Draper and McMichael (2002) remark, one appointment to an acting post in a school can cause a whole sequence of acting posts as the vacancy created by one acting post holder is filled by another acting post holder. Where one acting post holder comes from another school, this sequence can affect more than one school. This offers a further possibility of trying to ensure that such developmental opportunities do not happen randomly but that there is some attempt to ensure equity and plan benefit to particular individuals.

Whilst appointments between schools may need the assistance of LEAs, headteachers can plan appointments to acting posts in their own school. The focus here has been on replacing post holders who are temporarily unable to do their job but this can be supplemented by creating a new post for a fixed length of time. This can both serve a school need in terms of the work to be accomplished in the job and also provide development for the post holder. Although this has gone on in some schools it probably has greater potential to be used in more schools.

When considering the developmental possibilities for acting posts, whether these are replacements or newly created temporary posts, it is important that the development of the individual is planned. This involves the staff management activities of selection and induction but also requires development in the post at a more accelerated rate than need be the case for permanent appointments. The acting post is a learning opportunity but if the results of this are to be maximised there need to be arrangements for the person to reflect on their experience in an organised way and to be able to talk through their decision-making with a more experienced colleague. Like all mentoring activities this will involve extra effort from the person who is acting as mentor but this may also have learning benefits for them in terms of questioning what they do and how they do it. Whilst intuitively everyone knows that they gain from new experiences we do not know enough about the totality of the gains from this and how to bring them about.

Acting headship in Scotland

The data we have on acting headship is that from Scotland (Draper and McMichael 2002). Although the system is different with local authorities playing a much larger part in the management of schools, the data is recent and systematically collected. Thus it may provide some guide to the situation in England.

There were about ten acting heads in each of the 22 responding LEAs in a year. This affected more than 10 per cent of primary and secondary schools. Formal acting capacity was most likely after an absence of 20 days. About two-thirds of the posts were created for temporary reasons. Of these over 40 per cent were due to illness and a further third due to secondment with maternity leave accounting for 6 per cent.

The permanent absences were due to: retirement (40 per cent), resignation (about 30 per cent), promotion (14 per cent), other, including death, (15 per cent). Of the range of reasons for creating an acting post the expected length of absence of the headteacher was the most frequently mentioned.

Most posts were filled internally with assistant headteacher filling 8 per cent and deputies filling 92 per cent. This was usually the next most senior person. Not all primary schools have a deputy. Internal advertisement and selection was used where there was no obvious candidate. For 16 per cent of acting heads there was external advertising and selection.

Based on these figures, some 40 per cent of temporary and permanent absences were probably foreseeable and hence some degree of planning was possible.

The authors have carried out a series of small scale investigations on senior posts in Scotland. As these were not carried out on representative samples the figures should be interpreted with caution but the qualitative comments give good insights into how these post holders view promotion and the influence of acting posts.

In a study of 37 primary heads in Scotland (Draper and McMichael 1998a) a fifth had spent a period as acting head and of ten secondary heads three had acted up before headship (Draper and McMichael 1998c). Of 87 deputies 10 per cent had acted up (Draper and McMichael 1998b). Respondents reported that 'acting up' gives a taste of the post without the same pressures of being expected to deal with long-term problems. It can also give prominence for a short period which may aid applications for headships later. The authors speculate that the personal development effects on those acting may be greatest where leadership in a school has not been collaborative or the acting head comes from another school.

An acting post may either increase the desire to seek a headship or help form a decision not to do so. But in any event the career decisions are more informed. In view of the need to attract headship candidates this suggests that acting heads may need support if the role is not to put people off headship unnecessarily.

Acting posts at lower levels may have similar effects (Draper and McMichael 2000). The authors showed that of those acting as assistant heads (AHTs), two-thirds would apply for such posts. Whilst of AHTs acting as deputies, half would apply for deputy. There is no data on the pre-existing intentions of these groups which would indicate whether an acting post had caused any of them to change their minds although there are indications in the data that some did so.

Case studies of acting headship: two schools with four headteachers in two years

The following brief case study examples in England of the second reason for appointing an acting headteacher, i.e. the needs of the school, provide very poignant illustrations of the difficulties of either acting in such posts or following on as substantive headteacher.

> This is the case of a medium size primary school in a mixed catchment within an affluent area. The school is a church school with the vicar as chair of governors. A long-serving headteacher retired. An inspection report on the school before he finished was equivocal about work in the school. An outside appointment of permanent headteacher was made after a selection process in which the sitting deputy had been a candidate. The new head tried to make changes against determined opposition. Some

teachers took the inspection report to endorse their work and so saw no need to change, regarding the new head as over-enthusiastic. After two terms the new head took ill-health retirement following overwork.

A head from another school was brought in to stabilise the situation for two terms before advertising for a new substantive head. The sitting deputy was again a candidate but was not appointed. The new head came in to find some concerted opposition from a few staff; some being overheard to say that if the new head tried to make changes she would be 'seen off' like the last one.

This was an exceedingly difficult situation to change. Determined action from the head with some staffing changes and threats of capability procedures eventually broke the impasse. Stabilisation by the acting head had not provided a springboard for change and the new head was not provided with sufficient support to move on what was beginning to be recognised as a difficult school.

This was a primary school in challenging circumstances where the head-teacher had been ill for some time and the school had done very badly in an inspection (Crawford 2002). An acting head who was an experienced headteacher of another school stabilised the situation for two terms before he had to return to his own school for an inspection. He was replaced by another acting head, also an experienced head of another school, for two terms. He had a different approach but carried on 'keeping the show on the road'. When a substantive head was appointed she had to begin the improvement process all over again. There was little progress to show for the two periods of acting headship.

These two examples have been included to show that when schools have problems, either internally or as a result of external intervention, more is required of an acting headteacher than a safe pair of hands if the situation is to be improved sufficiently for a new permanent head to come in with a reasonable chance of success.

Implications

Acting headship can be of enormous developmental benefit to an individual as a foretaste of what headship will be like. It is more like a caretaker role than the full headship role but it can provide an experience which courses of training cannot. Where an acting post can be planned it should be possible both to meet the needs of the school and also to select a candidate who will benefit from the experience. There appears to be untapped potential to do this to a greater degree than is being done currently. However, there are occasions where the needs of the school require more than a safe pair of hands and the choice of acting head-teacher has to be made with more of an intervention in mind. Not all experienced headteachers can provide the right kind of intervention.

Training and qualifications

A survey of professional development provision for senior staff in schools and colleges in 1980 (Hughes *et al.* 1981) erected a distinction between longer award-bearing courses and short courses. That distinction has become increasingly fuzzy as education and training for management and leadership have evolved. However, we want to preserve a conceptual distinction between the two. We shall use award-bearing courses for those which involve reading the literature, grappling with theory and taking a critical and reflective approach to practice over an extended period, and which lead to an academic qualification. We wish to differentiate this kind of activity from the more pragmatic training, for example, which is offered for a national qualification, which is being offered in preparation for headship and may be offered at middle management level in the future.

From what we have said about the value of organisational analysis and the development of knowledge frameworks we believe that an extensive study of leadership and management at middle management level can be very beneficial. Some management experience is necessary to fully appreciate ideas in practice and to recognise the tensions between idealised prescription and the realities of practical situations. Middle management level is a formative stage when ideas about how to lead and manage are more fluid than later when a pattern of behaviour has become established and theoretical ideas are used to defend practice rather than to investigate it.

As was briefly mentioned in chapter 1 there has been increasing training for headteachers and others since 1983. Central government finance was made available for 20-day and one-term courses as training opportunities for senior school staff. In 1985 the regulations for financing full-time secondments for teachers were changed and they became financially unattractive for individuals and LEAs. There followed extensive training to deal with LMS, staff appraisal and the National Curriculum.

Finally in the mid-1990s a course of preparation for headship was devised by a newly formed Teacher Training Agency (TTA) before being revised and taken over by the National College for School Leadership. This began with such unrealistically high aims and untried and unproved methods that change soon became necessary. This kind of preparation before headship is clearly wise, particularly when it involves project work in school to demonstrate leadership capability, albeit in a different school from a likely headship and in the presence of a headteacher. The Scottish Qualification for Headship was set up a little later with the involvement of researchers who have been studying the learning of the course members and this should produce new knowledge about how mature professionals learn to practise leadership and management.

The pre-headship qualification is intended to become a requirement before headship and so an outline of its current shape is included here with a website reference. This is based on preparing candidates for the National Standards for Headship in England.

Qualification for headship

The National Professional Qualification for Headship (NPQH) was set up with a twofold role. It was to provide training for headship and also act as a pre-selection mechanism. The possession of an NPQH would indicate readiness for headship. Assessment was to take place in two stages. There was to be an assessment before training to assess whether candidates were ready for training and there was assessment at the completion of training to assess whether training had been successfully completed. It was this final assessment that was to indicate readiness to take on headship.

The stages were to be:

- Assessment of suitability for training
- NPQH training
- Assessment of success of training and readiness for headship.

The training for the qualification has been almost continuously revised since it was introduced. The course was being devised as the first group of candidates undertook the course and the materials were revised in the light of experience and a major review was undertaken, which was never published, of the early experiences. The course was formally revised and was to be made mandatory for future headship appointments at some date to be determined in the future. The current requirement is that it will be mandatory from April 2004 for all first-time heads to hold NPQH or be working towards it. Once in post, they must gain the NPQH qualification within four years of their appointment (http://www.dfes. gov.uk/headship/).

In addition to training, candidates were to draw up a portfolio of evidence of their leadership and managerial work. Increasingly this has focused on evidence of leading a development in their own school.

Although the possession of the NPQH was originally intended to give a guarantee that the possessor had the skills required to be a successful school headteacher, there are two obstacles in principle to this. First, the practice which the candidate is judged upon is as a deputy head or other post holder and not as headteacher, and second, for most candidates, the headship to which they are appointed will be in a different school. Thus for most candidates there are two transitions between the possession of the NPQH and headship – changing post and changing school.

It should be remembered that these two obstacles are in addition to all the usual provisos about training. Some of these are: the extent to which it captures the principal skills required, the extent to which these are validly assessed at the time and the extent to which these same skills would be exhibited on subsequent occasions. Another major issue for this particular qualification is its lack of relationship to academic qualifications and its own atheoretical formulation and development. Groups of practitioners drew up the content with guidance from TTA officials. There is little formal academic reading required to undertake the course, and the course operates outside the higher education system and is validated by government agencies. This suggests that such a course is unlikely to encourage critical thinking.

When the National Professional Qualification for Headship was established by the TTA in the mid-1990s, national standards for headship were established and these were updated in 2000. These have been covered in chapter 3.

Applications for headship

Application and selection

Application and selection are complementary. Selectors can only do their job if there are applicants who have provided evidence on which to select. Each party needs to appreciate the perspective of the other. If applicants are aware of how the selection process operates they can play their part and provide selectors with appropriate evidence and do themselves justice. Selectors also need to appreciate the time and effort involved in making applications if they do not wish to reduce the number of initial applicants.

Application

Candidates for headship need to decide what posts they will apply for. Some examples and guidelines for choosing are contained in chapter 9. For those anxious to secure a headship there are two extremes – apply for all within a geographic radius or apply selectively. A major limiting factor is the time required for the process of writing applications. Although word processors have speeded the process this is only for storing and reproducing previously written material. Thus a standard CV can be produced but it will take time to tailor this for any particular application and the writing of an individualised letter of application or a response to particular requirements of the selection process will require *time*. Applications which are very general and have not been tailored to the particular school and application requirements are easily spotted and are not usually very impressive. They may be seriously considered if there are few applications or if other information makes the candidate a likely contender for the post. Since some of the selection group may see applications for more than one headship, blanket applicants may be noted and be seen as frivolous applicants or acquire that notoriety.

To carry out serious background research on a post and create a tailored application for a particular headship could take a great deal of time. Whilst undoubtedly this would be seen by selectors as the ideal course, from the candidate's point of view, if lots of applicants all do this and only one is to be selected, this is very inefficient. Thus a three-stage tailoring of applications might offer a compromise for both candidates and selectors.

First stage

Choose general criteria to limit the number of applications to a manageable number. The criteria might include location, size and type of school and local reputation. The details of these posts could be obtained and scrutinised.

Second stage

From the further particulars some of these posts could be selected for application. The application should be tailored based upon the details given in the further particulars. Any extra information or responses to particular requirements will need to display the professional judgement of the applicant as this is likely to be one of the discriminating features by which the long-list and short-list are created.

Choice of referees

The choice of referees is always tricky. There are differences depending on how many are requested and whether the applicant is already a headteacher. For those who are not heads, one referee should be the headteacher of the current school. The selection group will want an opinion on current performance and potential for headship from someone who knows the requirements and has direct knowledge of current practice. Further referees from the same school are unlikely to add significantly to such knowledge and so a headteacher from a previous school or an LEA adviser should be sought. Where a deputy has worked significantly with a governing body committee and the chair of that group would be able to assess and write about that contribution that might be worthwhile as a third referee if one is required. Other possibilities for a third referee are an NPQH trainer if there has been significant interaction or an HE tutor if a recent academic course has involved significant contact and assessment of academic ability.

The situation for headteachers is more difficult. Two principal requirements for information from referees are judgements about professional performance as a head and also about relationships with the governing body. The chair of governors is in a position to give an opinion on work with the governors but there is no direct line manager able to give a professional judgement. There may be an LEA link adviser or officer who knows the professional work of the head well but this may depend on LEA arrangements and the type of school.

Third stage

This is the stage at which an applicant is invited to attend selection procedures. Here all information on the school and how it operates needs to be obtained. Some may have been sent with the further particulars but there will be additional details. In addition it may be the case that the further particulars have been selective and thus finding the exam performance over a longer period or both the present and previous OFSTED reports would provide a more complete picture. The OFSTED reports contain factual information about results and finance in addition to the judgements obtained during the course of the inspection visit.

This research is necessary on two counts. If this trawl uncovers information which makes the headship undesirable then it may suggest that withdrawal from the selection process is necessary without going any further. In any case this kind of research is necessary as preparation for the next stages of the selection process. Any attempts by the selection process to bring out prior experience or to ask for suggested actions can be made more effective if the context and situation of the new post are appreciated.

Applicants need to envisage the selection process as seen by selectors so that they can appreciate better how to present themselves and their skills and experience. The list of ways of discovering evidence on different aspects of performance (see chapter 6 on selection) and potential should help candidates to judge where to include different aspects of their experience and skills.

Finally, our advice to candidates is that if they are short-listed and do not get the job they should continue to apply. Short-listing should only have included capable candidates but since there is only one job not everyone could be given it. The evidence from the research by Morgan *et al.* (1983) is that candidates who kept on applying were judged suitable for some jobs and not others. Thus persistence pays off.

The comparable advice to candidates who are offered the job is to take only a headship where they feel that they have the particular skills, experience and personal attributes to make a difference and be successful in that particular school. There are examples of appointments where the successful candidate is less than confident when they take on the post but goes on to be a successful headteacher. But there are also ones where it is possible to trace failure back to an unsuitable appointment. It should be remembered that it takes two to make an appointment. Whilst a post may be offered, an appointment can only be made if the candidate accepts.

8   The career of headship

Introduction

A number of scholars have suggested frameworks which facilitate a study of headteacher careers. Such a framework allows a comparison of what has happened to a large number of different heads. However, those who have collected data from headteachers about their careers before and during headship have expressed reservations about whether all headteachers pass through the same stages and whether there is a clear transition from one phase to the next. The framework that we have put together at the end of this section has helped us organise the examples we have gathered from contemporary headteachers in chapters 9, 10 and 11.

The frameworks have been proposed as a result of interviewing a number of headteachers at different stages in their careers. These have covered both primary and secondary heads and have not generally suggested a different pattern for the two phases. Some research studies have been carried out at points in time when there have been large scale changes in the school system such as teachers' industrial action in the 1980s and the changes consequent on the Education Reform Act in the late 1980s and early 1990s. It then becomes a matter of judgement to decide which findings may be particularly affected and may not have been found if the research had been conducted at a different time.

The published accounts of research generally do not give a coherent account of different groups of headteachers in terms of their success and failure. Although most accounts do cover success and failure these are interspersed and so it is not possible to identify patterns which distinguish the two groups. In our discussion at the end of this section we try to make this differentiation.

Headship in four stages

A conceptual model of headship which encompasses the period between the formative influences on individuals in early life through headship to leaving headship (Gronn 1999) has the following four stages:

- Formation
- Accession

- Incumbency
- Divestiture.

Formation

This starts with the person's early life – they are born in a period, in a country and in a position in a society which shapes them. The period of formation includes all the above influences and the earlier career as a teacher before becoming an aspirant to a leadership position. This encompasses all the influences which shape personality, character and outlook. It begins to form the self concept and a preferred working style.

Accession

This refers to the stage of grooming or anticipation in readiness to apply for leadership positions. It can also be the stage where potential leadership capacity is tested.

The two aspects of this stage are (1) gaining experience to show leadership ability or potential and (2) self-publicity to be accepted into the field of contenders for headship. Gronn (1999) emphasises that an individual needs self-belief. This has two aspects:

- Belief in one's capacity
- Self-esteem or positive feelings of one's worth or value.

He intimates that many potential leaders have self-doubts which makes this difficult.

Then comes the application process and appointment.

Incumbency

The leader is in post and performs as a headteacher. In doing the job for the first time there is a rapid period of learning. This is the period that we develop in more detail in subsequent models. There are two alternative patterns during the early stages of headship:

- Career progression as potentially negative and destructive
- Career progression as potentially progressive and creative.

For those who fall into the second group, there usually comes a period of disenchantment towards the end of the period of incumbency. Ribbins (1999) and co-authors (Ribbins and Marland 1994; Pascal and Ribbins 1998) have suggested that there may be a long period of 'enchantment' with headship for some headteachers. The nature of their research subjects – high profile head-teachers – may have played a part in emphasising the frequency of this finding.

Other longitudinal and more representative findings (Earley *et al.* 1990; Earley *et al.* 1995) have suggested that keeping motivation and innovation high after about ten years in the same job becomes more difficult.

Divestiture

This is the stage of 'letting go' whether voluntarily or involuntarily. There may be creeping disillusionment with headship from those who were initially successful as time passes. Whilst in the past divestiture would lead to retirement from work, Ribbins (1999) has suggested an addition to this stage in England – 'moving on' to a new and different professional life. This may involve divestment or 'reinvention'. However, this generally involves giving up aspirations of leadership since most moving on is to posts of consultant or adviser, etc. which give few possibilities for leadership.

Value of this model

This four stage model draws attention to the formative influences in the early life of headteachers which shape their character. These influences are traced as the source of the values which guide them in terms of their aspirations for their school once in headship. The nature of such research does not allow any conclusions about whether there are different influences on potential headteachers compared to teachers in general. Similar influences before teaching and in the early stages of a teaching career will have shaped the behaviour of all teachers and it is not clear whether headteachers are unusual in this respect.

Whilst it is clear that some individuals are very ambitious and work at becoming leaders as fast as possible, to many others it is only in retrospect that a path through to headship can be traced. Gronn (1999) draws attention to the way in which those who have gone on to headship have gone through 'critical turning points and transitions' (p. 28). There may be initial prerequisites in terms of qualifications and further professional development which open up further possibilities, but further progress depends upon:

- Seizing opportunities offered by each post occupied
- Help from 'patrons and sponsors' or mentors.

For accession, leadership potential must have been demonstrated. This is easier if there are significant others who can give advice on career openings, promotion and present opportunities in which leadership can be practised. This provides a chance to gauge the reaction of followers and to practise impression management.

Four phases within the period of headship

For prospective headteachers and those in post, the period of headship is the one that needs further elaboration. Following a survey of secondary headteachers in the early 1990s by Day and Bakioglu (1996), four stages have been proposed. These will be explained before a more detailed discussion of the first years of headship from other researchers.

- Initiation
- Development
- Autonomy
- Disenchantment.

Initiation: idealism, uncertainty and adjustment (0–3 years)

This was made up of two key processes: the first was learning the job and could take a variable time depending on the problems which heads encountered; and the second was the realisation that although they wanted to make improvements these had to be made within existing structures and frameworks.

Two kinds of start were possible:

- *Simple easy beginnings*
  Typically when the school had a good reputation, good community relationships and the new head felt comfortable as there were few problems to deal with. Staff were positive, innovative and active and assisted the new head. If the new head had the same management style as the previous one, no change of style was required whereas if the previous head was not popular there was a welcome for the new head.

- *Difficult beginnings*
  These were sometimes associated with a legacy from the previous head, e.g. decisions on redundancies, results after the merger of two schools, falling rolls and associated budget reductions, no promotional payments. Sometimes it was external circumstances which contributed, e.g. externally imposed changes, LMS, industrial action (in mid-1980s). Whilst these could have affected many schools, it was the combination of them in particular schools or the way that they were handled which contributed to the difficulties.

In this phase heads wanted to make their mark and tended to make changes regardless, it seemed, of existing cultures. They appeared to have preconceptions of how good heads would act.

All (of the small number) of the newly appointed heads in the sample disagreed with their predecessor's management style, which was described as autocratic. They saw their own as consultative. A timescale for the changes which heads attempted is not given but one example shows this residual effect two-and-a-half years after the arrival of the new head. In the second and third years they began to realise the discrepancy between their ideal and what was possible in their particular school. A lot of changes had been made in the first year and in retrospect this was seen as too many and they were mainly small insignificant changes. Their enthusiasm was high and they devoted effort to learning the job. The first-time headteachers experienced more uncertainty than they had experienced in their career before. This characterises the subphases – idealism, uncertainty and adjustment – as they come to terms with their original expectations.

Those who had been pastoral deputies found that the posts were similar to their previous experience but, as head, at a more senior level. They appeared to experience fewer problems than other new heads. They all noted that they had more responsibility than previously and generally greater parental, staff and pupil involvement than previously and a more social role. For the first time they were responsible for other people's careers and development. A second concern was how they would deal with a problem that they faced for the first time. For some this led to feelings of inadequacy, especially in the first year. A third pressure was the longer hours required and the greater variety of tasks.

For some the expectations of the SMT were not in tune with their own and some found it irritating to be constantly compared with the previous head.

Gaining the respect of staff and children and learning all aspects of the work could take almost three years according to the heads interviewed.

Development: consolidation and extension (4–8 years)

Heads were still enthusiastic and enjoyed their work and wished to continue but their enthusiasm changed from time to time depending on their self-esteem and their own assessment of the success of their work. This was the 'most active, most satisfactory, most rewarding' phase (Day and Bakioglu 1996: 212). They knew their schools and moved them in the direction that fitted their vision. Some areas were left unchanged but others were prioritised. At this stage they tended to report fewer problems. Although there is reference to constructive self-questioning by some heads there was also a feeling by the authors of possible overconfidence on the part of the heads.

Features of this phase were more planning and increased effectiveness. However, it is not clear if this is due, at least in part, to external changes at the time or whether this would have happened in any case. As a result of retirements, heads usually had the opportunity of appointing new members to the SMT. Developing the SMT and improving the public image of the school were features of this period. Heads saw themselves as delegating more, showing they valued staff and involving them in the work of the school. They were also able to change responsibilities and give more to those they thought deserved it. Heads tended to respect the expertise of their colleagues and did not interfere. They generally felt that the schools were clearly moving forward. They were more confident in dealing with staff including discipline and competency.

Although they still had ambition this was a relatively comfortable stage. There were two alternatives – continue in the same school or seek a bigger school. A period of secondment was also used as an opportunity to think about future possibilities.

Autonomy: single loop learning

Two kinds of response were reported in this phase: less enthusiasm was reported because there was less stimulation or the imposed external changes were seen as undesirable; but heads were still self-confident based on their learning from experience.

A quote from one head (p. 216) identifies some changes accomplished at the start of headship as a combination of naivety and enthusiasm. In retrospect heads could make this kind of assessment based on their increased effectiveness and understanding. A number of quotes from heads were to the effect that they felt experts in educational management but this was often tinged with less enthusiasm if not laziness. Although the respondents didn't use the phrase, 'being in charge' might be a suitable description.

Various causes of dissatisfaction were mentioned, e.g. philosophy of external changes. Some saw this as an attack on their control. Six heads saw a need to revert to a more autocratic style in view of the external changes. The authors make the comment that this view seems to be more dependent on the head than the state of readiness or competence of the staff. They make the comment that this phase is about 'actions ... designed to maintain what is rather than develop what might be' (p. 219). This they liken to single loop learning (Argyris and Schon 1978).

Disenchantment

Declining confidence, enthusiasm and increasing personal 'fatigue' were characteristic of this phase. There were complaints about a variety of things – children's behaviour and external impositions. If the work plateaued this was accompanied by stress, emotional and physical sickness and deteriorating staff morale. The lack of confidence in external change was sometimes accompanied by giving staff the choice of whether to implement the initiatives or not. The authors suggest that this may be tempered by the heads' own fatigue and the effort which it would take to implement the changes. When asked about their educational philosophy this tended to be bound up with themselves and there is literature to suggest that retreat to the self is a consequence of ageing (Storr 1988).

As a consequence of the pressures many heads suffered illness (mental and physical). They reported that when they returned after a long illness they 'felt they had lost their control over the school' (Day and Bakioglu 1996: 220). In this section liaising with governing bodies is mentioned for the first time. 'The feeling of being under the control of governing bodies led to early retirements of some headteachers' (p. 220).

The feeling of losing control is reinforced as this leads to pressure which causes illness which leads to more feeling of loss of control. Most of the heads said that they had been planning to retire before their 60s. 'School improvement became less of a consideration as personal-life considerations and concerns increased' (p. 221).

The feelings of disenchantment may have been particularly strong at this time in the early 1990s as the major changes involved in moving schools to be more consumer-driven and the standardisation of curriculum (Fidler and Bowles 1989) were alien to many headteachers. The number of early retirements increased at this time as a number of heads decided they would rather quit than operate in ways which they did not find philosophically conducive.

Frustratingly it is not clear if those headteachers who experienced difficult beginnings went on to success or whether, as other later accounts in this section suggest, they may have reached an accommodation with staff and others as to the extent of their power to control the school.

The first years and their consequences

The study which produced the previous four stages within headship collected data from heads who had been in headship for varying lengths of time and there were only a small number in the early years of headship. There have been other studies which have specifically looked at the early years of secondary school headship in England and Wales (Weindling and Earley 1987a, 1987b; and follow-ups, Earley *et al.* 1990 and Earley *et al.* 1995) and high schools in the USA (Parkay *et al.* 1992). Another study of primary and secondary heads in England, Scotland and Denmark (Reeves *et al.* 1997) provides experiences of headship including the early years. The discussion in this section is largely based on these three sources.

Although preparation for headship has improved over the last 20 years, new headteachers still remark how traumatic their first experiences of headship were. In some ways we can appreciate from the earlier distinction in chapter 3 between 'knowing about' and 'knowing how to', that actually practising headship for the first time will be a seminal experience. In part this is due to acting in such a position for the first time – professional socialisation – but it is also, for most new heads, because they are moving to a new and unfamiliar school which they need to begin to get to know and understand – organisational socialisation.

Unless new heads hear of the experiences of other new heads they may be unaware of how far their own experiences of these two processes are similar to those of others. Whilst their own experiences may be challenging and disconcerting, it should be of some consolation to find that these emotions are not unusual in new heads. Thus this section tries to convey some of the experiences and emotions which may be encountered and to provide some pointers to likely scenarios and how they may be understood. The range of organisational models which were introduced in chapter 3 provide a range of approaches to analyse organisational experiences. In particular where conflict and opposition are experienced, the political model may offer a way of making sense of what is going on.

The following five stages of development in the first three years of headship were derived from a detailed study of 12 new high school principals in the USA

(Parkay *et al.* 1992). The findings of a study of new heads in England and Wales in the early 1980s have retrospectively been found to fall into similar stages.

- Survival
- Control
- Stability
- Educational leadership
- Professional actualisation (see Table 8.1).

A number of findings emerged from this three year study which may have relevance to new heads in England and Wales:

- Principals begin at different stages of socialisation
- Principals move through the stages at different rates (and some do not progress)
- A range of factors affect progress
  - State of school: a principal appointed to an award-winning suburban school moved further than a principal of a conservative rural school
  - Predecessor: a principal following a legendary principal progressed further than one following a head who had 'retired on the job'
- Principals may operate at more than one stage simultaneously
- All principals are initially concerned with curriculum and instruction (educational leadership) but other considerations may override this concern.

Two additional findings were:

Table 8.1 Stages of principalship (based on Parkay *et al.* 1992)

Stage	Indicators
Survival	Shock of leadership – personal concerns and professional insecurity – may feel overwhelmed
	Sorting it out
Control	Setting priorities – constant fear of losing control
	Getting on top of the situation – developing a 'normal' routine and assessing what significant others consider normal
Stability	Frustrations become routinised
	Management tasks become more efficient and effective
	Difficulties of change are understood – having struck a 'bargain' or compromise with teachers the principal is less concerned with change
Educational leadership	Focus on curriculum and instruction
	Confirmation comes from others – staff and external sources
	Behaviours are 'legitimated' by personal power
Professional actualisation	Confirmation comes from within
	Focus is on personal vision

- All principals reported that they came in with unrealistic expectations of change which became more realistic
- The stage reached at the end of the first year is a good indicator of the likely progress reached by the middle of the third year – 'the writing is on the wall'.

Learning at the initial stages

We want to analyse the initial surprises and sensemaking of the first stages of headship in order to bring out the differences between those who are promoted in their own school to headship compared to those who come to the school for the first time as headteacher. We know that about a quarter of heads are promoted internally.

The initial stages of learning are likely to be concerned with:

- Forming a personal cognitive map of the new situation
- Acquiring information by observation, interviews, reading documents
- Evaluating differences and the reasons for them.

Although the surprises on entering a new school cannot be eliminated the extent can be minimised. The sources of the surprises can be characterised as personal change, new school, difference in expectations:

- personal – acting as headteacher
- working personnel – working with new colleagues
- organisation – different culture and ways of operating
- expectations – vision of how the new school will be.

These can be examined to see which could be reduced and how:

- a period as acting head can reduce the personal surprise at headship
- working in a number of schools and working with a variety of colleagues can reduce the surprise of moving schools
- appraising the new school as early and thoroughly as possible can make expectations more realistic.

The surprise which it is most difficult to reduce is the comparison with the previous school and there are reasons to assume that this is likely to be high in many cases. Deputies are likely to be promoted who have worked in good schools and are likely to take over ones in need of improvement. Indeed it is comparisons with the previous good school which are likely to flag up the most evident areas in need of improvement.

Table 8.2 below differentiates the 'surprises' likely to occur for a deputy promoted in his or her existing school compared to a deputy from another school.

An expectation of the nature of the likely surprises should lead to an anticipation of surprise and hence lessen its effects.

Table 8.2 Comparison of promotion in the same school and changing schools

	Promotion from deputy head in existing school	Promotion from another school
Personal	Move to headship	Move to headship, unfamiliarity with new school context and situation
Working personnel	New relationship with *existing* personnel	New relationship with *new* personnel
Organisation	Existing school	New school to compare with previous school
Expectations	Expectations of how personnel will respond to new leader	Expectations of what new school will be like – staff, children and parents – and how they will respond to a new leader

Socialisation for different groups of new headteachers

Although the extent of socialisation will depend on individuals it is possible to distinguish three groups who, by their background, will experience socialisation differently. The largest group of appointments is of first time headteachers from another school. These will face both professional and organisational socialisation whereas deputies promoted in their own school will be largely concerned with professional socialisation and those who have previously experienced headship will largely experience organisational socialisation (see Table 8.3). For this latter group organisational socialisation can be expected to be less as they will probably have experienced it previously in another school and so the process will be more familiar.

A composite set of career stages for headship

Different researchers who have investigated the career stages of headship have dwelt upon particular stages and facets of headship. Table 8.4 is an attempt to

Table 8.3 The relative extent of professional and organisational socialisation for three groups of new headteachers

	Promotion of existing deputy	Promotion of a deputy from another school	Existing head from another school
Initial professional socialisation	M	H	L
Organisational socialisation	L	H	M
Continued professional socialisation	H	H	M

Extent: L = low; M = medium; H = high.

piece together a series of stages which most heads go through based upon a number of research studies.

We have synthesised the findings from the studies in Table 8.4 into ten phases and tried to indicate some common patterns of progress through these phases and also some less usual and rather less successful experiences. The vignettes in chapters 9 and 10 illustrate current examples of these stages.

- Formation
- Preparation
- Encounter: surprise, adjustment and survival
- Taking hold: getting on top of the situation and setting priorities
- Stabilisation
- The crunch
- At the summit: plateaued/time for a change
- Plateaued – disenchantment
- Letting go
- A fresh start.

Preparation

Professional socialisation begins on preparation for teaching and entry into teaching but this is followed by socialisation for leadership and management (Hart and Weindling 1996). This will involve preparation and includes:

- Courses
- First hand experiences
- Modelling and social learning by observation (and interaction) both positive and negative
- Deliberate mentoring.

Encounter: surprise, adjustment and survival

This covers the first term as headteacher and deals with the surprises as features of the new school and its staff are uncovered. It is the differences from previous schools which occasion the surprises. Initial ideas about what is possible at the school will need to be adjusted in the light of the discoveries made and a personal assessment of the current state of the school. The combination of discoveries, issues which come up for decision and staff expectations is likely to make the new head feel inadequate. It is at this stage that survival first becomes an issue.

This is the stage at which an initial assessment of the senior staff will be crucial. The reaction of other staff may be a good indicator of those in whom they do not have confidence and expect changes. The staff's views of the previous head will need to be assessed. His or her good points should be sought so that if possible continuity can be arranged. There may be the first signs of any opposition to changes.

Table 8.4 A composite set of career stages for headship

Stage	Fiddler and Atton (2004)	Gronn (1999)	Day and Bakioglu (1996)	Hart and Weindling (1996)	Parkay et al. (1992)	Weindling (1999)	Reeves et al. (1997)	Gabarro (1987)
Early life and career	Formation	Formation						
Preparation for headship	Preparation	Accession				Preparation	Warm up	
Headship	Encounter: surprise, adjustment and survival	Incumbency	Initiation: idealism, uncertainty and adjustment	Encounter and confrontation	Survival: shock and sorting it out	Entry and encounter (first months)	Entry (0–6 months) Digging the foundations (6–12 months)	Taking hold Immersion
	Taking hold: getting on top of the situation and setting priorities		Development: consolidation and extension	Accommodation and integration	Control: setting priorities and getting on top of the situation	Taking hold (3–12 months)	Taking action (12–24 months)	Reshaping Consolidation
	Stabilisation				Stability	Reshaping (second year)		Getting above floor level (24–36 months)
						Refinement (years 3 and 4)	The crunch (24–60 months)	

Stage	Fidler and Attom (2004)	Gromm (1999)	Day and Bakioglu (1996)	Hart and Weindling (1996)	Parkay et al. (1992)	Weindling (1999)	Reeves et al. (1997)	Gabarro (1987)
	The crunch				Educational leadership			
	At the summit: plateaued/time for a change		Autonomy: single loop learning	Stabilisation	Professional actualisation	Consolidation (5–7 years)	At the summit (48–120 months)	Refinement
	Plateaued – disenchantment		Disenchantment			Plateau (8+ years)	Time for a change (60–120 months)	
Preparing to finish	Letting go	Divestiture						
Continuing working life	A fresh start							

Channels of communication to staff and students should be clarified. This should indicate the kind of consultative machinery which is in place and whether this should be changed.

This is the stage at which an initial assessment of the staff's readiness for change will be needed. If there is a readiness then this should be used to plan some worthwhile changes. Without such a readiness, moves will need to be more circumspect. Small changes which will not provoke opposition and which will be successful and well received should be attempted. Weindling and Earley (1987a, 1987b) noted a 'honeymoon' period after the arrival of a new head when staff were often more receptive to change than in later years.

This is the stage at which, when under pressure, new heads may abandon the formal skills and knowledge that they have acquired in preparation for leadership and conform to existing patterns that they have experienced at the hands of their leaders in the past (Hart and Weindling 1996). Indeed leaders may initially have to conform to the expectations of their staff before they are in a position to operate as they would wish.

Taking hold: getting on top of the situation and setting priorities

After the first term there is time to take stock and plan for the next term. There will be fewer surprises and more familiar features leading to a feeling of greater security. There will be allies and supporters. From a better assessment of the current state of the school some clear immediate priorities will emerge. There may be some problems which need to be tackled but a timescale can be set up by which the more difficult and those which need a specific opportunity will be postponed until the time is right.

There should be more certainty about the assessment of the readiness for change and indications of how change should be handled. There may be general agreement on priorities particularly if these involve students and are clear to everyone. There may be external pressure to make changes and these can be mobilised to influence insiders. The account from Reeves *et al.* (1997) of small scale and minor changes initially, may be more difficult in the current situation in England because of the pressure on school improvement and on failing or serious weakness schools; the two phases of action may have to be telescoped.

Any weak staff and any opposition should be clearer and will need action plans to tackle them at an appropriate time. Reeves *et al.* (1997) noted that 'timings of staff changes did seem broadly to coincide with periods of conflict/ resistance' (p. 53).

Stabilisation

Urgent actions will have been put in place and medium-term priorities can be planned. Reeves *et al.* (1997) noted the idea of freeing up and letting go after the initial making of the head's mark. Where there is a competent and supportive senior team the future should be looking more promising. However, this is the stage when if either of these are lacking or there is confrontation from some staff or more general opposition, the stability can seem very fragile and could develop into a stalemate where only certain changes are likely to be successful and more radical change impossible. Reeves *et al.* (1997) noted that some heads had got stuck at the minor changes stage and 'had settled for a situation where they had reached a *modus vivendi* but had not gone on to have a fundamental impact on the school' (p. 55).

Any accommodation with opposing staff will need to be assessed as either dependent on forces outside the head's control or to be tackled in a suitable way in the future. A permanent antagonism is very wearing for the head and ultimately leads the school to run down. Heads may react by becoming more autocratic, 'New leaders often fear losing control and being labelled ineffective. As a defence, many rely on formal authority and sources of power' (Parkay *et al.* 1992: 328).

The crunch

This is the stage at which any log-jam caused by a previous accommodation is broken or the first major change is attempted where smaller ones have been completed successfully. This is a testing of the water which determines whether the head is fully in control of what goes on in the school.

At the summit: plateaued/time for a change

Having achieved control and carried out the major changes which were needed, this is the stage of either continuing on this plateau or feeling the need for another challenge and a new headship or other post.

There are a number of indications from research on schools and headteachers that there may be optimum lengths of time in a particular post and that certain lengths of time become disadvantageous. A finding from the research on effective primary schooling suggests that the effect of the head is most positive when they have been in post between three and seven years (Mortimore *et al.* 1988). They are less effective until they have completed three years whilst heads in post for eleven years or more were less effective especially for non-cognitive outcomes.

At the early stages of their career the new headteachers in 1982 thought that ten years would be the length of time that they would like to stay in post (Weindling and Earley 1987a). In the event, many of them stayed beyond that length of time. The follow-up studies indicated that generally heads who were still in their original school were less satisfied with their situation than those who had moved to a second headship (Earley *et al.* 1995).

From ten case studies of successful schools, Day *et al.* (2000) found that their findings appeared to agree with the previous findings on phases of development depending on the length of time that the head has been in post:

> the best time was at the end of five years. A lot had been achieved.
>
> [primary head]
> (Day *et al.* 2000: 58)

In the leadership survey of Earley *et al.* (2002) almost a quarter of the heads had been in post for ten years or more. Most heads expected to stay at their current school until they retired and only 30 per cent were expecting to move on to another headship.

Finally, in the survey on stress in headteachers in the late 1980s (Cooper and Kelly 1993), males who had been in post longest were more likely to have the highest levels of dissatisfaction with their job.

All of this suggests that more movement between headships, after a suitable period of time in post, would be beneficial to headteachers and to schools. Some of the six heads in their second headship in the study by Reeves *et al.* (1997) noted a similar pattern of development in their second headship. Some saw the timescale as speeded up whilst others felt their second headship had been more difficult as 'contextual factors meant that transfer of learning from one situation to another was not necessarily straightforward or helpful' (p. 50). They gave first hand evidence of the contingent nature of leadership.

Plateaued – disenchantment

Too long on the plateau without a new stimulus is likely to begin to lead to disenchantment to some degree. Where the previous stages have not been accomplished too successfully the position may be very stressful leading to a deterioration in health. Where there has been previous achievement and the position is more comfortable it is likely that the school will slowly begin to drift downhill.

Letting go

Letting go can either be voluntary and planned or can result from some trigger. This can be some weakness in the performance of the school which precipitates a crisis or the governing body becomes critical or there is a breakdown in personal health (see chapter 12).

A fresh start

Where the letting go has been voluntary there may be plans to take up further work after headship. There is a range of inspection, consultancy and advisory work which can be taken on part-time. By taking on a range of these a portfolio career can be built up. There are a range of agencies which offer such work and these have an internal structure which needs staffing.

9 Life cycle of a head

Becoming a head

This section explores the features unique to each stage in the life cycle of a headteacher and the characteristics required to negotiate them successfully.

The moment of conception in the life cycle of a head is when the decision is taken to apply for headship. We can see from the research analysed in chapter 8 that from that point through to the aftermath of retirement there are several stages which can be separately defined but whose length depends on the personality of the head and the circumstances of her headship. Broadly, these stages are the following:

- Preparation for applying
- From appointment to taking up the post
- The first term and first challenges
- Settling down
- Keeping moving
- Seeing it out.

This chapter explores the first two of these stages.

As seen in chapter 8, the role of a head is not constant throughout the tenure of the post. Each period has its unique set of features and these need different skills if they are to be managed successfully. A head new in post may successfully bring about a change in policy by simply being unaware of the historical issues that have prevented it happening earlier. Five years later she would not have that sort of freedom, but would then have a different advantage, that of knowing how best to manage change by dealing appropriately with the individuals involved.

Preparation for applying – *choosing a headship or choosing a school?*

In chapter 7 we explored the general preparation for headship through career planning and job specific qualifications such as the NPQH. Here we are looking at choosing a headship. A colleague just taking up a third headship said that when seeking his first he was looking for a headship, but that for the second and third he was looking for a school. What he meant was that, having decided he was ready to move on from successful deputy headship, he applied for most schools within his geographical range in the hope of being appointed to one of them, thus 'making it to headship'. Having proved he could do the job, for his subsequent posts he was looking for schools that offered him a specific challenge (in the first case the amalgamation of two underperforming schools and in the second case a Fresh Start school).

Earley *et al.* (2002) found that most heads seeking a second or subsequent headship said they were looking for a 'coasting' school or a country school and that few wanted to take on a challenging school. This was not the impression we gained from our interviews with those who were already in second or third headships. This is explored further in chapter 11 under further headships.

It would seem that in general terms there is more likely to be a mismatch between the appointing school and the head when it is the latter's first headship. Whether real (for financial reasons, perhaps) or self-imposed (to be seen to reach the top in your profession), the pressure to be a head can lead to wrong decisions being made. This wrong decision can be made on either side of the interview table.

From the perspective of those hoping to make an appointment: An LEA adviser who had recently been involved in unsuccessful attempts to appoint heads in three primary schools in his area commented that the temptation to appoint unsuitable candidates grew with each advertisement – strong candidates were immediately snapped up by successful schools, leaving potentially weaker applicants to be interviewed in less successful or more difficult schools. He defined as 'weaker' those whose career and references contained some area of doubt – this ranged from lack of management experience, through lack of good interpersonal skills to the quality of their teaching.

From the perspective of those hoping to be appointed: One head only discovered that the school budget was heavily in the red after he had taken up the post: wise governors and candidates would have ensured that this information was known before the job was offered and accepted, for how else were they to judge whether they would be able to work together to ensure future financial stability? It seems that the governors had chosen not to make the situation clear because they feared frightening away potential candidates, and the new head had been so focused on being offered the post that he had not really investigated what the principal challenges of the actual job might be. It was difficult after that for him and the governors to build an open and trusting relationship and far from a good start to his new role.

Due to demographic changes an LEA had the enviable opportunity to develop a brand new school in a multi-ethnic area. It was genuinely a new establishment, not an amalgamation or a Fresh Start school so there were none of the problems associated with these – divided loyalties, anxieties about job security, low morale. A powerful group of governors was collected to represent all interest groups, with high expectations of the head they would appoint. The first head appointed was already seen as a successful head elsewhere, was a member of the largest ethnic group within the local community and had been encouraged to apply for the post. It seems that the governors had expectations that he would be a high profile leader of their flagship school. Unfortunately for everybody concerned, his style was undemonstrative and low-key. By the end of the first term governors were openly expressing their disappointment and staff too were complaining about lack of communication and direction. At the end of the second term he was asked to leave and did so – in fact he did not return to the school from the day he received the letter from the governors expressing their concerns.

There are many issues arising from this vignette:

- The pressure on an individual to be representative of a specific community group – the governors had probably chosen him more for what he represented than for what he was. So not only did he carry all the expectations of anyone taking up a headship but also the expectation that he would take a lead for the ethnic groups in the community as well. This is a great deal to ask one person to do.
- The mismatch of style and expectations – how had the selection panel chosen the successful candidate? They had not taken into account the very different circumstances under which the head of the new school would be functioning compared with those of his academic and comparatively sheltered previous post.
- Once problems began to arise, relevant people may have failed to deal with them at an early stage for fear of being accused of racism. Where issues of ethnicity are concerned there may be a failure to apply rational principles and deal with difficult issues.
- Post-appointment support – was there anyone to help him move successfully into this role? No other heads in the borough had any experience similar to his, nor did he have a predecessor who could advise him on ways of working successfully with the new school's governors.
- The role of the LEA – they had obviously had a major role in setting up the new school, so what was their role in the appointment of the head and support thereafter?
- The justice of his dismissal – obviously he had made his own decision about applying for this particular post and the onus was on him to brief himself as fully as possible on the likely problems of the role but it does seem that both the governors and the head acted very precipitately, the former behaving in a high-handed, unethical and probably illegal manner and the latter responding instinctively by removing himself immediately from the situation.
- What happened to him next? Having been encouraged to apply for this headship because of his success in a previous post, was this the end of his career?

There are further issues about starting a new school: The gradual change in size makes it difficult to know how the culture is developing – can one be created that is suitable for the original small school and still be maintained when the school reaches its final size? This is the one occasion where there is no existing culture to inherit.

Similarly, the head's natural leadership style may be more appropriate to the intimate, personal approach of a small school and have difficulty adapting to the more distant executive role as head of a large school. Or vice versa.

There are difficulties (and opportunities) in possible lack of management experience amongst the staff. There are limited role models available within the establishment. This can of course be a source of great excitement for a new head – the rare opportunity to develop a style throughout the school which reflects her management philosophy.

Succession planning

There is a tension between succession planning in terms of preparing someone to take over a specific headship and the legal requirement to advertise the headship nationally. In a smaller school the most likely candidate is the deputy head, but what would happen in a larger school with two or more deputies? In at least two cases we are aware of, the designated second deputy was appointed to the headship, even though, in one case, the first deputy had had a period of acting headship in the school and had also applied for the substantive post. In this scenario it was possible to find a new role for the unsuccessful candidate in developing the specialist status of the school. More usually there is little scope for a satisfactory way forward and the only solution is for this deputy to move on.

In one LEA there have recently been two schools where the head was planning to retire within the year and there has simultaneously been a vacancy for a deputy head; the governors decided to advertise for a deputy with the stated intention that the successful applicant should proceed to the headship on the current head's retirement. This caused great unease in the personnel department and among other headteachers. They felt that such an advertisement would deter many possible heads from applying (as they would not wish to spend a year as deputy if they already had this experience), that no serving heads would apply and that there was no way out of the situation if it proved unsuccessful. In fact the adverts attracted over ten applications each (more than most headships), including one serving head. In one school the timing of the post was perfect for a person who had previous headship experience but was moving areas for personal reasons and was delighted to have the opportunity to take stock of the school and the area before taking up the headship itself. In the other school the governors appointed a serving deputy who will work alongside the head for a year as head designate. In both cases the governors responded to the concerns about the situation being unsuccessful by pointing out that any appointment could be unsuccessful but in this case they would be able to ensure all possible support and training was in place at the earliest possible stage. So far it seems to have worked very successfully in the schools concerned, enabling the transition to be made smoothly but without denying the new head the opportunity to set out her own expectations for the role.

Second or further headships

When a mismatch happens in second or third headships there are examples of heads being unsuccessful in their first appointment and taking a second headship as a way out of a developing problem. Sometimes the same problems develop in time in the next school. The more optimistic scenario is when the head has acknowledged the lessons to be learnt from the first school and made sure the same mistakes do not recur or has chosen his second school more carefully to match his own style and skills. We also found that there were often problems when someone was working through a third headship. Particularly in primary schools, it is likely that people appointed to headship in their thirties would be expecting to make several more moves in their career. They had developed their skills in the first post, and enjoyed putting them into practice in the second. The third no longer offered a challenge but a feeling of repeating what they had already done before, so they became demotivated. This is further explored in chapter 11.

Knowing what you are applying for

Therefore there is more to applying for headship than filling in an application form accurately. It is important to read between the lines of the information sent with the form and also OFSTED and PANDA reports (if not included), the school website and information about other schools in the area. Where does the school currently fit in the local 'pecking order'? What skills will a new head need to raise its status if it's near the bottom? Is the challenge realistically achievable? Good leadership will only transform a weak school if there are also the resources available to put new strategies into action. These resources are not only financial – if the demographic trend locally is to fewer children of school age in the school's natural catchment area, how will the new head succeed in attracting pupils from other areas where the schools are already successful? If it's already very successful, how will a new head keep it at the top? How will the leadership team react to a new style? Is the school financially secure? It makes sense to have as clear a view as possible of the likely reality of taking on the headship of a specific school.

The importance of self-awareness

It is also important to have an equally clear and realistic view of one's own strengths. Pre-course preparation for heads starting on the Leadership Programme for Serving Heads, now taken on by the National College for School Leadership, includes a questionnaire on the head's leadership style to be completed by a range of colleagues and by the head herself. Many heads who think themselves to be highly consultative and good at delegating are surprised and disappointed to find that their colleagues perceive them to be more autocratic and coercive. They then use part of the course to try to develop the skills to become the type of leader they wish to be. Heads may then survey the same groups later to see how successful they have been in changing this perception. It does not necessarily follow that they were better or worse at their job with the original styles, nor is there any objective evidence that their new style is more appropriate or successful. Psychometric tests are regularly included in the selection process. An aspiring head would find it useful to have already completed one of these as part of the preparation for headship: in general they give an extra dimension to the view of a person's preferred professional style. But it is also useful to know beforehand what areas may be seen to be weak, or less developed, and to be ready to discuss what strategies have been adopted to counter any weak areas. Some interview panels will assume that, for example, someone whose psychometric test printout shows a lack of interest in fine detail or the completion of projects will therefore automatically be weak in these areas. In practice, however, it is very likely that a good manager will have devised ways of ensuring that details are accurate and projects are completed and it is important to make the panel aware of this.

Knowing what we don't know

Many of the scenarios in this book describing unsuccessful headship experiences have come about as a result of a poor decision being made on appointment. Headship is more likely to turn out successfully if those on both sides of the interview table have as honest and clear a picture of each other as is possible: until someone has had experience of the reality of doing a job it is not possible to know exactly what any aspect of it means in practice. We cannot consciously know what knowledge we are lacking. For example, we can know all the detail of job descriptions, performance management and so on, but it is harder to imagine how we will respond in practice when dealing with an individual person. The theory of human resource management does not help us motivate an exhausted staff at the end of a long term. Can it help us know how to restrain the exuberant new member of staff who wants to change everything without demotivating her? Can it help us deal with the member of staff who resolutely refuses to change? It is important that the prospective head can imagine her responses to these questions, using examples from her past to create a framework for action, and has confidence that she has the inner resources necessary for success.

From appointment to taking up the post

First impressions

The cliché that you only get one chance to create a first impression is nowhere as true and important as in teaching. The first time you walk into a classroom your new pupils make a decision about you and the behaviour they will adopt. In headship the first staff meeting and the first assembly are when staff and pupils form their initial opinions about the new headteacher. Having formed a first impression, they will then test this out, looking for evidence that it was right. It is therefore better to have enabled them to form a good impression and start on a positive course than a bad one that takes a long time to set right. If these opinions are not positive or are different from the impression the new head hoped to give, it will be very difficult to change them. Even earlier the new head designate will have been asked to give opinions and make decisions that could have implications that reach far wider than they first seem to.

The first decision one newly appointed head was asked to make was whether to replace worn out hymn books with more copies of the same or to choose one he preferred. His personal reaction as one who had rarely taken a lead in assemblies as a deputy head would probably have been to dispose of all of them but, conscious of his new role, he had to reflect further:

- How important to the culture of the school was hymn singing in assemblies?
- Was this a part of the culture that he wished to perpetuate?
- If not, how was he going to communicate this?

The way the question was framed assumed continuation with the status quo but with perhaps a change in the style of hymns chosen. If he opted just to make that minor change he would lose the opportunity to make a major one and would then have to decide on his own role in hymn singing assemblies. His reply would also give messages to different groups within the school, perhaps seeming to favour a small, conservative group when the vast majority hoped to see changes. But, if he seemed to be opting for a change in policy without consultation he could equally give unintended messages about his leadership style ... The question itself was not of major importance but the head's response would be symbolic because it had an impact that far exceeded the scale of its importance when assessed rationally.

The person on the administrative staff responsible for ordering diaries and reprographic stocks had asked the question innocently. A certain number of hymn books were replaced annually and she had thought it simple courtesy to ask the new head's agreement to the order.

Staff appointments

Before taking up the post the new head is very likely to be involved with staff appointments. Providing, of course, that there are candidates for the vacancies, the new head will have choices to make but without a good knowledge of the teams within which the vacancy falls. Trust in the rest of the selection team may be well-placed but potentially restricts the new head's opportunities to bring about change: maybe the department concerned is very traditional and needs someone with a different perspective to move it on but the governors selecting the new member of staff see the department as stable, solid and dependable and do not want to risk causing discontent. One secondary head remembers very ruefully being involved in the appointment of a technology teacher just after her own appointment. On the day she accepted the retiring head and governors' opinion but felt ill at ease about the successful candidate; she had expected him to produce a portfolio exemplifying his pupils' work and to be as smartly presented as the technology teachers she had been used to in her previous school. As no one on the interviewing panel was a subject specialist they had taken on trust that the quality of his work was acceptable. By the end of the next year she was putting capability procedures in motion and had learnt the hard way to trust her instincts even if she did not know the rest of the picture.

Governors' meetings

The head designate is also likely to be invited to any governors' meetings taking place after her appointment. These can be fraught with potential for disaster:

- The governors want to see that their new appointment has leadership potential but the 'old' head is still there and it might be very undiplomatic to press for changes that might imply criticism of her leadership
- Pressure groups, lobbies and powerful minorities will want to use this opportunity to ensure the new head is aware of their case and, if possible, on their side
- Disappointed acting heads or deputies may be a powerful presence with supporters on the governing body
- There will be pressure for decisions to be made; the new head is the person at the meeting who may be least able to contribute to the debate but who will eventually have to implement the decisions made.

In spite of this, the opportunity to attend any such meetings is of tremendous value in enabling the new head to acquire an early understanding of the working style of the governing body and relationships within it. It would be even better if she is able to have a meeting with the chair of governors before the main meeting so that both can have an awareness of the potential problems and develop early strategies to deal with these. There are clear advantages in being able to attend these meetings as an observer: the head designate or the chair of governors can explain to the rest that, as an observer, the new head can only have limited participation in discussions. She can thus delay others forming impressions of how she will act when in post until she is ready to present herself to them. She will then be able to plan her own way of working with them from the start of her headship. A good relationship with the governors, especially the chair, is essential to being successful as a head and can help provide that support which is so difficult to find elsewhere.

10 Life cycle of a head

Being a head

The first term and first challenges – setting up relationships and expectations on first taking up post

Internal appointments

The experience of the first term will be very different for the substantial percentage of heads who were appointed to the headship from being deputies in the same school. The main effect will be the removal of most of the opportunities afforded by making a first impression, though the first action or decision made in the new role will probably be very important in impressing on everyone that this is now the head. Furthermore, the honeymoon period will only exist whilst the new head makes the journey away from the role (perhaps mediator, buffer, protector) previously played as the link between the head and the staff. A deputy who has been very popular with staff because she listened to them and relayed their concerns to the head without having the responsibility of making decisions relative to these concerns may find the exigencies of the new role difficult to adjust to. In spite of this, most deputies appointed to headships internally will already have a strong mandate from at least one powerful section of the school community and everybody starts off with real knowledge of the situation. Added to this the new head has already a depth of knowledge of the school and its community that should allow her to take up the post with a clear view of the developments she wants, with strategies already in mind for making them happen.

In the section on working with the leadership team (see chapter 5) this role is seen from the opposite perspective: the deputy who had assumed the role described above could be a strength for the new head, enabling her to learn very quickly about the emotional and political affiliations in the school. With a different agenda, however, the same deputy could make the new head's role more difficult by withholding such information or using it to create an alternative set of alliances.

Trigger points

There are a number of points during the early stages of headship which may trigger a chain of events whose eventual effect can be quite dramatic. They test the ability of the headteacher to see beyond the presenting problem to potentially deeper issues and to respond appropriately. This response will shape future decisions and have an important effect on other stakeholders' attitudes to the head.

Many of these are not important in themselves but the head's response will state her intent in terms of leadership style and the school culture. They can therefore be seen as symbolic. Such initial events include:

- Initial expenditure
- Dealing with the first serious pupil discipline problem
- First formal meeting with parents
- Choice of which meetings to attend or to delegate.

We will look in more detail at the first two of these.

Initial expenditure

SYMBOLISM 1

Some simple cosmetic changes to reception areas and offices can give a clear message about the new head's style and intentions. In a school where the retiring head seemed to have lost touch with some of the developing problems or who had become so familiar with the imperfections that he had accepted them as unalterable, the new head's first action was to move his office from the far end of the administration corridor to the room adjacent to reception and to make access available from both the administration side and from main reception. By doing this he stopped visitors to his office being filtered by several other people before he was able to choose whether to see them directly or not. It also advertised his intention to be welcoming and available. At the same time a head in Kent who was to see her school figure at the bottom of league tables before she (literally) disappeared had done exactly the opposite of this – she closed off the main entrance of the school and made it impossible for anyone to enter the newly created area without reporting to the receptionist at a small hatch. This deterred many potential visitors wanting to drop in to share good news with the head and led to only the very determined or very angry insisting on seeing her.

Whatever moves are made will be interpreted for their significance and staff will seek for underlying meaning to the changes. The above scenario suggested that accessibility is good, inaccessibility is bad; neither is intrinsically good or bad – the issue is whether the change has been explained and whether a suitable infrastructure is in place to enable effective two-way communication. What is important is that changes are part of a properly thought through pattern and not just convenient assumptions (a way of shutting one's eyes to problems and trying to pretend they do not exist). Most new heads will pay some attention to the decoration and layout of their office, even if it is not something they see as a first priority. Will they keep it as it was under the previous incumbent? (A male head one of us knows still looks rather incongruous after three years based in an office papered in a Laura Ashley print and with flowery festoons at the windows.) Will they take the opportunity to order new furniture, reasoning that they will be spending a lot of time there and need it to be as comfortable a possible? Will they then realise that there was no money in the budget to pay for it? Will they decide to leave things as they are, thinking it's more important to settle in before spending valuable and limited resources on their own office and then realise that adopting a non-confrontational style is impossible in a small room dominated by a huge desk and swivel chair?

SYMBOLISM 2

Making changes to pupils' uniform is very often the first major decision taken by a new head of a low achieving school. This is a sign to the outside community that something is being done to change the image of the school; to the inside community it gives a feeling of new smartness and care for the place and the people in it. This has to go alongside a genuine clean new start. There is no point in coming to school in a smart new uniform if the rooms are dirty and graffiti is everywhere. This is sometimes accompanied by refurbishments to the staffroom for the same reasons.

Dealing with the first serious pupil discipline problem

Dealing with the first serious pupil discipline problem is generally seen as a marker in the new head's establishment of her presence in the school. It was clear from heads who had chosen to take headships (especially if for a temporary period) in schools in difficulty that one of their priorities was to give a clear message that pupils behaving inappropriately would be dealt with firmly.

> A head who had taken over a school in special measures told us, 'I spent every possible minute during the first fortnight out in the corridors dealing with swearing, pushing, kicking, etc. and excluded fifteen pupils who I caught repeating the same offence. I didn't sit down in my office until I was confident that pupils knew the rules and that staff were consistently applying them. Then I could begin to look at teaching and learning.' This was in a school where it had been clear that learning had often been rendered impossible for the majority of pupils because the poor behaviour of some pupils had not been effectively dealt with.

> In a very different type of school – it had once been a boys' grammar school – the pressure on the new head was somewhat different. The leadership style of the long-standing previous head had been autocratic and peremptory,

tending towards confrontation. Although the staff had been very unhappy at never being consulted by him about curricular or staffing issues, they had been used to any small infringements of school rules being dealt with summarily. They therefore responded very angrily to what they saw as lack of support by the new head. His view was that all sides should have the opportunity for their view to be heard before a decision was made. This resulted in more of his time than he had expected being spent on pastoral matters, working with the pupils and their parents, and then working with disgruntled staff complaining that discipline was disappearing in the school. He persevered with this, feeling sure that relationships overall in the school would improve when it became clear that everyone would receive a fair hearing.

Governors and leadership team

Before taking up the post the new head will have been able to begin to make her assessments of how she will set up relationships with governors and she has probably already some views on the likely attitude to her of members of the leadership team. The governors have been involved in selecting her so will in general be predisposed to support her, but deputy heads may have a very different attitude. Those who have been in post for a long time and who were happy with the leadership style of the retiring head will understandably be anxious about likely changes and re-establishing their position. This anxiety could show itself in hostility and an initial unwillingness to support the new person. The possibility of a hostile attitude is stronger when the deputy head was also a contender for the headship. Several heads have told us of the difficulties they encountered with disappointed deputies and we were told of at least two others who never managed to overcome the barriers set up by deputy heads between them and the rest of the staff. In these scenarios the deputies subtly subverted the head's attempts to make any kind of change. Without any support amongst the most senior staff the head was deprived of much power to lead. These were extreme examples, but there are many where the new head has had to find ways of working round a senior member of staff or successfully encourage them to leave before she has been able to move the school forward in the way she wanted.

One head reflecting on his first year in post had been pleasantly surprised by the support he had been given by the long-standing senior team he had inherited and had only realised in retrospect how much his success had been dependent on their positive attitude since his arrival in post.

In reality most people want to work as comfortably as possible with their colleagues and, once they feel reassured that the new leader wants that too, their initial anxieties will subside. If the new head understands this and is not too impatient to impress her mark but to emphasise that they all have the same aim in mind, the problem should be minimised.

In building up relationships the new head should also be very aware of her administrative team. Managing the work of the office staff is an area of expertise she has probably not encountered before. This may be the first time she has had her own secretary, financial procedures may be totally new and dealing with the vast amount of paperwork requiring responses can be bewildering at the very least. The administrative team is crucial to a head's success. For many heads their personal assistant is a great strength to them; this person usually has unequalled knowledge of the people working in and closely involved with the school. She (it usually is a woman) can forewarn the head of impending internal problems and find ways of dealing with external ones as well as managing the head's diary and post. Because of the closeness of the working relationship it can be difficult for a new head to take over, but this is the one area where she can admit her lack of competence and win over the person she most needs to help her to succeed.

First major challenge

The next opinion-forming occasion is when the new head has to respond to a first major challenge. How it is dealt with will set the scene for success or failure in the future. Some of these challenges will be unexpected (as the scenario below) but others will have been foreseen and even used proactively.

> The southern comprehensive had agreed the date of its sports day the previous year and the PE department was relieved that the weather forecast was good. But in late June that particular year there was a heatwave. The sports fields were attractively situated at a short walk from the school with oak and chestnut trees bordering their north and east perimeters. Straight after morning registration the staff and pupils made their way down to the fields and sat on the ground or on benches around the running track. There was no shade anywhere on the field. An hour later the first pupils began to complain of feeling ill and before they could be returned to the school more and more succumbed to the symptoms of sunstroke. Ambulances were called, parents were contacted but very quickly the school's telephone lines were jammed and pupils were being treated on the spot in every available ground floor space.
>
> The next day a national newspaper ran a front page article about the effects of the heatwave and featured the school's sports day. This could have been embarrassing and difficult for the school's head, who had only taken up the post at the beginning of the term, but his actions were praised: he had ensured beforehand that letters had gone home to parents telling them of the details of sports day, inviting them to come to it and asking

them to ensure that their children brought hats and drinks with them. He had dealt calmly with the problem and immediately afterwards praised the emergency services and others who had helped look after the children so well. His instinctive deflection of a potential health and safety scandal into an opportunity to praise others turned a potential public relations disaster into a success.

New curriculum for new school

A larger first challenge was to the new head taking over a newly developing school which would be offering Key Stage 4 courses for the first time the following year. This coincided with the revised requirements for this key stage, giving the head and governors the opportunity to be very creative with their new curriculum. This is the kind of challenge that most heads would dream of, it is so rarely that a totally fresh approach is possible. It also opens up ways of working with middle managers to use their creative talents and so motivate the staff to produce some new and exciting courses. This is the opportunity to be brave. It might also be the defining moment that typifies the successful heads in the survey commissioned by HTI (2002).

They are all prepared to make decisions or take actions in spite of opposition from parents, governors or the LEA. Although it is interesting to read of maverick behaviour with successful outcomes, there are surely at least as many heads who lose confrontations with important stakeholders. More importantly, there are many, many more who work harmoniously with different groups and run very successful schools. The important thing is to have a clear vision for the future of the school in the short-, medium- and long-term. This will be the guiding star for any decision-making, taking some of the uncertainty out of being brave.

Underperforming staff

Dealing with underperforming staff is an early challenge that requires decisive and consistent action. It also requires agreement and support from governors – we see later what can happen if decisions are inconsistent and governors waver in their commitment to the agreed action. There is often a substantial changeover of staff when there is a change of headteacher. Sometimes this is because staff who have been happy under the old regime think it is time to move on, sometimes it is dissatisfaction with the new regime that causes movement. Sometimes, if the school is not seen as particularly successful, the new head is appointed with an expectation that some staffing changes will be made.

Another head, taking over a grammar school that seemed to be 'coasting' (LEA description), dealt with poor performance directly and by the end of her first year in post was in the process of dismissing or seeking early retirement for ten members of staff. Her first step was to ensure that detailed job descriptions were in place. She made her expectations very clear for the fulfilment of these jobs, including an early version of the performance management system that is now the legal requirement in every school. This gave her a benchmark for expected performance based on each member of staff's role, experience and targets set. Pupil performance was a prime consideration: in some departments pupils' average GCSE grades were not as high as in the comprehensive schools in the next county. Having made the lowest acceptable achievement very explicit to classroom teachers and expected management functions equally explicit to heads of department and other middle managers, she regularly monitored progress and immediately questioned why anyone was not meeting her criteria.

By Easter it was becoming obvious which members of staff were not performing to the standard set and some were on the informal stage of capability procedures. The rigorous approach had been taken in order to raise standards, but it had the double effect of also providing all the evidence necessary when she needed to dismiss someone. Even more important, she was able to show that the same criteria had been applied to everyone working at the school and could not be accused of victimisation.

Some time later an ex-member of staff appealed against her dismissal. At the ensuing industrial tribunal the panel found that the school had acted totally properly in all instances.

Most heads would not have such a big problem to address. Now, in the recruitment crisis in the south of England, an extra pressure would be the anxiety about being able to find a replacement for an underperforming teacher. Some heads feel it is better to keep a less than adequate teacher than to risk having no one to teach the class.

Change of leadership style

One head in his third term in post reflected that the biggest challenge for him had been following on from someone so different in style, a conscious appointment on the part of the governors. All decisions had previously gone through his predecessor, whereas the new head wanted to consult and involve people. As in an earlier case above, the previous head's role included all matters of student discipline, which he too seemed to have dealt with summarily, whereas the new head's inclination was to understand the students' point of view (he wondered if he was perhaps too understanding!). This then created a real danger that he was spending a great deal of time seeing all the difficult pupils, whilst some staff, often vociferous and sometimes cynical themselves, wanted simplistic 'exclude them, punish them' solutions. Even a normally positive staff, working hard and getting tired as the term wears on, easily becomes demoralised when they feel that they are not being supported in matters of pupil indiscipline in the way they were used to. Moving the debate on to what constitutes real learning and good teaching is a vital part of the job but which can so easily disappear under everyday pressures. He has found his new leadership team to be extremely supportive and remarkably loyal, to both the school and to himself, yet can still feel isolated by the pressure to perform to received notions of discipline and behaviour which are unrelated to the quality of what happens in the classroom. Whole-school planning, monitoring, self-evaluation, structures for decision-making, and catering for all students' needs are areas where there is much still to be done, and that's what he wanted to achieve when taking up the post. The school needed and wanted a change, from centralised control to a wider base, and from anti-educationalist attitudes to openness by the leadership to new ideas about teaching and learning. He is at the stage in his development where he wonders if he ought to have come in harder, made his mark first, then started changing attitudes. He wonders if he may have been too open and unguarded. He knows that for him a consultative style is good, and being authoritative would have been harder to define and achieve. Decisions or changes which he believes are right sometimes have to wait until people can see the need for themselves, and are no longer scared of losing anything or taking risks to get there. It takes considerable confidence in one's own vision to come through this stage without wavering.

Settling down

Feeling at home

Once the first year has been completed the new head will have experienced all aspects of the role, and will have made some changes and some decisions about other ways forward in the future. More importantly, she will also have had time to get to know all the important players and have a fair idea how best to work with each of them. They too will now have this knowledge about her. All parties will now know each other's strengths and weaknesses. If they are all generally happy with these the head will be able to move forward with some confidence that she will be supported. Now will be the time for establishing working patterns and systems that reflect the head's style and vision for the school.

Many heads we work with seem to feel quite different in their second year as heads. They have often needed to review their first year (for performance management or for the school improvement plan) and found by looking objectively at aspects of the school as they found it on taking up the post and checking these aspects at the end of the year that they had succeeded in making more progress than they had realised. They could also see the satisfactory and satisfying relationships they had formed with, in particular, staff and governors. This is another opportunity to make it clear that this is the situation in the vast majority of schools. In this book we mainly show where problems have arisen – we cannot emphasise sufficiently that these are not the norm.

If the important players are less happy with each other's personalities it is now that difficulties will develop. Governors and senior staff may have originally claimed they were looking for strong leadership – they did not realise that they would not enjoy the reality of that and wanted the new head to be far more consultative. On the other hand they may have been hoping that the new head would take the difficult decisions and solve problems they themselves had been unable to solve – they are disappointed that all this has not yet been done. No longer content to say, 'Let her find her feet, give her time to settle in', they want action.

Reaping the successes of the first year

A head took over almost two years ago a junior school in a mixed semi-rural area. This school was the least popular in the area, had been suffering falling rolls and poor SATs results and was seriously at risk of closure. She chose this headship because she felt at interview that the school had many positives, including a nucleus of three excellent teachers who seemed to her to be being frustrated by the other problems in the school, and that she would be able to make an impact on it. An OFSTED inspection in her second term reiterated all the problems she knew were there but acknowledged that 'the newly appointed head was providing positive leadership and improvements had been made since the last inspection'. She felt that the learning curve during her first year had been increased by her lack of knowledge of school finances. She had not done the NPQH and, with hindsight, regretted the lack of an overview of all aspects of the role she was taking on. Because of her insecurity in this area she had felt it necessary to work slowly and carefully when dealing with any financial matters and this had resulted in some decisions, especially related to staffing, being made too late. She felt that this was then made worse by governors responding very slowly and not realising that she needed their response before she could take any action.

During her first year she had had to deal very firmly with the small group of teachers, including the deputy head, who she felt were not pulling their weight professionally. She had not had to invoke any formal procedures but had made it very clear what her expectations were and that anyone who did not agree with them should look elsewhere. By the end of the year two had found other jobs and the third had retired. (The two moving to other schools had been offered posts without the backup of her references – the recruitment situation made other heads prepared to take the risk of employing them.) She was given an unexpected solution to the late vacancies when a teacher with good references relocated to the school's area in mid-June and an NQT who had been waiting for her partner to get a job before she applied filled the other full-time slot. There was still a part-time vacancy which she had to fill herself for the next year. She had planned to implement a timetable of non-contact time for all the staff but was unable to do this whilst she had a substantial class teaching commitment. She found this was the major source of stress during the second year – it took away a lot of the time she had planned to use proactively, cut down on her ability to monitor teaching systematically, made her unavailable to deal with problems as they arose and left her working late into the evening trying to keep up with paperwork. But the improvements she had been able to set in motion during the first year had already stopped the fall in pupil numbers and a substantial increase expected this coming year has enabled her to advertise early for an extra full-time teacher. She now feels that she can see clear improvements in most areas and is confident that her insistence on high standards from the beginning is now paying off. She also feels that the governors feel more confident in their own role now they feel confident in her abilities. She is now able to look at improving such things as how governors' meetings are run (the chairmen of the committees lack the skills needed to run meetings effectively with the result that they sometimes go on until very late at night without clear outcomes) and to work on improving visual aspects of the school. She cannot speak highly enough of her staff team, especially the assistant head, and rejoices in the children and parents' positive attitude to the school. The 'down days' are when she has to deal with very difficult pupil behaviour problems as these sadden her. When asked if she thought she might go on to another headship she said she had far too much to do in her current post to think of moving for the foreseeable future.

The importance of secure systems

Whether they were taking over from a successful head or in a school where there were difficulties, all heads we talked to in the middle period of their headships felt that they were only able to feel confident and settled once they had set up very clear systems. In spite of the constant changes and initiatives, or, more likely, because of these, they had devised cycles, fixed times for certain activities, priorities, fall-back positions, clear guidelines and clear boundaries. They also resisted being put under pressure to appoint staff who they did not think would be right for the school, even though they risked having vacancies. These boundaries provided a secure framework both for their own management and for everyone else in the organisation and freed them up for proactive leadership. They simplified their role under three necessary elements – a clear framework, valuing people, putting children first.

Dealing with accusations of harassment

One head found herself dealing with accusations of harassment against a member of staff. She found it very stressful, but was able to use the systems she had set up to support her successfully through the necessary procedures. Under pressure to respond to the accusations she was able without difficulty to prove that her behaviour had been reasonable, consistent and in line with the guidelines she had set up after consultation with all the staff and governors. She was thankful that she had put systems in place when she was not under pressure so that they were there when difficulties happened.

Life cycle research shows that there is a point towards the likely middle of most people's lives where they reassess their situation and either continue to move on in their careers or change their priorities. This is the 'mid-life crisis' moment when they realise perhaps that their career and/or personal life has been less successful than they had hoped and that further promotion is not going to happen, or perhaps they decide that it is no longer important to them to compete or to commute, that there are things they would prefer to be doing and now want the time to do them. Also career pattern research suggests a similar cycle after each promotion – a highly motivated period of a steep learning curve followed by consolidation and a feeling of confidence, then a reappraisal as the motivation for repeating the same job diminishes. Even in second and subsequent headships the pattern is similar though the first stage is much shorter. If life cycle and career cycle patterns are overlaid the two coincide in headship. Established head-teachers are very likely to be in their forties (earlier in primary, later in secondary) and have as much time ahead of them before the formal possibility of retirement as some have had in teaching. How are they therefore to keep motivated and revitalised? The choices for those who decide to leave headship are discussed in chapter 11, but here we look at what can happen with those who choose to stay.

The sentence above suggests that leaving a headship (or any other career) is an active decision. In reality the time of starting and leaving is not very often exactly as planned. Perhaps it has taken longer than expected to have that successful interview, arriving therefore at the first headship slightly too late to have a high expectation of moving on to a second. Perhaps the opportunity to move on is limited by family commitments – a natural unwillingness to change location when children are at crucial stages in their own education or when partners' careers also have to be taken into consideration. Perhaps the desire to retire early is prevented by the very contemporary commitment to paying for sons' and daughters' higher education. Whatever the reason, there are many heads who cannot choose to move on or out and the next sections explore what ways forward there are for them.

At the summit

The Head of a very successful junior school for the last six years, Amanda is the epitome of the bubbly enthusiast. She sparkles and motivates her staff, praising them and encouraging them to get the best out of their pupils. A trainee teacher based in the school seemed at first to have the makings of a satisfactory but uncharismatic teacher: under the tutelage of Amanda and her professional tutor in the school this trainee blossomed into a great success, bringing a fresh and refreshing approach to her teaching. The OFSTED inspection in early 2001 found: 'The headteacher has a very clear vision of the future of the school, which is shared by the senior management team and the staff ... Staff feel valued in the new management systems recently implemented, and they work very effectively as a team. Staff morale is high.'

Amanda therefore seemed to be the ideal person to give a positive response to being asked, 'what keeps you going?' Her totally unexpected answer was, 'anti-depressants'. After a brief pause to let what she'd said sink in, she talked about the moment four years ago when she started crying and could not stop. She was exhausted by what she saw as the unremitting pressure especially of simply keeping up with reading the stream of documentation emanating from the DfEE/DfES, Qualifications and Curriculum Authority (QCA), LEA, etc. (even keeping up with the abbreviations was a struggle!). She felt that she needed to be well versed in it all if she wanted to lead her staff with confidence and not take any wrong turnings. She knew they were all working to capacity and felt that it would be very wrong of her to make decisions that added to their workload unless she was quite sure that it was the only way forward. She had no criticism of the support given by governors and senior staff: 'The governors and the senior management team are totally behind me. In fact that's exactly where they are – behind me. There is no one actually going along beside me. I have to lead everyone all the time and the whole structure fails if I'm not doing that. The LEA is very supportive, but only whilst I am succeeding. The head of the infant school is leaving at Christmas without another job to go to and the head of the secondary school we feed into has just left. We are all at the end of our ability to take any more pressure.'

Coping with isolation

The isolation of a school leader has been explored by David Mercer (1996) who suggests that professional isolation is one factor inhibiting individuals from applying for headships and quotes Weindling and Earley's (1987) comment that 'it is the loneliness of being the final arbiter upon whose word all sinks or swims. It is this power that isolates and daunts'.

How do heads deal with this isolation? Sometimes they find another head to share problems and frustrations or to bounce ideas off, sometimes the chair of governors fulfils that need, sometimes the support is provided by the spouse or partner or through membership of a sports club or some other hobby. Some heads take a break: they have left school leadership temporarily for advisory posts or secondments to such bodies as professional associations, or business education partnerships; others moved out of education altogether and found jobs in different commercial sectors such as insurance, marketing and even hotel, leisure and tourism. Some will have made a success of this and their subsequent stories have not come back to us. Others decided to return to education, and to headship. Those who returned had discovered that many of the outside pressures were the same – keeping up with change, constant need to improve the product or the strategies used, long working hours. They also found that the result of not keeping up would ultimately be dismissal. Added to this were the difficulties of working to very stressed managers who were also striving to meet high targets and strict deadlines. They missed the camaraderie and teamwork and the constantly refreshing contact with children and young people. In spite of the constraints, demands and pressures, headship still offered more opportunities for using a wide range of skills and for independent decision-making as well as real enjoyment.

Comparing working life in and out of teaching

The head of a small primary school in a very rural area had an unusual path to headship that has given him a different perspective on the role. Having trained as a teacher, spent some years in the classroom and some as an advisory teacher, he decided to leave education to work in industry. His background was in design technology so he found a job in toy design. Although he enjoyed the work he found the pressures far greater than in teaching: performance targets had to be achieved and deadlines had to be met, otherwise you lost your job. He saw people come to work in their company cars and leave half an hour later without a car or a job. This pressure was exacerbated by dependence on other departments also meeting their deadlines and having no way of ensuring that they did. The worst thing of all was the lack of holidays. He felt that the company owned him. Eventually he was made redundant and during his time out of work he was asked if he would like to take on the acting headship of a local primary school. He was successful in returning to teaching and coming straight back into a leading managerial role. He then applied for the permanent headship but was not offered it – there were disagreements among the governors – so he found himself out of work again. So when he was offered his present post he was again coming into a headship from being unemployed.

He has now been at the school for ten years. Although there are few children in the village itself, the school has a good reputation and attracts more than three-quarters of its pupils from other villages in the area. He has thought of moving on but cannot see the value of moving – it would be a bigger challenge but not a new challenge and not worth the difference in salary. He has, however, kept his interest in advisory work. He regularly delivers courses for his LEA and has been building an international portfolio with links in the United States and elsewhere. This prevents him becoming isolated within the school and provides an external focus. He knows of many heads who have decided to leave because they feel unable to maintain the energy levels required to keep on top of all the new initiatives and the accompanying paperwork. Two are now doing supply teaching and are very happy to have relinquished their headships. He believes the difference in salary between a classroom teacher and the head of a small school is insufficient to encourage anyone to take on the responsibilities of running a school. This is especially so if the head has to teach as well.

He compares his present headship post with his time out of teaching in Table 10.1.

Seeing it out

Although many heads move on to second headships and to other posts, there are still a large number who choose to stay in their first headship for the rest of their career. Several, when asked why they had not moved on, replied that they had vaguely thought they would move but there was always something else that needed doing in their current school, something that had kept them motivated, and the time had passed so quickly they had not really realised how long they had been there. There are also the advantages that come with long experience – detailed knowledge of the community and its people, an understanding of the decisions made earlier and the successful reputation already built up.

One particularly sad situation is that brought about by a head being in post for too long, especially if appointed pre-1988. Many cases were brought to our attention of heads in their fifties but not yet quite old enough to go, who had been very effective leaders for many years, had done their best to keep up with all

Table 10.1 Comparing headteacher and product design manager

Headteacher	Product design manager
Can't be made redundant (though the school could close)	Vulnerable to redundancy
Can be dismissed for misconduct or incapability	Can be dismissed for not meeting targets over an extended period
Responsible for the work of team of staff	Responsible for the work of team of staff
Fixed salary within prescribed range	Salary plus bonuses and expenses
Responsible directly to board of governors who have no financial stake in the school	Responsible indirectly to board of directors who have financial stake in the business
No line manager	Direct line manager
Responsible for deployment of agreed budget	Negotiates budget for project, then responsible for working within this
Inflexible and long working hours with constant interruptions	Flexible, but could be long, working hours with uninterrupted time on task
Wide range of interactions	Limited interactions
Highly visible, representing the school at all times	Inconspicuous – sales and marketing departments represent the company externally
Bottom line – pupils are successfully educated (how is this defined?)	Bottom line – the end product makes a profit for the company (clearly defined)

the changes, to keep motivated and motivating, but who gradually had run out of energy. The early retirement opportunity offered in 2000 and 2001 to those over 55 who felt unable to implement any more initiatives provided a way out for a substantial group but many more found themselves carrying on until continuing poor examination results or a disappointing OFSTED inspection triggered action. The background to several of the scenarios above is of a head who was appointed when the school seemed to need particular skills in its new head, but whose skills are no longer appropriate to the current demands of the school or of headship in general.

The need to provide support for heads in difficulties, or schools temporarily without heads, has led to the development of consultant heads. These are usually retired, successful headteachers who go back into schools on a temporary or part-time basis.

One of these had spent her whole teaching career in the same school: one extremely successful inner London primary head had started her working life with the then Greater London Council and had studied in the evenings for a teaching certificate and then a degree before working for twenty years until her retirement in the same school. She said she never had time to get bored or to need new challenges as the job itself was constantly changing: the school had a very varied intake and as soon as families found their feet they moved on. There were boat people, Somalis, many different Africans, latterly Portuguese and South American Hispanics. She put her success down to having a very clear idea of what she wanted and communicating this equally clearly. It was also clear that she cared deeply not only about the children who came through the school but also their families and she often fulfilled the role of mediator or conciliator in local and family disputes. Whilst she was head the school had two highly successful OFSTED inspections and she decided to retire when the school amalgamated with the junior school on the same site.

Since then she has worked with several newly appointed heads in difficult schools to help them devise strategies and act as a sounding board and mentor. She is strongly in favour of the idea of mentoring new heads because she has a unique position:

- She can really be a critical friend as she is genuinely not carrying any other agenda
- New heads daren't admit that they've got problems to anyone else in the system because of the destabilising effect this could have on the school as well as the risk to their own reputation.

She has been mentor to the head of a primary school in special measures who was used to being deputy head in a school where the head was regularly absent. She was mature and reasonably confident but needed help in working out her priorities in her new school. It was a 1930s building, almost derelict to look at. Although she was delighted that a lot of parents were supportive and were willing to help in practical ways, she was concerned about having the energy she needed to be around all the time showing people how to do things.

She also mentored another head just back from maternity leave who felt very out of touch and anxious about getting back into the rhythm and pace of school life.

Another head who had taken slightly early retirement was coaxed back to work three days a week as acting head whilst helping the deputy develop the skills to take on the headship. This situation had arisen because of the sudden decision of the substantive head to leave immediately after his leadership of the school was criticised by OFSTED inspectors. This is similar, but on a much smaller scale, to the development of the Lichfield Foundation in Wolverhampton.

'This is the story of a novel response to a school in difficulty' is the beginning of the school's own story of its regeneration. The Regis School in Wolverhampton was deemed to be failing whilst the nearby St Peter's Collegiate was highly successful. The first move was for the head of St Peter's to take over the other school for two terms whilst it re-established itself as The King's School under the Fresh Start initiative. Then he returned to his own school but retained an influential role through the development of a partnership between the two schools. At first he was director of the partnership alongside his role as principal of St Peter's, with an associate head at the King's School. This partnership became the Lichfield Foundation with the principal of St Peter's as the principal of the foundation as well. When he moved on to a different role, he retained his position with the foundation whilst each school appointed its own head. He retained a part-time consultative and support role.

As the number of applicants for primary headships, especially in the London area, has diminished, so a new style of *itinerant head* has emerged. Inspired by industrial project management and short-term manager contracts with very specific briefs, one of the larger supply agencies started recruiting senior managers to work on short contracts in schools. This has grown as other agencies took up the idea. Then new ones developed specialising in this area, using heads and deputies who had taken early retirement and who were prepared to take on work for a term or so but no longer (because of the effect on their pension and/or because of the personal commitment that a longer-term post would require).

In a different scenario, the head of a Roman Catholic primary school had seen the school through a complicated building programme and a highly successful OFSTED inspection early in the autumn term and decided to retire (early) at the end of the Easter term. Just after she handed her notice in, her deputy was successful at interview for another local headship. Although neither Sue nor the school governors had voiced this, they had all felt it quite likely that the deputy would have succeeded Sue in her own school and this was partly why Sue had felt comfortable with her decision to leave mid-year. Unfortunately the first advertisement for her replacement attracted only one applicant, who was already known to be unsuitable for the post. There was now no one else already in the school who had the experience and ability to take on the headship, however temporarily, so Sue decided to defer her retirement for a term. She did not know what she would do if there was still a problem finding a suitable replacement, but at least by then she would have been able to develop key people in the school to take on senior roles.

Not every headteacher is desperate to retire

Not only do some heads work comfortably through to the normal retirement age of 60, there are even some who stay on till they are 65. One of these took up his second headship aged 45, never imagining that he would remain in the job for twenty years. He had expected to move on one more time and retire at 60 but found there were always challenges to keep him occupied and time passed so quickly he only realised it when it was too late to move on.

The school he spent so much of his career in was in a very deprived urban area. He had come from headship of a more typically mixed school and experienced a great shock on discovering the economic and social poverty of the families in his school's catchment area. It was the challenge of helping these children to make better lives for themselves that motivated and engaged him. It was clear that twenty years later he still felt strongly about them.

When he was appointed to the headship the school was going through a particularly difficult time. The previous head had been very prominent in local politics and was involved nationally in his professional association, with the result that he was either not available or not really interested in problems in the school. The deputy head had lost interest in running the school in his absence. He was also perceived as being very unsympathetic – an ex-sergeant-major – and not easily approached by staff (or anybody else) with problems. The staff were therefore very demoralised and frustrated and those who could move on did so.

The new head found he had a positive force in this frustrated young teaching staff. They were very happy to have a head who was interested in their work and the school generally and were, in his words, 'the making of the school'.

He had already learnt in his first headship that staff were always prepared to work hard provided that he remembered that everybody had another life outside school. He respected this and they respected and worked harder for him. It was obvious on talking with him that this was a man who really understood people, both young and older, and treated them all with courtesy and respect whilst making it clear that he expected everyone to try their hardest: staff for the benefit of the pupils in their care, and pupils for their own achievement.

He had been helped in making a success of his job over the years by good relationships with his deputy heads (three in 18 years, all of whom went on to be successful heads themselves). The deputy in post when he arrived had retired within two years so he was able to appoint someone sympathetic to his philosophy very early in his time in the school. He was therefore able to share concerns and explore ideas with them. He had also appreciated the support of other local heads. They had always been linked by the problems common to schools in difficult areas and not divided by competition for pupils or positions in league tables. They shared problems about social issues – for example the anxieties surrounding decisions by social services to use a particular development for rehousing problem families. He was proud that his school was a stable and secure place for these children, probably the only consistent element in their lives. An OFSTED inspector described the school as 'an oasis in the desert'.

There was only one OFSTED inspection during his time as head; this was obviously quite late (only three years before he retired). Although he felt he was fortunate in the inspection team he had and the resulting report was very positive, he was unhappy about the amount of stress it caused. One teacher was physically sick on the morning the inspection started and all were exhausted afterwards. He had tried to keep the pressure off them and not cause extra stress but they put themselves under enormous pressure.

He had also always had supportive governors, though he had found it very annoying when he was first the head, that so many governors saw the role as a political status symbol and arrived at meetings without reading the paperwork and having no real interest in or knowledge of the school. The first chair of governors had been the local mayor and did not really have the time to take a proper interest in the school. The next one was a local clergyman. He was an excellent person to have as he knew the problems of the area very well and they were able to work together to try and improve the school, and therefore the opportunities for the children. His third chair was also a local person, living and working with the same families whose children came to the school. He felt her knowledge and support were invaluable.

Although he had always deemed the paperwork a 'curse' it eventually became more of a burden. Towards the end of his time as head he began to feel that he no longer had the energy to be as proactive as he had been. He also began to be stressed by the difficulty of getting staff – either supply cover or teachers to fill vacancies.

He knew that he had genuinely been fortunate in the people he had had to work closely with over the years and could give many examples of colleague heads who had moved, resigned or taken early retirement because of problems with staff or with governors. There were also colleagues who had resigned because of the effect OFSTED had on them and their staff. But it was clear, however, that the success of this head was really more to do with

- his positive attitude to change
- his understanding of the pupils and staff and
- his ability to leave the job behind when he went home.

Part III
Playing longer

11 Keeping moving

Successive headships, revitalisation and work after headship

Introduction

As we have commented several times in sections above, many heads go on to second and third headships. Since many achieve their first headship in their late thirties or early forties it is very likely that they will want at least one change of environment in the twenty years' career still left to them. Some now take a break between headships, a strategy that in the recent past (and in some LEAs currently) would have had an adverse effect on the head's career, and there may still be some resistance by governors and other selectors to appoint if candidates are over 50. What then are the options for those who have been in the same job for some time?

- move on to a further headship
- revitalisation in the same post
- work after headship.

The second and third options are for those who do not wish to move to another headship or do not think they will be given the opportunity.

The first section examines the possibilities for second or third headships. The following section assembles a range of possibilities for existing headteachers to consider. Any planning for their development and further career progression has to be undertaken by heads themselves. Thus they should both be aware of this range of possibilities and consider it in the light of their own personal circumstances. These circumstances will involve both their personal situation and also the current state of development of their school. The impetus for any change may come from a combination of their wish for change and a recognition that the school needs a different kind of spur to its further development than they could provide.

Such speculative planning needs to be opportunistic. This has two elements:

- Seize opportunities
- Have a range of possibilities in mind.

Heads need to be ready to seize opportunities if they present themselves. Although there may be an ideal time to take on new tasks or to move on from headship, any possibilities on offer may be transitory. If the head has begun to be sensitive to opportunities because he or she has a longer-term plan for their own development, then suitable opportunities can be followed up when they are available. Some may be around for only a short period of time.

Opportunities which satisfy the needs of particular individuals may be quite rare particularly if they also have geographical restrictions. Thus heads need to have a range of possibilities in mind that they would be willing to consider. It should be fairly obvious that the more specific the range of options that have been considered in planning, the less likely they are to be available at the right time. This fact may be overlooked when very deliberate planning has been done and the most desirable possibility has monopolised thinking. Thus a range of possibilities need to be borne in mind so that the chance of a match between timing and desirability is maximised.

Further headships

'Dropping in and out' – a flexible approach

Alex was very proud of the fact that in his first permanent headship in his mid-thirties he took the school out of special measures. To do this he had had to confront and resolve many personnel issues under very stressful circumstances. When he considered the job to be complete, he resigned and took a year out travelling round the world – something he had never been able to afford to do before. He viewed this as valuable experience and that he would come back reinvigorated and ready to take on another challenging headship. On his return he was offered an acting headship, again in a school in special measures. The school's improvement was measurable but he was not offered the permanent post. A second acting headship reflected the same scenario and in the feedback from the LEA after the interview for the permanent post he was told that the governors were unwilling to take the risk of appointing someone who seemed to be 'dropping in and out of the profession'.

In LEAs like Lambeth, for example, the scenario described above would not happen: their view is that a period out of headship is valuable and sometimes essential and that taking time out positively should be seen as a healthy way of keeping revitalised. This is the attitude of some LEAs faced with the desperate shortage of applicants for headships, especially for those schools in the most challenging circumstances, who are looking at more flexible approaches to appointments. In Lambeth, where the local authority acknowledges the fact that few people can be expected to run a challenging school for an indefinite period, fixed term contracts are being used – the head is appointed on a higher salary than would be normal for the size of the school, but for a predefined period. A future application from a head following this with a term or so out of school would be viewed positively.

Richard took over an expanding school that had been very much the bottom of the league tables. The previous head had done much to improve the school's status in the community, by achieving Technology College status for it and by vastly improving the morale of its staff and pupils. He was very much an enthusiast with excellent interpersonal skills and the right person at the right time for the school. It was thanks to him that the school avoided closure: three schools geographically close in an ageing area of very mixed urban development from the 1960s and with a dwindling school population – there were not enough pupils for them all. It was at this pivotal point that Richard took over. He continued the progress made but began to put systems in place to embed the changes made and to restructure the management of the school. By then it had become clear that another of the three competing schools was having problems recruiting and retaining pupils and staff – not surprising considering the unstable situation and its reputation as the least successful in the area. The LEA decided to close the other school and let the head take early retirement. Richard had therefore the challenge of managing the integration of the two schools over a three year period. He had to make decisions about each member of staff – who would be needed in the enlarged school, who was a good teacher but in an already fully staffed department, who he deemed not a good enough teacher to work at raising standards in the new college.

Progress on this front was delayed by difficulties with one particular member of the governing body. Richard took legal advice and sent him an official warning that he would be taken to court if he did not refrain from the aggressive and inappropriate behaviour that he had been displaying. Afterwards Richard felt that the challenges of managing the amalgamation of the two schools to the satisfaction of the majority were less stressful and wearing than the problems caused by this one governor.

Whilst this was taking place, the future of the lowest achieving school in the county where Richard had previously been a deputy head was under discussion. As there was still a need for the pupil places in the surrounding area, it was agreed to close the school down and reopen it under the Fresh Start initiative and with private funding. The first round of advertisements for the headship of this new school did not produce a candidate whom the governors felt would be right for the post so applications were encouraged from people already known in the county. Richard was one of these and decided that the time was right for a move. His application was successful. He had one term in post before the school reopened with new governors, staff and pupils on a refurbished and revitalised site. This time the challenge will be to raise pupil achievement within the target timescale but with plenty of resources to deploy as he thinks most appropriate.

Choosing a second headship

In applying for a second headship Richard weighed up different priorities from those when approaching his first job as a head. The first time round he had been willing to apply for most headships occurring within quite a wide radius from his home. The school he first took over was more than an hour's drive away. At the point of applying for that post the important thing in his mind was to succeed in obtaining a headship. The second time around Richard weighed up the challenges of the new role – were they going to provide him with new experiences or simply the same problems but in a different context? He also included in the equation the distance of the school from home – he wanted to use the time taken up by travelling for something more profitable, and to avoid arriving home at midnight after governors' meetings.

Earley *et al.*'s 2002 research into heads' attitudes will suggest that, when deciding to move to a second or subsequent headship, they look for a post which will not be too challenging. Those we spoke to who were not in their first headship did not seem to endorse that view: they generally seemed to have been looking for schools which would provide them with a new challenge. One had been particularly annoyed after an interview for the headship of a school in special measures (no one was appointed to the post following that round of interviews) to be told casually at a later date by a member of the interviewing panel that they couldn't see why she wanted a difficult school at her stage – they had not asked her that during the interview. The young woman who took Rutlish Boys' High School out of special measures and turned it into 'a good school' moved quickly on to another London school in equally difficult circumstances and was genuinely enthusiastic about the challenge of transforming this second school too.

The difference in the findings may be because Earley *et al.*'s interviewees are describing their future intentions and they may not move on to second headships, but our interviewees were those who had already moved into their second or third post.

Development of the executive head

A new (2002) development is to extend the role of the 'successful' head to be in charge of a cluster of less successful schools, thus sharing the leadership skills which have made the first school successful. This was pioneered by Peter Crook, executive principal of the Lichfield Foundation, whose story is described in more detail in the previous chapter. This may prove to be a successful device for improving schools. The fear, however, is that the skills needed to bring a school out of serious difficulties are quite different from those required to lead a school whose success in part derives from its ability to attract pupils who are more likely to perform highly. The highly successful, and highly selective, girls' grammar school in Reading has recently become a beacon school with a mandate to spread its good practice to the less successful schools around. But what can teachers in schools in the least favoured areas of Reading learn from the good practice of this beacon school? This is not to detract from the quality of the grammar school's success but to suggest that the role model is not the right one.

Businesses that have put this model into practice have encountered difficulties as it has proved impossible for the leading manager to use complex skills or help develop them in others. This is because his time has been taken over by the need to be aware of too many issues without having the time to work on any of them in any depth – this has to be delegated to the managers of the various subsidiaries.

Rise and fall of the 'superhead'

This development of the 'executive head' has taken over from the old model of the 'superhead'. When Calderdale LEA drafted in a high profile experienced head in the highly publicised aftermath of the OFSTED inspection of the Ridings School, this was probably the beginning of the idea of the 'superhead'. Since then there have been many examples of a similar scenario:

1   A school was in difficulties
2   So it was strongly criticised after an OFSTED inspection
3   The current head resigned, was dismissed or disappeared
4   The LEA funded a large injection of funds for the school and for a new head's salary
5   The headship was advertised at a much higher salary level than would have been either affordable or permissible until this action was triggered
6   A 'superhead' was appointed with much publicity and high expectations for the transformation of the school.

After this point there was a pause whilst the new head got to work. In some cases little more was heard of the school, but in others the next burst of publicity followed the resignation of the head who had found it impossible to fulfil the expectations that accompanied her appointment. Not all 'superheads' have been surrounded by publicity. The majority have quietly moved in and set about the necessary transformation with energy and determination but without the extra pressure of being in the public view. The more interesting question is to ask what happened next – how did the next head manage to make improvements stick, had the problems causing the original problem been eliminated or had they re-emerged once the publicity and extra funds dried up? Research carried out in Australian schools and in challenging schools in the UK suggested that the perceived 'superhead' style leads to a dependency culture: more successful leadership is achieved through teamwork, support and consensus and this takes time.

A recent article in *The Economist* (2002: 73) reinforced this suggestion by stating that the boards of big companies in difficulties have an 'unreasoning faith in the ability of an outsider ... Hiring a high-profile outsider can destabilise the firm and destroy the loyalty of senior managers, including good internal candidates. It rarely restores the firm's fortunes.' The article goes on to suggest that the qualities required of someone who will restore faith in the company have less 'marquee value' and more integrity; 'quiet, workmanlike, stoic leaders bring about the big transformations'.

A further nail was put in the coffin of the 'superhead' idea by an article in *Headship Matters* (2002: 12) which began 'The superhead is extinct. This must surely be one of the shortest lived species in the history of the planet'.

Revitalisation

We shall consider two possibilities:

- Reinvigorating headship
- Professional work after headship.

The first of these covers taking on additional roles and responsibilities whilst still in headship with a view to generating stimulation and revitalisation such that headship can be pursued with renewed vigour and insights. The second prepares for active professional life after headship has been given up. The two may be connected in that skills, experience and contacts built up in reinvigorating activities may be taken up and provide the basis for professional work after headship.

Reinvigorating headship

The need for such stimulation and development outside school should increasingly be considered to be an expectation for heads. There is abundant evidence that long periods in the same post lead to deteriorating satisfaction and performance. Many commercial organisations recognise that performance in post rapidly plateaus unless there is additional stimulation and development. This should not be regarded as a weakness of a particular headteacher but as an expectation of need for the individual and the school. We do not wish to suggest that undertaking major change projects or other school activities may not be very stimulating, but instead to suggest that a balance between activities in school and ones outside can be particularly valuable. Hence we concentrate on ones here which involve activities outside the head's own school.

An issue in some schools is the willingness of governors to grant release for a period and in some there may also be financial implications. As release depends upon a governors' decision, it will be important for them to be aware of their obligations to the development and continuing motivation of their headteacher. Governors need to recognise that they have to balance short-term and long-term needs. Whilst they may perceive a period of absence of the head as a short-term sacrifice, they also need to recognise the long-term benefits of enhanced performance from a headteacher with enhanced skills and motivation.

There are a number of planning steps which need to be taken as a longer-term preparation for a period of this kind:

- Pattern of work
- Preparing governors
- Acting head and logistics.

School and personal life have a pattern. The school year has a number of predictable features and there are times which are more favourable to periods away than others. Similarly personal circumstances may mean that there are favoured and less favoured times to take on different and possibly supplementary tasks. This should lead to the identification of periods when opportunities would be most welcome. For longer-term plans, the rate of development of the school and periods of consolidation under an acting head may indicate particularly desirable times for alternative activities by the head.

Over a period of time the chair and other governors need to be prepared by the head to accept the necessity of reinvigoration activities. If the principle is accepted and that this will need to happen at some stage, it will be easier to make a case for a particular timing. The extent of the period of getting governors to accept that such activities are a normal part of headteachers' careers may be different in different schools and heads will need to gauge this. More effort and preparatory activities may be needed in some schools including enlisting the help of the local authority to make the case.

An important part of general planning should be a consideration of whether an acting head will be required and, if so, who should be offered the opportunity. This may also require further acting posts if the deputy acts as head. Where these are particularly desirable, they may help make the case for a period away. In any event these will need thought including any financial implications of a period away.

There are a range of possibilities for taking time out, either full-time or part-time, with the intention of returning to the same headship:

- Secondments
- Consultancies
- Inspections
- LEA temporary posts
- Mentoring
- Professional posts
- Academic courses and other training
- Acting headship in another school.

There may be significant differences in terms of the effect on the school and the possibilities for a deputy or other person to act as headteacher whilst some of these are being pursued. A prolonged period away from school by the head will offer an opportunity of acting headship whereas the same time taken as short periods is unlikely to present the same developmental opportunity for an acting headship.

Secondments

There are a variety of secondments for limited periods which can be taken up. For example:

- Industrial secondments
- National College for School Leadership
- Research scholarships to universities.

These have the advantages of being time-bounded, creating an acting headship opportunity at school and providing a new absorbing interest for a period. Such an interest may have direct spin-off benefits for the school in that the experience is directly relevant or the benefits may be indirect because of the renewed enthusiasm with which the head returns.

In some cases there will be financial issues as secondments do not have sufficient finance attached to compensate the school for the loss of the headteacher's salary. However, detailed planning can often show that the actual cost is quite low as there are some acting allowances to be paid and a number of teaching periods to be covered in secondary schools rather than the full cost of the head's salary. Whilst this may also be the case in large primary schools, in smaller schools the cost will be higher. Earmarked funding for the professional development of headteachers as alternatives to the Leadership Programme for Serving Heads could remove the financial problems for these secondments.

A secondment which is known about in advance can provide a planned period of acting headship for a deputy and make a major contribution to their development.

Consultancies

There are a variety of part-time activities at the present time which serving and former teachers and headteachers can take on. For example:

- Threshold assessors: check a sample of the threshold assessments made by headteachers
- Performance management advisers: give advice to headteachers on the implementation and operation of performance management for teachers
- Headship performance consultants: advise governing bodies on the performance and targets of headteachers
- Fast-track teachers assessors: there are assessors for the performance of fast-track teachers and also separate assessors for the school-based projects to be tackled by fast-track teachers

- Graduate teacher schemes tutors and assessors: also those overseas trained teachers who are qualifying to teach in England have both advisers and assessors
- NPQH tutors and assessors: there are tutors who teach NPQH and there are also those who assess NPQH candidates
- AST assessors: teachers who apply to become Advanced Skills Teachers have to have their teaching assessed to be eligible to be appointed as an AST
- Headship appointment consultants: many schools employ consultants to help them select their next headteacher
- Consultants for schools in special measures: consultancy is often a part of the support offered to schools in special measures.

The schemes to which these various posts relate are generally organised by private consultancy firms and these take on appropriately experienced and qualified professionals to perform the tasks. Almost all tasks involve specific prior training and some may also involve periodic updating.

Almost all tasks will develop skills and experience which could be an asset to a headteacher and most involve visiting other schools and analysing and advising on an aspect of their work. These provide a headteacher with additional experience of other schools which should provide comparisons with his or her own and a more analytical approach to schools as an outsider would see them.

Inspections

Inspection teams in both the state sector and the independent sector can have members who are serving headteachers. This involves training before being eligible to join inspection teams. This training may be valuable in its own right as it includes training in systematic lesson observation which may be generally useful in schools. Although taking part in inspections is very demanding and concentrated work, it exercises analytical skills and involves seeing how another school operates at close quarters. In addition to the function of inspection this provides a comparison for the headteacher and should help to sensitise a head to how outsiders see his or her school.

LEA temporary posts

There are a range of LEA temporary posts which are created from time-to-time for specific purposes. These are often filled by seconded headteachers. When new tasks are passed down to LEAs by central government and this is an additional responsibility for which full-time LEA officers and advisers do not have spare capacity, a short-term measure is often to second a headteacher to run the scheme. This happened with the performance appraisal of headteachers in the 1990s.

Such posts may be filled by a succession of headteacher secondments or the secondments may be a temporary measure until a full-time LEA appointment is made. This also may provide an alternative to headship for some candidates.

Mentoring

As we have seen, mentoring of new headteachers is a valuable activity from the perspective of the new head and may also be invigorating for the mentor. The mentor probably will have to undertake some training for the role, will probably be part of a network of mentors who interact and may be a valuable source of communication on other issues too. Finally, the actual mentoring role provides a close working relationship with another head and a requirement to analyse another school context and situation in order to offer appropriate support and advice to the new headteacher.

Professional posts

There has been a long tradition that headteachers serve on LEA committees and working parties. Some may serve on national committees and working parties. A number serve in some capacity in local headteacher associations and a number serve on national and regional committees of headteacher associations.

The recent launch of schemes to revive parts of inner cities with multi-professional activities has provided another opening for headteachers to take part on the committees and other consultative bodies which advise and oversee the work of such schemes.

Academic courses and other training

We have not left this suggestion until nearly the last because we think that it is the least valuable, but because we think that the other activities have been rather underused for their value to the individuals undertaking them. They have tended to be seen for their value to those who are direct beneficiaries of the activities. Academic courses and other training and development courses, on the other hand, are seen as of benefit to the individuals undertaking them. Increasingly this has been interpreted as being demonstrated by what changes they will make on their return to school. However, as we have suggested, changes to the thinking of the headteacher and their perception and evaluation of school activities and how to change them may be much more significant in the longer-term.

Acting headship in another school

As an activity for heads to consider this is a possibility which is far more prevalent than it has been in the past and so needs more discussion here and we have collected a number of recent examples of this in practice. Here the perspective is that of headteacher; the previous discussion of acting headship in chapter 7 examined it from the perspective of a deputy or the school.

In looking at reinvigoration earlier in this chapter, one of the opportunities is to serve for a limited period in another school. Almost inevitably the situation in the other school is challenging in some way. Often those in LEAs ask heads they consider have the right kind of skills whether they would be willing to take on such acting roles for a temporary period. Many heads who had not thought of such tasks are flattered to be asked and seriously consider such requests. Such tasks have a number of advantages which should be considered. They

- are time-bounded
- provide a complete change of school and situation
- may call upon skills which are not in current use
- will provide a challenge
- are likely to be of great benefit to the receiving school
- provide an opportunity for an acting headship by a deputy in the original school, who may be enabled afterwards to obtain a headship and bring about a change of senior colleagues.

For those who fear that they are slipping into a rut and feel they need revitalisation, these are a considerable set of reasons to consider such an invitation. Clearly before accepting, heads need to weigh up whether they feel that they have the skills and the energy to take on the acting role. They need to be clear about the length of time such an acting headship should last. As we have seen in the vignettes in chapter 7, when helping a school in difficulties there is a lot to do and the task of preparing the school to be handed over to a permanent head may seem an unending one. It is much better to agree a timescale and stick to it. If the task is not completed this may provide an opportunity for another head to move in for a temporary period. Though this has implications for the school's reputation and staff morale.

When returning from acting headship the original school is likely to be seen through fresh eyes. This may suggest improvements which need to be made and provide a fresh impetus to tackle previously sidelined problems. The period out of school will have created a planned period of acting headship for a deputy or other colleague. The deputy who has been acting head will have new insights into being a headteacher and the issues at the school. This should mean that he or she is a more informed and empathetic colleague with whom to talk through issues.

The range of reasons for appointing an acting head that we have obtained details about, include one or more of the following:

- The previous head is suddenly not there and confidence in the school needs maintaining whilst decisions are made about the school's future development (holding role).
- The previous head had not been perceived as a good leader/manager so an experienced head is brought in to re-establish a direction for the school, establishing internal confidence and ensuring necessary structures are in place.
- An experienced practitioner is given the opportunity to analyse the school situation realistically to help governors work out their vision for the school.

- The experienced head is brought in by LEA because the governors themselves are unable to work together – the previous head has left because of this. All parties want to avoid a similar situation recurring.
- The school is in special measures. An experienced head is needed to make immediate changes.
- The school is due to close. An experienced head is brought in to manage especially the personnel and morale issues surrounding the closure.
- Serious changes are perceived to be needed in the school. An experienced head is brought in to make these changes (capability procedures, redundancies, etc.) to clear the way for a new head to develop a new team.

Although all of the list above are seen from the receiving school's perspective, are conceived in order to help that school improve and do not necessarily require the temporary secondment of another head, they all are scenarios which are advantageous to experienced headteachers – they provide opportunities for developing and using skills which may be needed later in their substantive post, they provide the possibility to try out a different leadership style, and, perhaps, to see that what is successful in their 'own' school may not work in a different school culture. (The successful head of a highly selective grammar school was the first to admit that her secondment to a local school in difficulties was not successful: very different skills were needed.) They also give a period of distance from their usual environment, enabling some time for reflection and refreshment, even though the demands on them for the length of that secondment may be very high and unsustainable over a longer period. Each of the scenarios is explored in more detail with case studies below.

THE PREVIOUS HEAD IS SUDDENLY NOT THERE AND CONFIDENCE IN THE SCHOOL NEEDS MAINTAINING WHILST DECISIONS ARE MADE ABOUT THE SCHOOL'S FUTURE DEVELOPMENT (HOLDING ROLE)

The most tragic situation for any school is when the headteacher dies whilst still in post. Heart disease and cancer are as prevalent amongst teachers as any other sector.

> We heard of one school in which two successive heads had fought cancer whilst in post; one had retired and survived for a while, the other had still been in post until almost the end of his life. In another school one head retired because of ill health, died almost immediately and was succeeded by the first deputy who moved on after two years. His deputy was then appointed to the headship, was almost immediately diagnosed with cancer and died not long after. One can only imagine the traumatising effect such events could have on the staff and pupils.

In such cases it has been important to have someone sensitively taking over the day-to-day management of the school whilst the school community in its widest sense has been able to grieve and come to terms with the bereavement. These situations bring out the best in terms of loyalty to the school but still require someone to guide the school forward whilst motivation and energy are low. There has also been some reluctance, superstitious and illogical perhaps but very understandable, from others to apply for these jobs and it took longer than would be expected to find suitable replacements.

In the first case the remaining deputy took over as acting head for two terms and was then appointed to the permanent post. In the second case an experienced local head moved over to the school until the new head was appointed. In another similar scenario the school was run jointly by another local head and the deputy head, the deputies having responsibility for the day-to-day management of each school whilst the head provided strategic direction for both.

THE PREVIOUS HEAD HAD NOT BEEN PERCEIVED AS A GOOD LEADER/
MANAGER SO AN EXPERIENCED HEAD IS BROUGHT IN TO RE-ESTABLISH A
DIRECTION FOR THE SCHOOL, ESTABLISHING INTERNAL CONFIDENCE AND
ENSURING NECESSARY STRUCTURES ARE IN PLACE

This would be difficult for an inexperienced head.

> The small rural comprehensive had had a period of decline when it became apparent that the skills of the head were no longer appropriate to marketing a school in a very competitive environment. Jim had been appointed because of his interest in architecture and the main school building was a listed building in a state of disrepair. The governors at the time of his appointment were very anxious about the future of the old building and wanted someone who would understand the architects and historians when plans for its restoration were being made. Ten years later it was still deteriorating, and so were the numbers of pupils on roll. There was no development plan for the school, as opposed to the building, no staffing structure and a power struggle going on amongst members of the senior management team. There were also personality clashes among the governors. Many of the problems were long-standing, involving very strong personalities, and needed addressing firmly and with confidence. This would be difficult for a new, inexperienced head coming into the school without an understanding of the background to the problem (see page 65).

Local authority advisers suggested to the governors that, before advertising for a new headteacher, they bring in an experienced local head to resolve some of the problems. The head chosen to do this had been in post eight years. He had originally been chosen at interview because the panel felt that he would be the candidate most able to deal sensitively with some difficult personalities in the school's senior management team. His style was to work slowly but determinedly, avoiding confrontations and gradually bringing people round to his point of view. In his time in his own school he had solved the staff conflicts and turned the school from one that still had remnants of its old secondary modern ethos into one of the most highly performing in the county.

AN EXPERIENCED PRACTITIONER IS GIVEN THE OPPORTUNITY TO ANALYSE
THE SCHOOL SITUATION REALISTICALLY TO HELP GOVERNORS WORK OUT
THEIR VISION FOR THE SCHOOL

Alison received a telephone call from a senior adviser at the very end of the summer term. The following scenario was described to her and she was asked if she would be prepared to leave her school for a term to go and help the governors of this school devise strategies to help the school move forward. She had been in post five years, her own school was running smoothly and she had a deputy head who would both enjoy and benefit from having the opportunity to have a term as acting head.

A smaller comprehensive in an adjacent area of the county had had an OFSTED inspection earlier that academic year which reported weaknesses in leadership and management despite the headteacher being 'a role model of courtesy which has a major effect on the good behaviour of the pupils and the good relationships in the school'. The main problem seems to have been lack of consultation and strategic direction. Although it was clear that problems existed before the inspection, the findings struck a major blow to the head's self-esteem and he took an increasingly less active role in running the school. This resulted in the two deputy heads, who had never worked successfully together, developing their own power bases and staff aligning themselves to one or other of them. Lack of consistency in decision-making and forward planning bred dissatisfaction and the turnover of both teaching and support staff was huge. There were also a small group of staff whose work had been deemed unsatisfactory by the OFSTED inspectors but who were receiving no support or monitoring of progress. Departmental planning was only as good as the relevant head of department and there were no whole-school strategies to support them.

The incumbent chair of governors during the inspection had become a close friend of the head over many years. He had not been aware of potential problems and had not kept up-to-date with the legislation relevant to governors' responsibilities. This too was the subject of some criticism in the inspection report. Under pressure from other governors, this man resigned. In the same way as the deputy heads took the opportunity to extend their individual influence, so some governors reacted by involving themselves in internal politics in the school and further complicated the increasing problems.

THE EXPERIENCED HEAD IS BROUGHT IN BY LEA BECAUSE THE GOVERNORS
THEMSELVES ARE UNABLE TO WORK TOGETHER – THE PREVIOUS HEAD HAS
LEFT BECAUSE OF THIS. ALL PARTIES WANT TO AVOID A SIMILAR SITUATION
RECURRING

This situation was brought about by problems emerging in the governing body at the time of the recent head's appointment: one section of the governors had felt very strongly that they should appoint a particular internal candidate to the vacant headship, another section felt equally strongly that they should not appoint this person and went ahead with the appointment of an outsider. When the newly appointed head took up her post she found that certain governors seemed to be acting obstructively and that governors' meetings were rendered impossible by the refusal of some members to work with her or with others on the body. She found the situation very distressing and, although she was trying to find ways of solving the problem, when the headship of her previous school became vacant she applied successfully for it.

Not wanting a recurrence of the same problem, the school's advisers suggested that the governors accept a temporary, experienced head whilst they resolved the issues of the previous appointment. This time the head brought in was very experienced and had been involved in governor training, so was already known to the governors of the school. Her role was to help the governors agree on the person specification for the next head and to ensure that they understood and displayed the behaviours expected in the role of school governor.

THE SCHOOL IS IN SPECIAL MEASURES. AN EXPERIENCED HEAD IS NEEDED TO
MAKE IMMEDIATE CHANGES

Drafted in to take a primary school out of special measures, Geoff had been a successful head who had moved into the LEA advisory team. He arrived in the school mid-November – the previous head having disappeared virtually overnight. Staff morale was low and pupil behaviour poor. The atmosphere of anxiety and barely suppressed aggression was almost tangible as you walked through the front door. Staff were shouting and pupils were shouting back. Geoff's first task was to establish a sufficiently calm environment for teaching and learning to start happening again. His next priority was to ensure that systems were in place to provide the framework for continued improvement. He did this, and more, with the result that the next inspection visit found the school to be satisfactory and better in most areas, leadership and management being reported as a strength of the school.

A year on Geoff is wondering how much longer he can keep up the pace. Constant staff changeover means that the new vision needs constantly restating. Because of lack of continuity in the senior management team, Geoff feels that he cannot step back from being a constantly visible presence around the school. The new culture of success is in place and systems are there to support it, but these all need time to become embedded and that remains a serious challenge whilst staff shortages continue to be an issue. Geoff is not sure that he wants to remain in post for the amount of time he feels is needed.

THE SCHOOL IS DUE TO CLOSE. AN EXPERIENCED HEAD IS BROUGHT IN TO MANAGE ESPECIALLY THE PERSONNEL AND MORALE ISSUES SURROUNDING THE CLOSURE

There were too many pupil places in the town and it seemed likely that one school would have to close. A steep decline in pupil numbers as a result of the problem described below had led the LEA to choose the school for closure.

When Tony, the current head of the school, first became aware of problems at the school he also was a local authority adviser. He too had moved from headship to an LEA post, originally on secondment but then with a permanent contract. This was when one model for headteacher appraisal comprised a chain of peer appraisals. He had been contacted by the head who had been designated Henry's peer appraiser. She had arranged interviews with staff at the school appropriate to the focus of appraisal decided by Henry and had been shocked by the negative response of the two deputy heads. They had nothing good to say about Henry. She therefore contacted Tony to discuss the problem.

The staff had raised lots of issues round such things as delegation and communication. It was difficult for her to know who to contact about the problems and she found it very stressful.

Weaknesses described to her included inconsistency of practice and lack of structures – it seemed that people were awarded extra points if they went and asked for them. There were no budgeting policies, no capitation formulae or monitoring of expenditure. In fact there were few policies of any sort in place and there was no school development plan. There were no formally scheduled SMT meetings. Action tended to be taken on an ad hoc basis by whoever felt like doing it.

Accommodation was allocated by request – the head of a minor department had a huge room with settee, etc. but a faculty head had a tiny space. The head's office was hidden away upstairs. The impression was given that Henry was always hiding and had no presence around the school. It was felt that he was a very nice person who offered no threat and avoided confrontation. Even the site manager made unilateral decisions re access to the school, including by the headteacher.

Henry had come into teaching from industry and had been instrumental, as deputy head at another local school, in managing a huge rebuilding programme there. The chair of governors at the school was aware of this and wanted someone with those skills. In the meantime, one of the school deputies was very hopeful of getting the job himself. He was very disappointed and it was felt that he did a lot to undermine Henry's position when he took up the post.

Henry suddenly left at the half-term at the end of October. Staff only discovered this at a staff meeting on the first morning back. An OFSTED inspection was scheduled for two weeks later. A senior LEA adviser took the school with almost no notice, running it for a term and gaining everybody's respect by her leadership of the school through the inspection.

There were two very powerful influences in the school: one was the very powerful personality of the chair of governors, who even had his own separate telephone line in the head's office. The second was one of the teachers' professional associations, which had a very active membership in the school and a national official was on secondment from the school. This led to many problems for staff. They felt very uncomfortable with both of these as they were unable to predict how any comment, critical or otherwise, might be used. It also led to much insecurity in the senior management team, resulting in a decision by one deputy to leave teaching and the other to retire early. Other senior staff, both teachers and support staff, also left in a short period of time.

Tony was then appointed to the headship of the school. He inherited a budget deficit, no senior management team – two acting deputies – a new secretary, no finance officer and no site manager. He felt that, through no fault of his own, Henry had been appointed on a false ticket, with the wrong sort of experience for the job, because of the governors' narrow focus on the proposed building programme. His experience had been very limited – short-term management of a major building project – and included little practice in managing people and developing the broader range of skills needed in senior management.

Sometimes it is as a result of an inspection that action is taken but in this case the OFSTED reports did not reveal the problems: in the first inspection the school was seen as sound in most areas, including leadership and management. This perhaps reflects the quality of the senior adviser's work more than the internal reality of the school. The same was the verdict in the next round, with some criticism of progress since the previous inspection.

Tony's brief had been to manage the closure of the school but he had so successfully changed the culture within and the perception people had of it in the local community that the decision to close it was changed. It now functions as a successful school and two other local schools have been amalgamated.

SERIOUS CHANGES ARE PERCEIVED TO BE NEEDED IN THE SCHOOL. AN
EXPERIENCED HEAD IS BROUGHT IN TO MAKE THESE CHANGES TO CLEAR
THE WAY FOR A NEW HEAD TO DEVELOP A NEW TEAM

A very experienced inner London primary head worked for one term as an interim head. The school was in special measures and the previous head had walked out. Pupil behaviour was very challenging, especially in Year 5, and the school was not fully staffed. There was no deputy head. Her role was to calm the situation down, stabilise people, give the staff their confidence back and bring pupil behaviour back to being manageable. The governors were very supportive but at a loss as to what to do. They were very grateful for her input and this enabled them to start rebuilding confidence in the school with a new head. The improvements visible in the school also helped when recruiting a new head – people were willing to apply and give the school a try.

She felt that her own success was down to being very clear what she wanted and therefore very able to articulate it in a way that ensured others also knew what she wanted and they could all work together effectively. She also felt her background in office administration and finance made her at ease in these areas so she was able to get systems working as smoothly as possible and then focus on the people involved in the school. In her own school she seems to have acted as auntie, counsellor and mediator for the parents and was obviously an important figure in the community serving the school. The head of a neighbouring school described her as 'an institution', so it was clear that the governors of the school she took over for a term would be able to feel utterly confident in her ability to make the important difference to their school.

Considering the benefits

The variety of opportunities which may prove reinvigorating for headteachers is substantial. Most of these could be justified as being of benefit to the headteacher as developmental and refreshing and also may involve the acquiring of specific skills which will be of value in schools. However, only schools in relatively stable circumstances are likely to have a headteacher who feels he or she could take up such opportunities and whose release governors would also approve. Further, there is a danger, and some of our examples demonstrate it, that these external activities begin to take over the interest and time of a headteacher eventually to the detriment of the school in the longer-term. Thus there is a balance to be struck between the invigoration which can come from taking on these activities which will benefit the school indirectly, and the time away from school that they involve. Part of this judgement must involve a consideration of who will be in charge whilst the head is away, even if only for short periods for some opportunities. Acting headship can be of benefit to deputies and enhance the management of the school in the longer-term, but this needs to be evaluated rather than made as a 'convenient assumption'.

Professional work after headship

Decision to leave headship

When analysing their reasons for giving up headship (Draper and McMichael 1996) some heads have identified that there are two forces at work. One is the 'push' to leave headship and the other is the 'pull' of other possibilities in place of headship. The push may be due to the pressures and stress which headship involves or it may be that headship no longer offers the stimulation and enjoyment that it once did. In addition to the general pressures on heads there may be school specific reasons why headship no longer is perceived as attractive. No less important than any push to leave headship is the pull of more attractive alternatives. These may be plans for retirement from work and the increased leisure this offers or they may be some alternative paid employment full- or part-time.

Reasons to leave headship are complex and may involve personal and family circumstances. A spouse who is retiring, or not, often plays a large part in triggering any decision. Changing financial commitments and pension provision also are usually important determinants of any decision. Financial circumstances may also play an indirect part in any decision. If income is not a prime concern then the range of alternatives to headship is greatly enlarged. There may be long cherished dreams that can be realised. Finally, personal health and that of close family members may be contributory factors.

If leaving headship and not contemplating full-time retirement there are a number of initial choices to be made. These may depend on age, personal circumstances, partner's circumstances and a range of other factors. The major choices are between a full-time or part-time commitment and will the work be in education in some way or outside education. Although work may be full-time, each component may be part-time and there may be a portfolio of them. Many opportunities will have been opened up during headship. The range of part-time work additional to headship that we have introduced earlier may have created networks of contacts and established credentials which can be exploited after headship. Whilst this will partly be fortuitous, those who are on the look out for such possibilities are likely to recognise future opportunities.

What work is contemplated may be dependent on financial circumstances. There are clearly many more options if finance is secondary to job satisfaction since this opens up charity work and other unpaid or poorly paid jobs. It, of course, doesn't follow that part-time educational jobs need be financially un-rewarding if a new business opportunity is created. Coaching and additional tuition for children is an expanding opportunity and in addition to doing this oneself there are opportunities to organise others to do this and create a business opportunity. In the future there may be more opportunities of this kind – spotting services which schools, teachers or parents need and are willing to pay for.

A number of people initially want to work part-time but then find that they are sucked into working full-time. This comes about because there is a crisis of some kind that requires someone competent, 'a safe pair of hands', to step in at short notice who is used to managing people and budgets in a complex operation.

Part-time educational

At the present time the most frequent opportunities are part-time educational jobs. In addition to the range of opportunities which are available to those in headship which have already been listed, there is a return to part-time teaching. This may be either through a supply agency or a more regular commitment at one school. For those who like teaching and want employment only during term time this may have many attractions.

In addition to the posts open to serving heads, the professional associations employ field officers to advise headteacher members on school leadership and management and legal issues.

Full-time educational

There are moves to advisory jobs with LEAs or other moves which can involve moving on from headship at quite a young age which represent promotion, particularly for those from small primary schools. They may represent a considerable salary increase. There are a number of openings offering full-time but perhaps fixed term contracts in the many government schemes that have been created. These may offer openings at a later age than the posts which have been regarded as part of the normal career path after headship. In the past Technical and Vocational Education Initiative (TVEI) has offered such posts and the Excellence in Cities and other schemes currently offer such prospects.

There is the possibility of building up a portfolio of part-time activities from the list above for serving heads. Programming work becomes an issue and trying to preserve times to take holidays can be a problem. In some cases full-time openings arise from some part-time posts if an area of work expands and the consultancy firms need someone to manage a new area of work.

Part-time non-educational

This opens up a range of opportunities but the largest group are likely to be charitable or poorly remunerated posts unless the head has a specific interest which opens up opportunities.

Full-time non-educational

This probably is fairly rare except where it grows out of self-employment from starting a business of some kind. As commercial ventures there are a large range of possibilities. Headteachers' management skills are increasingly being recognised more widely: one successful secondary head moved straight from school to the management of a local Health Service Trust. Another was recruited by an interim management agency and is employed by small or medium sized companies to train managers or solve management problems by a short-term secondment to the company.

Choices after headship

In the past there were more conventional openings for posts after headship: LEA advisory posts, HMI, teacher training and university posts. Most of these have either reduced in number or are financially prohibitive. As salaries for headteachers have risen and some others have not, it is no longer possible to move on to posts that may utilise the skills and knowledge acquired by heads because the salaries of such posts would require the head to take a substantial salary cut. Such piecemeal changes appear to have taken place without any explicit consideration of what headteachers might do after headship if they were not to retire.

The current proposals to 'fast-track' teachers through their career into headship will, if successful, lead to the appointment of headteachers at a younger age. If their development before headship has been well-planned they may take on headship very successfully but there also needs to be thought about how long they will stay in headship and what they will do after headship.

Whilst a second headship may become the norm after 7–10 years in a first headship, for those appointed at a young age, this will mean either a very long period in a second headship, or moving to a third headship, if there are not sufficient attractive opportunities to progress to after headship. There are about 25,000 headteachers in England. There will be substantial numbers who are too young to retire and who do not wish to move on to yet another headship.

We have listed many opportunities which have arisen which heads could take on after headship. But these have arisen as a result of other needs rather than in response to the need for career progression after headship. At the present time it is difficult to get applications for many headships. Although many of the suggestions we have made in this book should lead to better preparation before headship and more awareness of the pitfalls which may occur in headship, a further element is needed to make headship more attractive. That is career possibilities beyond headship. These would need to encompass possibilities for the small number who are not successful in headship and the larger number who wish to see possibilities after successful headship.

12 Stresses and challenges

Trio of tensions – governors, school and head

Introduction

The pressures on headteachers that we have identified in earlier chapters place stress on headteachers. We have some detail about such stress and how head-teachers deal with it from a large-scale survey of heads in the late 1980s (Cooper and Kelly 1993). We supplement that by more recent findings which have investigated what headteachers find stressful.

In this chapter we also discuss the premature departure of headteachers from their post. This may be as a result of stress or a more clearly identifiable chain of events. It is some likely situations which provoke such a chain of events that we wish to analyse.

It is becoming increasingly common for some headteachers to leave their posts prematurely and with some degree of reluctance. The cases we have in mind are when heads

- leave suddenly and unexpectedly
- retire prematurely and reluctantly
- accept ill-health retirement under pressure
- move to a second headship under pressure
- are dismissed.

These are very different to those where heads move on to another school willingly or for promotion, or where they retire, even prematurely, but at a time of their choosing, or choose to take ill-health retirement.

The later analysis aims to examine the contributory factors which may lead to this state of affairs. These may range from the lack of success of the headteacher to relationships with governors or staff breaking down. We hope that this section will provide a framework for heads and prospective heads to recognise the forces at work in such circumstances when it may be possible to change the course of events. We hope that the later sections illustrating actions which have led to headteachers leaving in the cases cited above may prepare such heads for the likely procedures. These appear to be neither the officially recognised formal nor informal procedures.

Headteacher stress

A major study examined stress in headteachers in 1987/8 in the UK (Cooper and Kelly 1993).

Demographic data was collected along with measures of job satisfaction, mental health, job stressors and coping strategies. As one element of personal character-istics heads were assessed as showing type A or type B behaviour (Friedman and Rosenman 1974). Type A is characterised by 'extremes of competitiveness, striving for achievement, aggressiveness, haste, impatience, restlessness, hyperalertness, explosiveness of speech, tenseness of facial muscles and feelings of being under pressure all of the time and under the challenge of responsibility' (p. 134). Type B is other than type A: they are mutually exclusive.Coping strategies were categorised as one of three types:

- direct – involve yourself in work, deal directly with the stressful events and re-interpret the event in a more positive light
- diversionary – take exercise, pursue outside interests
- withdrawal – do nothing, avoid stressful situations.

Some of the principal findings were:

- Job satisfaction: primary heads were more dissatisfied than secondary and males more than females in primary and females more than males in secondary.
- Mental ill health was higher for primary than secondary heads. Male heads had higher mental ill health than the general population but only females in primary had higher than females in the general population.
- Type A behaviours were more likely to have higher mental ill health.
- Direct coping strategies appeared to increase job satisfaction whilst the other two did not and may even add to dissatisfaction.
- Job stressors: there were five factors with the first being much larger than the remaining ones: work overload, handling relationships with staff, resource management, the LEA, handling poor performance. These are reflected in the sections of this book dealing with the internal and external demands of the job.

A finding which relates to the time the head has been in post was that the longer male heads had been in their present post the greater their degree of job dissatisfaction.

Most at risk of mental ill health is the combination of: type A behaviours, experiencing work overload, having relationship problems with staff and attempt-ing to cope by palliative strategies such as drinking, smoking and tranquillisers. The same pattern is true for women but they are more likely to use diversionary strategies for coping and these appear to reduce stress.

The authors comment on the two principal stressors: work overload and relationships with staff. Their suggestion is training courses in time management and interpersonal skills. Whilst these are rational solutions they rather under-estimate the problems, their causes and hence the solutions. For example, a study on US high school principals showed no statistically significant relationships between the use of time management techniques and stress (Tanner *et al.* 1991). A small-scale study on primary heads in England showed similar results (Simpson 1994).

They note that the coping strategies generally being used do not appear to be effective and suggest a move from withdrawal and palliative approaches to more direct and diversionary approaches. They suggest stress management courses.

Recent evidence on stress comes from the case studies of Day *et al.* (2000) and the leadership survey of Earley *et al.* (2002).

A number of the heads gave warnings about the need to balance the expectations of the school and their own stress (Day *et al.* 2000):

> The job has no boundaries so you must impose your own to maintain your sanity.
>
> [primary head]

> I have to tell myself that I can't be all things to all people all the time and not to cross bridges before I have to.
>
> [secondary head]

> I have returned to school in the evening 40 times this school year for work purposes.
>
> [primary head]

> [The head] … Needs a 'critical friend' on whom he can off-load, especially when new initiatives come in rapid succession – deputy provides but it is a 'two-way street' between them.
>
> [primary deputy]
> (Day *et al.* 2000: 58–9, 71)

The nature of the frustrations was explored by Earley *et al.* (2002):

- bureaucracy and paperwork were most mentioned (over half)
- constant change (25 per cent)
- budget and resource issues (over 20 per cent)
- low status and negative media image (one in six)
- stress and demands of job (about 20 per cent)
- problems with recruitment (over 20 per cent).

A small-scale study of Welsh primary heads gave further insights into the nature of the stress which they felt and some ways of lessening it (James and Vince 2001). The weight of expectations which the heads carried, they referred to as the 'rucksack' on their back. These were the negative emotions but there was also passion and commitment on the positive side:

- Anger at 'carrying rucksack'
- Distress created by expectations of others on an overdeveloped sense of personal responsibility
- Anxiety with carrying out the role which led to overemphasising the positive
- Anger at the isolation and the expectation that they be perfect managers.

The heads suggested four areas to help develop headteachers' emotional understanding:

- Learning how to 'give back' the projections and expectations that the role attracts
- Learning how to make choices about what the role involves and to establish clear boundaries around what it does not
- Learning about the function of the role of headteachers in containing the emotions that are generated as an everyday aspect of organising
- Learning how to accept being 'good enough' rather than trying to be perfect.

Premature departure of a headteacher

The formal responsibilities of the headteacher in school are:

> The headteacher, with other senior members of staff, has responsibility for the leadership, direction and management of the school, within the strategic framework set by the governing body.
>
> (DfEE 1999: 7, paragraph 26)

Below we analyse the sequence of events which may lead up to the reluctant departures described in the introduction to this chapter and we have collected some empirical evidence, some of which is illustrated by vignettes in previous chapters. Although each individual case is unique we have detected common patterns and we have produced simplified models in this section to help understand the initial causes which trigger the sequence of events. As in our previous book we are particularly interested in the initial trigger for action rather than the final formal actions since we believe that the pattern is more easily influenced by the parties involved if it is detected early rather than when it has developed momentum.

In the following examples we make no judgement about the rightness of the actions of any of the parties involved. Indeed, it may be that no one is acting wrongly but the overall result is unsatisfactory and a school is not producing an acceptable education for children, e.g. if the headteacher is operating satisfactorily but this is not producing an acceptable impact in the particular circumstances. On the other hand, one or other of the parties may be acting unreasonably but all parties still have to deal with the situation.

We hope that our simplified analysis will help both heads and governors make sense of the situation they find themselves in, consider the consequences and take appropriate action. In our previous book (Fidler and Atton 1999) we drew attention to the fact that it was the responsibility of governing bodies to initiate appropriate action if they considered that their headteacher may not be competent. In community schools that would involve asking the LEA to conduct a professional assessment. Where governing bodies are unaware of possible incompetence in their head or they do not appear to be taking appropriate action they can have their attention formally drawn to a need to investigate by their LEA.

There is a far greater amount of information on the performance of schools and leadership in schools than in the past. In an earlier chapter we suggested that the performance of the headteacher and the performance of the school are connected but we have also made the case that a poorly performing school does not necessarily mean that the headteacher is doing a poor job. In Table 12.1 we indicate some sources of evidence and whether they give direct or indirect evidence on the subject. Direct means that this is the main focus of the source.

The sources may be using some of the same underlying data but the focus may be different. That they provide some evidence should not be taken to imply that the evidence is necessarily of the highest quality. Governing bodies will need to weigh the quality of the evidence from these external sources and take them into account along with their own experiences, visits to the school, and conversations with pupils, parents and staff.

This model attempts to simplify the actual situation and to produce a hierarchy of influences to study in the case of headteachers under pressure. The major contributory influences are assumed to be:

- Governors: governors appoint the headteacher. Thereafter they oversee the work of the school and approve policy.
- Head: the head will have a particular personality and have a range of skills and experience.
- School: the school will be made up of teachers, other staff, pupils and parents. It will have a particular performance.

Each of these is, of course, more complex than might be indicated by a single description. Below we give more detailed insights into the likely forces at work. However, the simplification above facilitates a description at the macro level. Each of these factors may play a part in leading to the headteacher coming under pressure.

Table 12.1 Sources of information on school and leadership performance

Source	School outcome	School processes	Leadership outcome	Leadership processes
OFSTED inspection report	Direct	Direct	Direct	Direct
League table of test and exam results	Direct		Indirect	
Performance adviser	Direct	Indirect	Direct	Direct

Governors

There appear to be a number of factors which determine the stance of the governing body. One is the historical role of governors in a particular school. This sets expectations which tend to persist unless some particular incidents upset them. Where governors have relied upon the headteacher to lead and manage the school and their main role is to approve policy presented by the head this will be very different to a situation where more independently-minded governors are very jealous of their prerogative to formulate policy. The particular stance is likely to be related to the extent to which governors feel that they have the skills and expertise to make policy independently of the headteacher.

It goes without saying that the chair of governors is a particularly influential position. Heads and the chair work particularly closely together. Most issues concerned with the school will be discussed between them. Depending on the personalities and the relationship this is usually a great support to the headteacher. However, there can be issues concerned with

- Dominant chair
- Opposition to the chair
- Change of chair.

Where the chair of governors has a very dominant personality or has very strong views about some aspects of the school, what might be expected in terms of normal rational decisions and ways of working may need to be reconsidered. Heads in this position are likely to find the micropolitical view of organisations introduced in chapter 3 of value, since it is power and who exercises it which is a key aspect.

There are two cases where there may be opposition to the chair and which may have repercussions for the headteacher. Other governors may consider that the relationship between the chair and headteacher is too close and that they are being excluded from much formative discussion. This may lead to general antagonism to the chair and possibly the headteacher. The second case is where the governors are factionalised and there are competing power bases. These competing groups will interpret any actions by the headteacher in their own way. Again the micropolitical view is most likely to help heads analyse what is going on and work out how to handle it.

Finally, a change of chair when a good working relationship has been established can be destabilising. The change can be either by a 'palace revolution' where governors decide against the wishes of the current chair that a change is necessary – this may be because the chair/head relationship is too close or simply that it is time for a change – or the change may come about because the previous chair has stepped down or left the governing body. Establishing a relationship with a new chair may be affected by the previous chair and their reason for leaving. Problems can be expected where the head is very closely identified with an ousted chair.

Where there are a series of changes of chair and they have different priorities, the position of the headteacher can become very difficult. Fortunately such cases are fairly unusual.

Head

Heads react to situations in individual ways and thus the same situation may be handled very differently. First, there are the rational factors such as skills and experience and the extent to which the head is dealing with what to him or her are familiar issues. This will affect the confidence of the head to deal with problems whether they concern issues in school or relationships with the governing body.

Second, and no less important, will be the personality of the headteacher. This will affect both their original perception of the issues and the way they initially react to them. Such factors as flexibility, persistence and resilience are likely to be important for success.

School

We consider that the state of the school will play a part in the timescale for issues to be resolved. A school where there are no obvious concerns about performance will allow time for changes compared to one where performance is poor or deteriorating.

Where school performance is generally considered to be good, problems are likely to arise from relationships with staff or governors or concern changes which the governing body or head would like to implement.

Where school performance is weak, deteriorating or not improving sufficiently rapidly, there are likely to be imperatives which speed up events. If a school may be judged to be failing or have serious weaknesses in a forthcoming inspection, this appears to be a time when the state of the school precipitates events. Related issues arise if a school has had such a judgement following inspection. Where leadership is criticised or does not appear to be capable of making improvement there is likely to be swift action.

The model

Whilst ultimately it is the governing body which has to initiate action in the case of poor performance by a headteacher, it is assumed here that initially the pressure arises as a result of strain between two components of the model. An initial assumption is that the strain will be between different components depending on the length of time that the headteacher has been in post.

The first years

The governing body has appointed the headteacher and is likely to have confidence in them and feel a proprietorial interest in their success. So it is likely

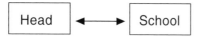

Figure 12.1 Model of strain in the early years of headship

that any source of strain will be between the head and the school (Figure 12.1).

This may be because of difficulties in implementing changes in the school or relationships with particular people or groups in the school. It may be that the approach of the new head is unsuitable or that his or her experience and skills do not match the requirements of the school. This could be a 'fit' problem between the head and school.

The governors can be brought into the picture if some individuals or groups of staff have a direct line to influential governors. In some cases deputy heads who were not appointed to the headship have their supporters on the governing body. The relationship between the head and chair of governors will be important and the standing of the chair within the governing body (Figure 12.2). These will be tested if issues are raised in the governing body about the head's conduct. This may be done subtly in a micropolitical way by taking a proxy issue on which to seek to defeat the head rather than a major issue.

Figure 12.2 Model of strain in later years of headship

Established heads

For established heads it is assumed that the cause of pressure will be relationships with the governing body. This of course may relate to the state of the school but it is likely to be pressure from the governing body which is the main focus of perceived pressure. Two cases are considered below.

Governor relationship

Pressure may arise when there are no particular school problems but the governing body are losing confidence in the head. This may be because the head resists changes which the governors would like to make or because the head's behaviour is becoming unacceptable to governors. Such a lack of confidence may come about slowly, often because there is a gradual change in the composition of the governing body. New members may bring different expectations and these may become larger issues as the number of governors with similar views grows. Heads need to be sensitive to such effects and be aware of the need to adapt. This may be particularly difficult if the chair continues to operate in an old-fashioned way.

School problem

Relationships with the governing body can come under pressure when the head appears incapable of implementing agreed changes and improvement in the school. The factors which governors are likely to use to diagnose a school problem are:

- Progress and results
- Staff morale/attitudes
- Pupil attitudes/behaviour
- Parental attitudes.

Any issues in school are likely to be influenced both by the initial state of the school and the rate of progress of any improvement, as well as the seriousness with which these are viewed.

Stages of increasing pressure

When the first signs of pressure are felt heads need to be aware of the importance of the trust and confidence of the governors. Once governors begin to question the actions of the head they are likely to notice any moves which increase their doubts. When they begin to question the frankness of the head the situation is likely to deteriorate. Heads need to consider how their actions and words may be perceived and take this into consideration when they decide how to proceed.

As pressure increases the sequence of possibilities moves from left to right in Table 12.2. After the first two stages have been passed there is no way back. At this stage compulsory procedures are either implied, threatened or used.

Table 12.2 Stages of pressure on headteachers

	Stage 1 Volunteer	Stage 2 Pre-empted	Stage 3 Forced out	Stage 4 Dismissed
Attitude	Has had enough: willing to leave	Willing to leave if suitable opportunity	Unwilling to leave	Unwilling to leave
Finance	Either no package or package is not critical	Package negotiated if no other job	Package to ease situation to prevent next stage of dismissal	No package
Action	Resigns or possibly puts out feelers for any enhancement	Looks for another job inside or outside education or financial package if early retirement is contemplated	Leaves under pressure with some financial inducement	Dismissed

In many recent examples OFSTED inspections have been a trigger for stages 2 and 3: Stage 2 generally in anticipation of an inspection or after an indifferent OFSTED inspection; Stage 3 may follow after a poor OFSTED inspection particularly when poor leadership has been flagged as a key issue.

Formal designations of leaving

In official statistics the designations under which data are recorded are:

- Normal retirement
- Premature retirement
- Retirement due to ill health
- Resignation.

Resignation may mean that they are moving to another job or ceasing employment.

We can examine official statistics to see trends in headteachers leaving their posts. The statistics come from different sources with slightly different definitions so it may be difficult to find exact continuity in these figures. However, the time trends from one source can be compared with those from another.

First there are statistics on the turnover of headteachers (see Tables 12.3 and 12.4). This means the number of headteachers who leave their post for any reason during the calendar year.

In both primary and secondary schools the large turnover is clear in 1997 when the terms for early retirements were changed. Current turnover rates for heads are now at higher levels than their long-term averages.

Table 12.3 Percentage turnover rates of primary heads, deputies and all staff

Primary	1990	1993	1996	1997	1998	1999	2000	2001
Heads	9.4	6.3	7.8	10.7	6.8	6.8	8.9	7.7
Deputies	13.1	8.8	10.9	13.8	9.7	10.3	12.1	11.0
All staff	14.2	7.6	9.4	11.7	9.0	10.3	12.8	13.0

Source: National Employers' Organisation (2002: Table 12).

Table 12.4 Percentage turnover rates of secondary heads, deputies and all staff

Secondary	1990	1993	1996	1997	1998	1999	2000	2001
Heads	8.1	8.4	7.8	10.5	6.7	7.8	9.3	9.2
Deputies	10.9	9.7	9.1	12.8	6.2	7.2	8.2	8.2
All staff	12.1	7.4	8.5	11.4	8.2	9.4	12.7	13.5

Source: National Employers' Organisation (2002: Table 12).

Statistics from the NAHT sample survey by John Howson of Education Data Surveys in 1998–9 showed the destinations of heads leaving primary and secondary schools (see Table 12.5).

More primary heads move on to another headship than secondary headteachers.

Statistics of Education (Teachers) from DfES give more information on the breakdown of retirements in England and Wales. The figures for 1996–00 from the Database of Teacher Records and Pension Statistics give the distribution of retirements as shown in Tables 12.6 and 12.7.

In both primary and secondary schools there are falling numbers of ill-health retirements but more premature retirements. Although early retirement became more difficult for most teachers after 1997 because of the financial constraints on local authorities, a scheme was created to allow headteachers to apply for premature retirement.

Table 12.5 Primary and secondary heads' destinations on leaving a school

Destination	Primary heads (%)	Secondary heads (%)
Another headship	29	21
Another post in education	13	10
Post outside education	2	2
Retirement at 60+	17	21
Retirement before 60	23	34
Other	16	12

Source: NAHT survey

Table 12.6 Types of retirement of primary heads in 1996–2000 (%)

| | | | Retirement | |
	Age	Ill health	Premature	Actual number
1996–7	14	29	57	1,610
1997–8	15	18	67	1,790
1998–9	33	33	33	690
1999–2000	28	24	47	720

Source: Database of Teacher Records and Pension Statistics.

Table 12.7 Types of retirement of secondary heads in 1996–2000 (%)

| | | | Retirement | |
	Age	Ill health	Premature	Actual number
1996–7	14	16	70	370
1997–8	20	9	67	440
1998–9	35	17	48	230
1999–2000	26	15	59	270

Source: Database of Teacher Records and Pension Statistics.

Heads leaving under pressure

We can draw on a recent study funded by the DfES on the operation of teacher capability procedures (Earnshaw *et al.* 2002). The project received minimum information from 61 per cent of LEAs. The figures may have covered only formal capability procedures and so the figures may be underestimates. The study concluded that about 1 per cent of heads were subject to formal capability procedures each year. However, the researchers discovered that for teachers generally, almost half of the cases were dealt with 'outside procedures' (either informal or formal). The project suspected that for heads an even higher percentage may be dealt with in this way.

From their 13 case study LEAs they studied six cases of headteacher capability but they suspected that these only covered those within established procedures. The six cases were all primary – three new to post and three experienced. In only one case was it felt that the head had been good in the past (others were in post eight and eleven years). Four cases were triggered by OFSTED and a further through pre-OFSTED LEA work. Five heads were in denial. 'We know from our interviews with LEA officers that, where possible, headteachers' cases are dealt with extremely quickly outside procedures' (p. 56).

The assumption was made that these cases were unlikely to be of that type and here procedures were used perhaps because of denial. Only one case here was dealt with quickly when the head accepted the problem. Another was a compromise agreement at the informal stage. The remaining four went to formal procedures and took 3, 6 and 12 months. One was dismissed and three resigned at the point of dismissal. In only one case were the governors acting, in the remainder their role was problematic.

The LEA perspective was that the difficulties of dealing with poorly performing heads were threefold (p. 97).

- Difficulty in identifying headteacher incompetence
- Problems implementing procedures
- Current shortage of good applicants.

The role of governors was almost universally problematic. Governors were not keen to be involved in the formal procedures for dealing with the poor performance of teachers and even less so in the case of heads. Some had inappropriate responses – 'some need persuasion to act, and others are keen to sack good heads' quote from LEA respondent (p. 97).

Suspension with the agreement of the governing body had been used in a number of LEAs.

It was generally felt that it was more difficult to identify headteacher capability, and that it was easier for a head to hide in a large primary or secondary. Additionally, in those schools with excellent results, it might take some time to identify a weak head, who could hide behind an effective management team. 'In one case, we had a head with an old-fashioned, shut-in attitude. He had been a head for over twenty years and it was hard to convince the governing body that there were problems. He kept long-established loyal staff on side, and got rid of others. The LEA had no powers, so had to be vigilant and wait to act'.

(Earnshaw *et al.* 2002: 97)

There were also other examples where governors were in the pocket of the head because he or she had been instrumental in bringing them on to the governing body.

Most LEAs agreed that it was hard to turn a head round. As one LEA commented

We can't think of a head who has improved; in general, there is no recovery. Some heads might dip in performance in a minor way, and we try everything to support them, partly because it is not easy to find quality headteachers. The job of the primary head is particularly difficult these days. We provide induction, monitoring, and 'ladybird' guides, but when we have done all that we can we refer the case for departure.

(Earnshaw *et al.* 2002: 98)

Although heads could step down, the research concluded that it was unusual for them to do so within the same authority. Most LEAs were able to second acting heads for short periods when there was a sudden vacancy. One authority had compiled a register of those who could be called upon giving the amount of time they were willing to serve and the geographic area which they would consider.

Most of the LEAs reported that headteacher cases were usually dealt with outside formal procedures. In most cases the Director of Education, or their delegate, would meet with the head to effect a compromise agreement and an immediate departure. It was felt that fast action was essential in order to prevent the school sliding downhill quickly. As one respondent noted, 'Where there is gracious acceptance of the problem, we can act quickly'. (p. 98). One authority said that it would use dismissal on the grounds of gross dereliction of duties where the school had been placed in special measures following an OFSTED inspection.

As the researchers commented

In fact, of the six headteacher cases which we looked at, only one was dealt with outside of procedures. However, this may be because the LEAs directed us to cases which used the procedures; and in five of the cases, the headteachers were in denial and were initially determined to fight the case.

(Earnshaw *et al.* 2002: 98)

A union official and an NAHT official listed four common cases:

a) They have had a successful headship for roughly five years, they transfer schools and in a year they are having difficulties. The reasons are complex – the governors could have recruited a head to do a particular job, for example, the staff are coasting and so the governors decide to get a dynamic head. The head finds resistance from staff and the head's relationships could break down.

b) They have been in the school for a long time and then they just cannot keep up with the initiatives.

c) They have just been appointed to their first headship and within a few terms they are struggling.

d) Heads who were appointed before 1988 and the Education Reform Act sometimes get into problems because the job has changed considerably since the Act, making heads managers of organisations and in charge of budgets.

(Earnshaw *et al*. 2002: 99)

The more hopeful cases were those caught early or those going through a bad patch.

Concluding discussion

As we have indicated it is action by the governing body which may lead to the early departure of a headteacher although it may be that the governing body is under pressure from the LEA. Heads may come under pressure because they are not successful or because their relationship with the governing body breaks down.

There are now an increased number of indicators of school success which give warning signs if school performance does not match up to that of comparable schools. Headteachers are expected to be aware of these and to be able to lead school improvements. If these are unsuccessful, heads are likely to come under pressure. Competent heads will be aware of the judgements being made about the school and the implications for how their leadership will be judged.

In the case where their efforts to improve the school are not as successful as needed, there may be the opportunity to apply for other more suitable headships. This is likely to become more difficult if they are seen to be unsuccessful in their current headship. Thus there is a narrow window when the head realises they must move and they also have an opportunity to do so.

When pressures come from the governing body this may be because of school performance but they may also come from deteriorating relationships either with the governing body or key members of it. If the cause of the deterioration is because of differences of priority or differences of style and it becomes an issue of who holds power, a micropolitical perspective may be the most useful for the head to use to analyse the situation and to plan his or her future actions. The tenure of the head in this case may rest rather on how effectively they enter into micropolitics with the governing body than on how they lead the school.

Early actions to try to reverse a deteriorating situation are far more likely to be effective than realising what is happening and its seriousness at a late stage. At a certain point the die may be cast and it may be an issue of how to negotiate terms to leave irrespective of the merits of the case. Examples from this chapter illustrate the range of possibilities before the ultimate stage of dismissal.

Part IV
Playing better

13 Where next?

The future

Introduction

In this final chapter we collect together what we think has emerged in the book as advice for groups involved in headship, headteachers and prospective head-teachers. However, we begin with an analysis which suggests actions for a little-mentioned group in this book, the Education Department of Central Government. There are some issues which need to be tackled to reduce pressures on headteachers and to support their success.

Most of the proposals are aimed at heads and prospective heads. They mainly emerge from the material in the preceding chapters. However, we have made one suggestion which we have not discussed previously, although the problem which it addresses has been discussed in a number of chapters, and this is fixed term contracts for headteachers.

In the final section we return to the gaming allusion that we began with and analyse what we have offered in those terms. We have also reiterated what are clear differences between the meritorious art of headship and games of any kind.

Recruitment crisis

We are aware that by pointing out many facets of headship which can cause problems we are in danger of making headship seem less attractive as a career option than it otherwise might be. This could have a number of adverse effects. There could be even fewer applications for the least desirable headships and there could be an increase in the proportion of applicants who apply as a result of power motivation rather than in the spirit of educational service, and this might not lead to the most desirable appointments.

We have said it previously, and it bears repeating, that headship can be exciting and immensely rewarding. There is abundant evidence from headteachers that they would not wish to have any other job. They have a great sense of worth because of the enormous impact which a well run school can have on the education of children and as a satisfying workplace for staff. We have devoted less space to stories which support this view of headship because there are many books and other sources which amply provide first hand evidence from headteachers. We have no reason to believe that these are not the typical reactions of headteachers. However, these other sources take particular headteachers at particular points in their career. The research evidence of a more longitudinal kind (Weindling, Earley and colleagues) and the cross-sectional data (Day and Bakioglu 1996; Reeves *et al.* 1997) provide a more mixed picture. For all headteachers at some point in their careers there are testing times and for some headteachers for long periods there are stressful challenges.

Learning

We have placed emphasis on critical incidents in the hope that prospective headteachers and headteachers new in post might be forewarned about the possibility of such events. There are so many more possibilities available if one has time to think about likely courses of action and their consequences well before an urgent decision is necessary. The alternative of having to make a rapid decision but then seeing the consequences unfold over a number of weeks and months is the least desirable one.

We hope that by examining the classes of knowledge which headteachers need to do their jobs the complexity of the knowledge base becomes more explicit. It is not just facts and other such propositional knowledge which they need. The process knowledge that they need to acquire including an awareness of their impact on others and their own emotional reaction to events are vital ingredients to their understanding. The complexity of the knowledge base leads on to a consideration of how such knowledge is acquired. The learning of headteachers has been under-theorised and under-researched. We know too little about how headteachers make connections between different classes of knowledge or how emotions impact on learning or the use of knowledge.

This examination of the knowledge and skills which headteachers need in order to do their job effectively suggests that their training and development before and during headship should be more carefully planned. In this way heads might be better prepared to deal with the situations they encounter. It should be borne in mind that many of the problems which new headteachers encounter are as a result of the legacy left by their predecessor. This may be due to a change of style, for example we have seen how difficult it is to follow a charismatic headteacher; however, more often the issues are not only concerned with style but what appears to have been neglect of developing problems in the school. This argues for both better preparation but also for continuing support and development throughout headship.

If headship is to be seen as more attractive and more manageable we believe that there are a number of changes which need to be considered:

- Reducing the demands of the job and providing more assistance
- Better preparation before headship
- Support and development in the job
- Recognition of the limited length of effective working life.

Pressure in post

The principal sources of pressures in the job are staff, pupils, parents, governors, inspectors and government. And for some, the LEA may be added to the list. Little is to be gained by listing again more detail of these. Our purpose at this stage is to see which of these sources of pressure are most susceptible to reduction and how that might be achieved.

What must be quite clear to a disinterested observer is that the government's 'ambitious agenda' for school improvement is a major cause of stress to headteachers and is becoming counter-productive. Of course we all wish to offer the best for children and a substantial element of this is provided by education in schools. That is not in question. What is in question is what this means and how it might be accomplished. There must be policy changes.

The desirability of the ends does not justify using any means to try to accomplish them: that is the moral case. There is an equally good pragmatic case. When the evidence shows that the prescribed means are increasingly ineffective, there is no justification. We consider that the seemingly relentless pressure to improve test and examination results in schools is of this kind. No other organisation has set itself and succeeded in such a relentless effort to improve results. This is because:

- the effort becomes channelled into the performance indicators which measure success and not the underlying aims;
- teaching and learning become repetitive and boring;
- there is an increasing tendency to cheat in such high stakes assessments;
- the pressure becomes self-defeating and only generates increasing anxiety which hinders performance; and
- other desirable ends are neglected.

Thus however desirable the ends, the means must be tailored to what is realistic and achievable. This must involve periods of pressure to innovate and improve followed by periods to consolidate and evaluate. This change of emphasis has to come from government. Expectations have been pitched at a level which will burn headteachers out if they conscientiously try to fulfil them. As one of us has written elsewhere (Fidler 1997) this pressure from government is transmitted to and reflected by others who also influence schools. So the relentless pressure has to be taken off and a more measured pattern of pressure and consolidation has to be proposed, understood and implemented. The alternative is to recognise the consequences for headteachers, expect many to burn out after a few years and to have remedial measures including finance in place to deal with the after effects. The pace of change has to be slowed and include consolidation.

A number of our recommendations concern the use of finance. To bring about more real decision-making on finance at school level there needs to be more transparency and realism about funding. It is not sensible to refer to funding increases for schooling in 'real terms'. This measure is most unreal. It refers to increases in comparison to the general measure of inflation, the retail price index.

This is not a very good measure of educational costs if they rise faster than the RPI. There is every reason to expect that educational cost will continue to rise faster. Salary increases need to exceed inflation if teacher recruitment is to increase and introducing non-teaching time in primary schools will increase costs. The present rhetoric from government about increases in real terms increases expectations of results from lay people whilst reducing the scope to make improvements at school level. Schools need increased funding in terms of an educational price indicator.

There was to be a five year moratorium on changes to curriculum at the time of the Dearing Review in 1995. In hindsight teachers were right to be sceptical of the chances that this proposal would stand the test of time. As each policy commitment is broken the trust which government needs from teachers is eroded. Thus it is more difficult to get teachers to accept that current proposals will be financed and implemented. This is particularly the case at the time of writing when yet again school budgets are falling when government is claiming to have earmarked extra money for schools. This is a debate which has gone on for at least 25 years and shows no sign of resolution.

The Appendix to the Implementation of the National Agreement of Teacher Workloads of January 2003 does address resourcing issues. However, a feature of government statements on resources in the past is that they haven't started from current spending but have dealt only with hypothecated spending and local authorities have regularly had to fund schools at a higher level. Thus plans have to start from current spending levels and take account of changes in pupil numbers and known changes to employment costs including threshold and post threshold progression of teachers.

Current moves to suggest that more clerical and other support should be provided for teachers and headteachers are welcome. This was a trend which was developing after the introduction of LMS but the financial squeeze on school budgets has been a major handicap. Many schools wished to go in this direction but could not afford to do so when resources to cover the cost of teachers left little room for manoeuvre. Workloads and financing of small primary schools is a particular pressure which the calculations on averages conceal. There are, however, some schools who even if finance becomes available may need a nudge in this direction otherwise they will seek to lower class sizes by spending extra resources on teachers.

This raises the issue of teacher supply. Whilst improving the working conditions and salaries of teachers can be expected to have an effect, if there are other attractive careers in a buoyant economy, there will be continuing strains on teacher supply particularly in shortage subjects. Schools have already been innovative in using classroom assistants to assist teachers in a range of ways and although some training for classroom teachers has begun to appear there appears to have been rather less consideration of the training and preparation needed for teachers to adapt to this new way of working. Increasing use of support for teachers is not being trialled and the results made available to schools, each school is having to devise patterns of usage for themselves. The use of classroom assistants to cover for absent teachers and to take on a pseudo-teaching role after advanced training is another proposal of this kind. There are no trials to discover effective ways of working which then make it easier for individual schools to take on, each is left to experiment. Yet a further pressure on headteachers.

The use of computers in school for administrative purposes has been left to the commercial sector. There has been no planning of how such systems might assist administration and management. Their use has evolved in a piecemeal way and there has not been the vital technical backup to deal with teething troubles and breakdowns. This has added to frustration rather than reducing it as it has the potential to do.

In Victoria, Australia, specially prepared software has enabled schools to use data from pupils, teachers and parents to identify and plan areas for school improvement. In England, schools have been presented with the results of analysis, carried out by others, of data only on pupils' test results. They have not been able to identify their own data needs and produce the results in a form which meets their requirements.

Length of working life

If prospective heads do not see themselves having to work through to 60 or 65 this will make headship more appealing. Thus either a permanent scheme of early retirements, or an expectation that arrangements can be made, is needed.

The current preoccupation with the leadership of schools and the expectations placed on headteachers both increase the burden on individuals and also make it more difficult for them to do other temporary revitalisation activities of the kind we suggested in chapter 11. If they are seen as indispensable for the success of the school everyone concerned will be reluctant to think of periods of secondment or part-time temporary activities since they will take the head out of school. But in the medium- and longer-term heads will be less effective if they are not developed and refreshed by these out-of-school activities.

Governors

A number of the changes which we have identified require a change of expectations and professionalism from governors. This is not the place to examine the desirability of having a governing body for every school with the extensive powers which they currently have. Whilst the majority of governing bodies act in a supportive way to their school, there are examples in our findings where individual chairs or governing bodies do not appear to have acted in the best interests of the school but from more personal motives.

School inspections have begun to examine the actions of the governing body and this should act as a check on its actions. But inspections are not frequent and there is no clear and speedy mechanism for action against governors or governing bodies found to be acting unreasonably. The provision of specialist advisers to governing bodies and joint training of chairs and heads together are steps which should help.

Solutions

Turning from solutions which need the impetus of government to succeed, we turn to more individual decisions which headteachers and prospective head-teachers can make themselves.

Better preparation during pre-headship career and less reliance on a course before headship

It is clear from any consideration of the forms of knowledge, including process knowledge, which are needed by headteachers, that preparation involves more than attending courses. It is also clear that this preparation needs to start well before headship. In the past, the discussion has polarised between the advantages of training courses compared to experience rather than recognising that many kinds of activities have their vital parts to play:

- Award-bearing courses
- Training courses
- Experience in schools (and reflection on it).

Substantial courses of education in management and leadership can provide theoretical knowledge, help develop more informed internal knowledge frameworks, share experiences of course members and aid more systematic reflection on experience to aid learning. Longer courses can allow course members within the group to develop new expectations of how schools should operate and sustain them even when their current experience in school is very different. Such courses are likely to be particularly formative if taken when course members are at middle management level in secondary schools or deputy head level in primary schools. They can be formative if their academic input is used to analyse experience and to develop robust mental frameworks to store new knowledge gained from experience. Heads and others who have experienced the benefits of this kind of development in their thinking need to speak out about its value and encourage junior staff with potential to recognise the importance of such development.

Training courses can introduce and draw attention to new knowledge. They can provide simulations and other experiential learning but the largest element of process knowledge is going to be acquired from on-the-job experience. Thus a major consideration should be how to acquire such knowledge in more effective and systematic ways. Here mentorship, coaching and other aids to learning on the job offer new opportunities – to aid reflection on experience and to offer advice. This probably requires some training for mentors also.

Whilst the advice given here is mainly intended for prospective headteachers, many of the possibilities require the active co-operation of existing headteachers. An overriding message to existing headteachers is that they have a crucial role in the development of their staff and particularly those with headship potential. Heads can:

- Provide experiences from which to learn
- Offer advice about stages and sequences of learning
- Encourage a culture of reflection and learning from experience
- Provide mentoring and coaching opportunities
- Actively mentor and coach senior staff themselves.

Moving from school to school at suitable opportunities during career progression to headship provides practice at organisational socialisation and widens experience of different ways of doing things. There are other requirements of well-rounded experience:

- Experience of academic leadership and pastoral leadership
- Experience of working with internal and external groups
- Working with governors.

The concept of a course of preparation before headship as represented by the NPQH is a welcome one, and the NPQH is itself described as providing a threshold standard of skills for entry to headship. But there is a danger that this will be seen to be sufficient preparation and detract from the longer-term, more integrated and deeper preparation for headship as identified in this book. It needs to be recognised that learning of this advanced kind is slow and often it is difficult to identify the sources of learning or the specific results.

Period of acting headship

A period of acting headship is highly influential. More such opportunities could be provided on a more predictable basis if it was an expectation that heads would be out of school for temporary periods as suggested for the development and reinvigoration of headteachers. As we have seen there are a variety of reasons why acting heads need to be appointed and almost always these are intended to serve primarily school purposes rather than developing headship potential. Nevertheless it is clear that there is greater potential for this to serve a learning purpose. Whilst being thrown in at the deep end because of a crisis may be very realistic for aspiring headteachers it is not the best learning experience and may put off some perfectly capable potential heads. So more planning and preparation where possible is needed so that the learning from the experience can be maximised. This learning is both of the process kind but also of the emotional kind in terms of what sort of headship would be satisfying and 'do-able' for a particular headteacher. Those who have the technical ability but not the attitudinal and personal qualities to succeed in a particular headship need to recognise this before they find themselves appointed to such a position. Acting headship is also a process of self-discovery.

Prospective headteachers need to push to be offered such experience. They also need to work out in advance what they hope to gain so that they can maximise the learning experience. Inevitably they will gain in ways that they had not predicted but a plan to learn will heighten their awareness of learning potential so that they are on the lookout for such opportunities.

Improved selection

It follows from the previous section that the fit between the headship candidate and the school is a critical one. The present process of selecting headteachers does not make the maximum opportunity of 'fitting'. Whilst it may be unrealistic to hope to achieve a perfect fit every time, it is certainly the case that the present selection process could be improved. This involves a diagnosis of school needs. This requires an assessment of immediate, short-term and long-term needs. As we have pointed out and return to later, these do not often coincide. The selection process should concentrate on the immediate and short-to-medium-term since if these don't come right there may be no long-term.

Improved selection requires a consideration of the 'technical fit' and the 'emotional and attitudinal fit' between the candidate and the school.

Improving technical fit

- Better diagnosis of school needs
- Better diagnosis of candidate strengths and weaknesses
- Understanding the nature of a fit which works.

Emotional and attitudinal fit

- Better information for candidates on the mode of working of the school and governors
- Better understanding by governors of the leadership style in action of the prospective head.

This is an issue both for selectors and for prospective headteachers. Prospective headteachers need to be aware of these issues so that they can

- decide which posts to apply for
- identify information they need so they can assess whether they are likely to be successful in a particular headship post
- decide whether to accept a post if offered.

Mentoring by trained heads

The value of mentoring of new heads by existing heads has advantages for both parties particularly if it involves choice and empathy on the part of the new head and training and networking for the existing head.

This is an organisational issue. In addition to support by new and existing headteachers there needs to be a group to organise the activity. LEAs are well-placed either individually or collectively to set up schemes to provide such support to new headteachers. They need to:

- select and train experienced headteachers with the right personal qualities to be mentors
- diagnose the needs of new headteachers, and
- offer a selection of suitable mentors to the new headteacher for them to indicate a preference for who they wish to have as a mentor.

Support for heads

When heads have problems either personally or in the school they need support. Heads may be able to engage consultants to help them but often the problems overtake them or financial constraints may preclude such help. In which case LEAs need to be able to diagnose the need and support the head particularly if the head is so engrossed with issues inside the school that they do not think to ask for external help. Heads may also be reluctant to ask for external help from LEAs when they think that this honesty may reflect badly on their schools and lead to them being categorised unfavourably. LEAs are playing a greater role in identifying and supporting schools likely to be experiencing difficulties – but the emphasis is on the school rather than the head – so heads need to be very aware of the particular style of their LEA before they risk admitting to needing advice or support.

Periodic refreshment and reinvigoration – sabbaticals

Although many heads may react adversely to the notion that they may need reinvigoration, there is much evidence that substantial numbers do. Whilst it may be unsafe to carry generalisations too far, it would be quite wrong to reject the notion because it affected the sensibilities of some heads and ran counter to espoused theory. The research evidence from heads is of slowing down and dis-illusionment and so many of our examples are of this kind. Whilst our examples are not representative we are constantly struck by others in the educational world reading our vignettes and identifying similar situations from their experience. These situations are common even if they are a small minority.

We see two processes which may be interconnected. First there is development which includes acquiring new knowledge. This could be of myriad kinds – new educational development, different approaches to leadership, etc.

The second is the remotivation or reinvigoration of heads who need an emotional recharging. This is valuable and should not be seen as a luxury which cannot be afforded.

In chapter 11 we have listed and briefly described a large range of activities. What is needed are expectations that such activities are part of the normal career of a headteacher and the resources to make some of them possible. Whilst the Leadership Programme for Serving Heads is a welcome start there needs to be a range of opportunities from which to select at national and local level and this should involve universities where research on leadership is being undertaken.

This proposal involves a number of groups – heads, governors, government and others – for it involves:

- Expectations about the continuing development and support of heads
- Financial support so that a choice of opportunities are available to individuals without cost to their school
- Knowledge of the range of opportunities and their benefits so that heads can select.

Fixed term contracts to facilitate movement

We mentioned at the selection stage that the longer-term needs of a school may not be the same as the shorter-term ones. In this case either the headteacher has to be capable of adapting or the fit between head and school begins to deteriorate.

The other argument from the previous section is that headteachers need a change from time to time. This is to refresh and recharge so that they can look at a school with fresh eyes and can be resensitised and remotivated to tackle issues which have been allowed to slide in the face of more pressing problems in the past. The temporary activities we have described may enable this but it is clear from the research evidence that a change of school can be extremely beneficial. At the start of headship most heads do not think in terms of staying at the same school for very long periods and many do move on. But many more do not and the evidence from their successors is that in their final few years the school made less progress than might have been expected.

Not spending too long in any one headship is partly a matter of expectations. And this means expectations from all parties – headteachers, governors, staff, pupils and parents. Whilst there has been an expectation in many small primary schools that the head would move on to a larger school since this would increase their salary, other more sideways moves (in terms of finance) have been less expected. The expectation should be gaining ground that headteachers do not spend all their headship in one school. We think there is a case for reconsidering the idea of fixed term contracts for heads as a way of making it 'normal' for heads and schools periodically to think about changing their headteacher. This will facilitate the moves of those heads that would wish to move on but do not have the opportunity under present conditions.

Any contracted period would need to be substantial since schools need a lengthy commitment and deep-seated educational change is slow. But the period cannot be too long if it is to facilitate movement. One possibility is to have a period of say five years which can by mutual consent be renewed once to make a ten year period, but not normally longer than that. There would need to be generous redundancy packages for those who could not find a further post or did not wish to do so.

Second headship

The advantages of a second headship have become clear although there are a number of examples where a second headship has been less successful than the first. So it is not to be taken for granted that successful first headship automatically leads to a successful second headship. Issues of flexibility on the part of the head and the selection 'fit' are equally important in second headships.

Early retirement

Finally, even if preparation and pressures in headship move in the way which we suggest, and even more if they don't, many heads will not wish to remain in post to the retirement ages of 60 or 65 or until sufficient years' pension has been earned for a full pension. There need to be flexible arrangements for heads to leave headship with financial arrangements that mean they can consider topping up their income by the kind of part-time appointments which we have identified but they are not forced to take any up in order to have a relatively comfortable retirement from headship.

Our contribution to the headship game in England and Wales

To conclude we return to the allusion to headship as a game and particularly its analogies with the game of chess. In these terms we hope that we have offered insights into:

- Opening up the range of moves
- Analysing situations
- The importance of analysis from different perspectives both theoretical and according to the individuals involved
- The sequencing of moves and their consequences
- The continuity from one move to the next both in preparation for headship and during headship – there needs to be an overall strategy as well as individual tactics
- Preventing fool's mate: we hope that we have identified potential pitfalls that may befall headteachers in particular situations. Preparedness for such situations offers the best prospects for success.

Finally, some obvious findings which do not fit the analogy.

Headship is challenging and stimulating work in pursuit of success for the school. This success has implications for so many people in addition to the head, most notably pupils and students, parents and staff. This leads on to a most significant difference: headship is a collective endeavour, it is not a solitary one although at times it may feel like that.

Headship is an enabling activity: it creates the conditions for teachers to teach and for pupils and students to learn. Headteachers cannot do this alone. There will be others in the leadership team who play a part in this. There will be others in leadership and managerial positions in the school and there will be involvement of teachers in making decisions and implementing them. This is not the place to open up a discussion of distributed leadership or even to write of the need to delegate responsibility to others, but to make the more substantive point that headteachers need to work collaboratively with others including the governing body not to be individual grand masters working alone.

References

Argyris, C. and Schon, D.A. (1978) *Theories in Practice* (second edn), San Francisco, CA: Jossey-Bass.

Ashburn, E.A., Mann, M. and Purdue, P.A. (1987) 'Teacher mentoring: ERIC Clearinghouse on teacher education'. Paper presented at the Annual Meeting of the American Educational Research Association, Washington, DC.

Barrick, M.R. and Mount, M.K. (1991) 'The big five personality dimensions and job performance: a meta-analysis', *Personnel Psychology*, 44, 1–26.

Begley, P.T. (1996) 'Cognitive perspectives on values in administration: a quest for coherence and relevance', *Educational Administration Quarterly*, 32(3), 403–26.

Blake, R.R. and Mouton, J.S. (1964) *The Managerial Grid*, Houston, TX: Gulf Publishing.

Blake, R.R. and Mouton, J.S. (1985) *Executive Achievement Making it at the Top*, New York: McGraw-Hill.

Bolman, L.G. and Deal, T.E. (1997) *Reframing Organizations: Artistry, Choice and Leadership* (second edn), San Francisco, CA: Jossey-Bass.

Bossert, S.T., Dwyer, D.C., Rowan, B. and Lee, G.V. (1982) 'The instructional management role of the principal', *Educational Administration Quarterly*, 18(3), 34–64.

Bottery, M. (1992) *The Ethics of Educational Management*, London: Cassell.

Boyatzsis, R. (1982) *The Competent Manager*, New York: Wiley.

Bryman, A. (1992) *Charisma and Leadership in Organizations*, London: Sage.

Bullock, K., Jamieson, I. and James, C. (1995) 'The influences on educational management learning', *School Organisation*, 15(3), 253–66.

Burns, J.M. (1978) *Leadership*, New York: Harper and Row.

Conger, J.A. and Kanungo, R.N. (1987) 'Towards a behavioral theory of charismatic leadership in organizational settings', *Academy of Management Review*, 12, 637–47.

Conger, J.A. and Kanungo, R.N. (1988) 'Behavioral dimensions of charismatic leadership', in Conger, J.A. and Kanungo, R.N. (eds) *Charismatic Leadership: The Elusive Factor in Organizational Effectiveness*, San Francisco, CA: Jossey-Bass.

Cooper, C.L. and Kelly, M. (1993) 'Occupational stress in headteachers: a national UK study', *British Journal of Educational Psychology*, 63(2), 130–43.

Crawford, M. (2002) 'The charismatic school leader – potent myth or persuasive effect?', *School Leadership and Management*, 22(3), 273–87.

Daresh, J.C. and Playko, M.A. (1992) 'Mentoring for headteachers: a review of major issues', *School Organisation*, 12(2), 145–52.

Day, C. and Bakioglu, A. (1996) 'Development and disenchantment in the professional lives of headteachers', in Goodson, I.F. and Hargreaves, A. (eds) *Teachers' Professional Lives*, London: Falmer Press.

Day, C., Harris, A., Hadfield, M., Tolley, H. and Beresford, J. (2000) *Leading Schools in Times of Change*, Milton Keynes: Open University Press.

Deal, T. and Kennedy, A. (1988) *Corporate Cultures: The Rites and Rituals of Corporate Life*, London: Penguin.

DfEE (1999) *Code of Practice on LEA-School Relations*, London: DfEE.

DfES (2001) *Statistics of Education 2000*, London: DfES.

DfES (2003) *Statistics of Education: School Workforce 2002 Edition*, London: The Stationery Office.

Draper, J. and McMichael, P. (1996) 'I am the eye of the needle and everything passes through me', *School Organisation*, 16(2), 149–64.

Draper, J. and McMichael, P. (1998a) 'Making sense of primary headship: the surprises awaiting new heads', *School Leadership and Management*, 8(2), 197–211.

Draper, J. and McMichael, P. (1998b) 'Preparing a profile: likely applicants for primary headship', *Educational Management and Administration*, 26(2), 161–72.

Draper, J. and McMichael, P. (1998c) 'In the firing line: the attractions of secondary headship', *Management in Education*, 12(2), 15–20.

Draper, J. and McMichael, P. (2000) 'Contextualising new headship', *School Leadership and Management*, 8(2), 197–211.

Draper, J. and McMichael, P. (2002) 'Managing acting headship: a safe pair of hands', *School Leadership and Management*, 22(3), 289–303.

Duignan, P.A. and Macpherson, R.J.S. (eds) (1992) *Educative Leadership: A Practical Theory for New Administrators and Managers*, London: Falmer Press.

Duignan, P.A. and Macpherson, R.J.S. (1993) 'Educative leadership: a practical theory', *Educational Administration Quarterly*, 29(1), 8–33.

Earley, P., Baker, L. and Weindling, D. (1990) *'Keeping the Raft Afloat': Secondary Headship Five Years On*, Slough: NFER.

Earley, P., Baker, L. and Weindling, D. (1995) 'Trapped in post', *Managing Schools Today*, 4(9) July, 30–1.

Earley, P., Evans, J., Collarbone, P., Gold, A. and Halpin, D. (2002) *Establishing the Current State of School Leadership in England*, London: DfES.

Earnshaw, J., Ritchie, E., Marchington, L., Torrington, D. and Hardy, S. (2002) *Best Practice in Undertaking Teacher Capability Procedures* (DfES Research Report 312), London: DfES.

Economist, The (2002) 'Bosses for sale – are headhunters to blame for the damaging cult of charisma?', 5 October 2002, 73.

Eraut, M. (1994) *Developing Professional Knowledge and Competence*, London: Falmer Press.

Esp, D. (1993) *Competences for School Managers*, London: Kogan Page.

Fidler, B. (1992) 'How to get the top job', *Times Educational Supplement*, 21 February 1992, 17.

Fidler, B. (1997) 'School leadership: some key ideas', *School Leadership and Management*, 17(1), 23–37.

Fidler, B. (1998) 'How can a successful school avoid failure?: strategic management in schools', *School Leadership and Management*, 18(4), 497–509.

Fidler, B. (2002a) *Strategic Management for School Improvement: Leading Your School's Improvement Strategy*, London: Paul Chapman Publishing.

Fidler, B. (2002b) 'The most important task for governors? A detailed look at the critical process of selecting a new headteacher', *School Governor Update*, 11, May, 8–9.

Fidler, B. and Atton, T. (1999) *Poorly Performing Staff in Schools and How to Manage Them*, London: Routledge.

Fidler, B. and Bowles, G. (eds) (1989) *Effective Local Management of Schools: A Strategic Approach*, Harlow: Longman.

Fidler, B. and Cooper, R. (eds) (1992) *Staff Appraisal and Staff Management in Schools and Colleges: A Guide to Implementation*, Harlow: Longman.

Fidler, B., Earley, P., Ouston, J. and Davies, J. (1998) 'Teacher gradings and OFSTED inspection: help or hindrance as a management tool?', *School Leadership and Management*, 18(2), 257–70.

Fiedler, F.E. (1967) *A Theory of Leadership Effectiveness*, New York: McGraw-Hill.

Firestone, W.A. and Wilson, B.L. (1985) 'Using bureaucratic and cultural linkages to improve instruction: the principal's contribution', *Educational Administration Quarterly*, 21(2), 7–30.

Friedman, M. and Rosenman, R.H. (1974) *Type 'A' Behavior and Your Heart*, New York: Knopf.

Gabarro, J.J. (1987) *The Dynamics of Taking Charge*, Boston, MA: Harvard Business School Press.

Gronn, P. (1999) *The Making of Educational Leaders*, London: Cassell.

Gunter, H. (2002) 'Teacher appraisal 1988–1998: a case study', *School Leadership and Management*, 22(1), 61–72.

Hallinger, P. and Heck, R.H. (1996) 'Reassessing the principal's role in school effectiveness: a review of empirical research, 1980–1995', *Educational Administration Quarterly*, 32(1), 5–44.

Hart, A.W. and Weindling, D. (1996) 'Developing successful school leaders', in Leithwood, K., Chapman, J., Corson, D., Hallinger, P. and Hart, A. (eds) *International Handbook of Educational Leadership and Administration*, Dordrecht: Kluwer Academic.

Headship Matters (2002) 'Demise of the superhead', 14 January–February 2002, 12.

Hellawell, D. (1997) 'Appraisal of primary school headteachers in schools in England: the perceptions of three LEA coordinators', *School Leadership and Management*, 17(2), 257–72.

Hersey, P. and Blanchard, K. (1988) *Management of Organizational Behavior: Utilizing Human Resources* (fifth edn), Englewood Cliffs, NJ: Prentice-Hall.

HMI (1976) 'Excerpts from the "Yellow Book"', *Times Educational Supplement*, 15 October, 1–3.

HMI (1978) *Primary Education in England (The Primary Survey)*, London: HMSO.

HMI (1979) *Aspects of Secondary Education in England (The Secondary Survey)*, London: HMSO.

Hodgkinson, C. (1991) *Educational Leadership: The Moral Art*, Albany, NY: SUNY.

House, R.J. (1977) 'A 1976 theory of charismatic leadership', in Hunt, J.G. and Larson, L.L. (eds) *Leadership: The Cutting Edge*, Carbondale, IL: Southern Illinois University Press.

Hoyle, E. (1986) *The Politics of School Management*, London: Hodder and Stoughton.

HTI (2002) 'No barriers, no boundaries', HTI 2002 Survey of ten successful headteachers carried out by the Hay Group.

Hughes, M.G. (1985) 'Leadership in professionally staffed organisations', in Hughes, M., Ribbins, P. and Thomas, H. (eds) *Managing Education: The System and the Institution*, London: Cassell.

Hughes, M., Carter, J. and Fidler, B. (1981) *Professional Development Provision for Senior Staff in Schools and Colleges: A DES-Funded Research Project: The Final Report*, Birmingham: University of Birmingham.

James, C. and Vince, R. (2001) 'Developing the leadership capability of headteachers', *Educational Management and Administration*, 29(3), 307–17.

Jirasinghe, D. and Lyons, G. (1995) 'Management competencies in action: a practical framework', *School Organisation*, 15(3), 267–81.

Jirasinghe, D. and Lyons, G. (1996) *The Competent Head: A Job Analysis of Heads' Tasks and Personality Factors*, London: Falmer Press.

Katz, R.L. (1974) 'Skills of an effective administrator', *Harvard Business Review*, 52 September/October, 90–102.

Kotter, J.P. (1990) *A Force for Change: How Leadership Differs from Management*, New York: Free Press.

Leithwood, K., Jantzi, D. and Steinbach, R. (1999) *Changing Leadership for Changing Times*, Buckingham: Open University Press.

MCI (1995) *Senior Management Standards*, London: Management Charter Initiative.

Mercer, D. (1996) 'Can they walk on water?: professional isolation and the secondary headteacher', *School Organisation*, 16(2), 165–78.

Mintzberg, H. (1973) *The Nature of Managerial Work*, New York: Harper and Row.

Mintzberg, H. (1983) *Structure in Fives: Designing Effective Organisations*, Englewood Cliffs, NJ: Prentice-Hall.

Morgan, C., Hall, V. and Mackay, H. (1983) *The Selection of Secondary School Headteachers*, Milton Keynes: Open University Press.

Mortimore, P. and Mortimore, J. (eds) (1991a) *The Primary Head: Roles, Responsibilities and Reflections*, London: Paul Chapman Publishing.

Mortimore, P. and Mortimore, J. (eds) (1991b) *The Secondary Head: Roles, Responsibilities and Reflections*, London: Paul Chapman Publishing.

Mortimore, P., Sammons, P., Stoll, L., Lewis, D. and Ecob, R. (1988) *School Matters: The Junior Years*, Wells: Open Books.

National Employers' Organisation (2002) *Survey of Teacher Resignations and Recruitment 1985/6–2001/2*, London: NEOST.

OFSTED/Audit Commission (2001) *LEA Support for School Improvement*, London: The Stationery Office.

Parkay, F.W. and Hall, G.E. (eds) (1992) *Becoming a Principal: The Challenges of Beginning Leadership*. Boston, MA: Allyn and Bacon.

Parkay, F.W., Curie, G.D. and Rhodes, J.W. (1992) 'Professional socialization: a longitudinal study of first-time high school principals', *Educational Administration Quarterly*, 26(1), 43–75.

Pascal, C. and Ribbins, P. (1998) *Understanding Primary Headteachers: Conversations in Characters, Careers and Characteristics*, London: Cassell.

Peter, L.J. and Hull, R. (1969) *The Peter Principle: Why Things Always Go Wrong*, New York: William Morrow and Company.

Pocklington, K. and Weindling, D. (1996) 'Promoting reflection on headship through the mentoring mirror', *Educational Management and Administration*, 24(2), 175–91.

Podsakoff, P.M., MacKenzie, S.B., Moorman, R.H. and Fetter, R. (1990) 'Transformational leaders' behaviors and their effects on followers' trust in leader, satisfaction, and organizational citizenship behaviors', *Leadership Quarterly*, 1(2), 107–42.

Polanyi, M. (1967) *The Tacit Dimension*, London: Routledge.

Reddin, W.J. (1970) *Managerial Effectiveness*, London: McGraw-Hill.

Reddin, W.J. (1987) *How to Make Your Management Style More Effective*, Maidenhead: McGraw-Hill.

Reeves, J., Mahony, P. and Moos, L. (1997) 'Headship: issues of career', *Teacher Development*, 1(1), 43–56.

Ribbins, P. (1999) 'Understanding leadership: developing headteachers', in Bush, T., Bell, L., Bolam, R., Glatter, R. and Ribbins, P. (eds) *Education Management Redefining Theory, Policy and Practice*, London: Paul Chapman Publishing.

Ribbins, P. and Marland, M. (1994) *Headship Matters: Conversations with Seven Secondary School Headteachers*, Harlow: Longman.

Roberts, N.C. and Bradley, R.T. (1988) 'Limits of charisma', in Conger, J.A. and Kanungo, R.N. (eds) *Charismatic Leadership: The Elusive Factor in Organizational Effectiveness*, San Francisco, CA: Jossey-Bass.

Rutlish School OFSTED inspection report July 2001.

Sergiovanni, T.J. (1991) *The Principalship: A Reflective Practice Perspective* (second edn), Needham Heights, MA: Allyn and Bacon.

Simpson, T.B. (1994) 'Pressures on headteachers of primary schools during the transition to local management'. Unpublished PhD thesis, The University of Reading.

Southworth, G. (2002) 'Instructional leadership in schools: reflections and empirical evidence', *School Leadership and Management*, 22(1), 73–92.

Spender, J.-C. (1998) 'The dynamics of individual and organizational knowledge', in Eden, C. and Spender, J.-C. (eds) *Managerial and Organizational Cognition: Theory, Methods and Research*, London: Sage.

Storr, A. (1988) *Solitude*, London: Harper Collins.

Stott, K. and Walker, A. (1992) 'Developing school leaders through mentoring: a Singapore perspective', *School Organisation*, 12(2), 153–64.

Tanner, C.K., Schnittjer, C.J. and Atkins, T.T. (1991) 'Effects of the use of management strategies on stress levels of high school principals in the United States', *Educational Administration Quarterly*, 27(2), 203–24.

Weick, K.E. (1990) 'Cartographic myths in organizations', in Huff, A.S. (ed) *Mapping Strategic Thought*, Chichester: John Wiley.

Weick, K.E. (1995) *Sensemaking in Organizations*, Thousand Oaks, CA: Sage.

Weindling, D. (1999) 'Stages of headship', in Bush, T., Bell, L., Bolam, R., Glatter, R. and Ribbins, P. (eds) *Education Management Redefining Theory, Policy and Practice*, London: Paul Chapman Publishing.

Weindling, D. and Earley, P. (1987a) *Secondary Headship: The First Years*, Windsor: NFER-Nelson.

Weindling, D. and Earley, P. (1987b) 'The first years of headship – towards better practice', *Educational Research*, 29(3), 202–12.

Yukl, G. (2002) *Leadership in Organizations* (fifth edn), Upper Saddle River, NJ: Prentice-Hall International.

Zaleznik, A. (1977) 'Manager and leaders: Are they different?', *Harvard Business Review*, 55(3) May–June, 67–78.

Index